SUPERMAN
FOR TOMORROW

VOLUME TWO

BRIAN AZZARELLO
WRITER

JIM LEE
PENCILLER

SCOTT WILLIAMS
INKER

RICHARD FRIEND
SANDRA HOPE
MATT BANNING
ERIC BASALDUA
JIM LEE
DANNY MIKI
TREVOR SCOTT
TIM TOWNSEND
JOE WEEMS
ADDITIONAL INKERS

ALEX SINCLAIR
COLORIST

ROB LEIGH
NICK J. NAPOLITANO
LETTERERS

SUPERMAN CREATED BY
JERRY SIEGEL & JOE SHUSTER

SUPERMAN
FOR TOMORROW

VOLUME TWO

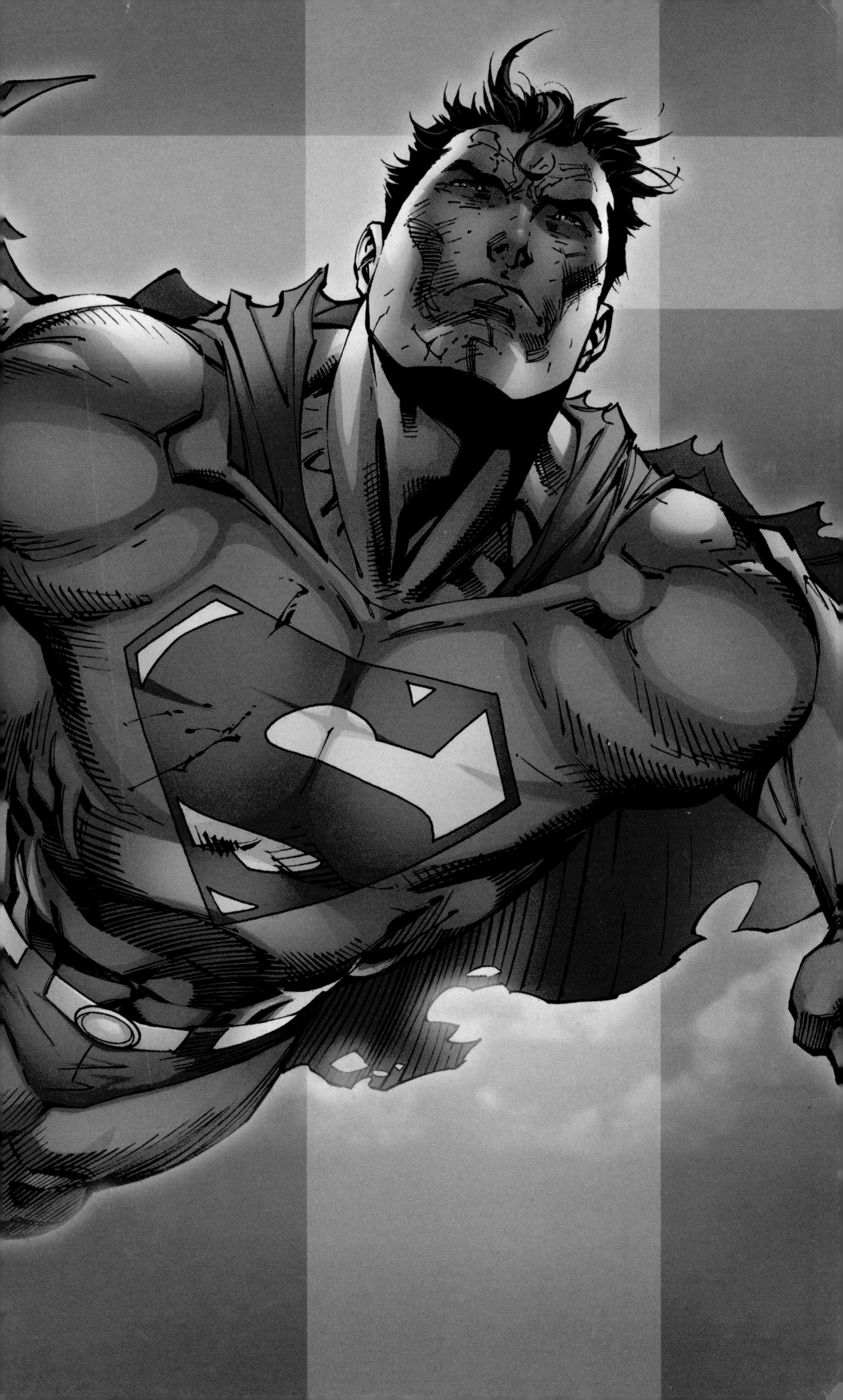

Dan DiDio
VP-EXECUTIVE EDITOR

Will Dennis
Eddie Berganza
EDITORS-ORIGINAL SERIES

Casey Seijas
ASSISTANT EDITOR-ORIGINAL SERIES

Anton Kawasaki
EDITOR-COLLECTED EDITION

Robbin Brosterman
SENIOR ART DIRECTOR

Paul Levitz
PRESIDENT & PUBLISHER

Georg Brewer
VP-DESIGN & RETAIL PRODUCT
DEVELOPMENT

Richard Bruning
SENIOR VP-CREATIVE DIRECTOR

Patrick Caldon
SENIOR VP-FINANCE & OPERATIONS

Chris Caramalis
VP-FINANCE

Terri Cunningham
VP-MANAGING EDITOR

Stephanie Fierman
SENIOR VP-SALES & MARKETING

Alison Gill
VP-MANUFACTURING

Rich Johnson
VP-BOOK TRADE SALES

Hank Kanalz
VP-GENERAL MANAGER,
WILDSTORM

Lillian Laserson
SENIOR VP & GENERAL COUNSEL

Jim Lee
EDITORIAL DIRECTOR-WILDSTORM

Paula Lowitt
SENIOR VP-BUSINESS & LEGAL AFFAIRS

David McKillips
VP-ADVERTISING & CUSTOM
PUBLISHING

John Nee
VP-BUSINESS DEVELOPMENT

Gregory Noveck
SENIOR VP-CREATIVE AFFAIRS

Cheryl Rubin
SENIOR VP-BRAND MANAGEMENT

Bob Wayne
VP-SALES

SUPERMAN: FOR TOMORROW VOLUME TWO

DC Comics, 1700 Broadway,
New York, NY 10019
A Warner Bros. Entertainment Company
Printed in Canada. First Printing.
Hardcover ISBN: 1-4012-0715-4
Softcover ISBN: 1-4012-0448-1

Cover art by Jim Lee &
Scott Williams with Alex Sinclair.

Special thanks to Scott Iwahashi
and Laura Martin.

Publication design by
Amie Brockway-Metcalf.

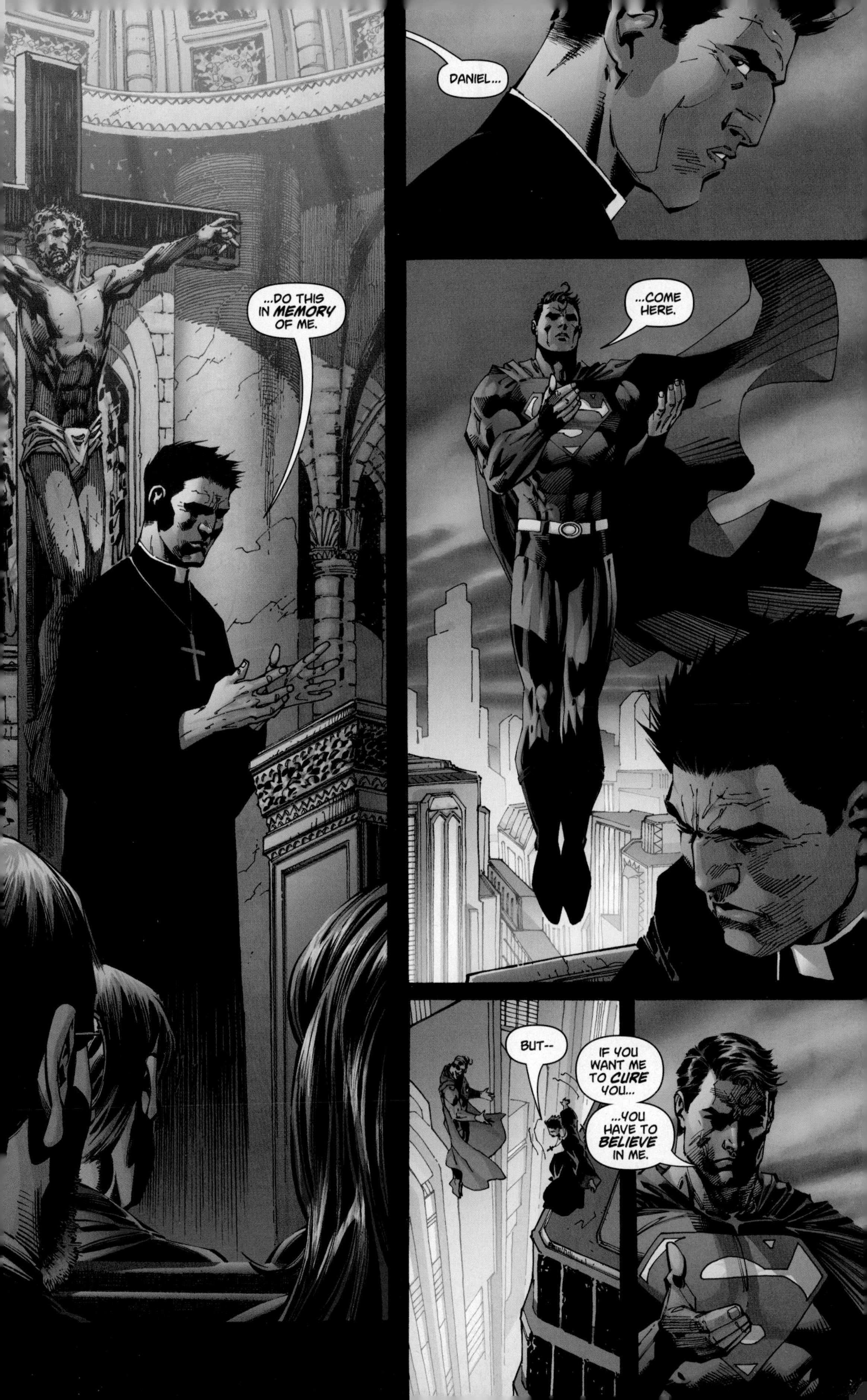

...DO THIS IN MEMORY OF ME.
DANIEL...
...COME HERE.
BUT--
IF YOU WANT ME TO CURE YOU...
...YOU HAVE TO BELIEVE IN ME.

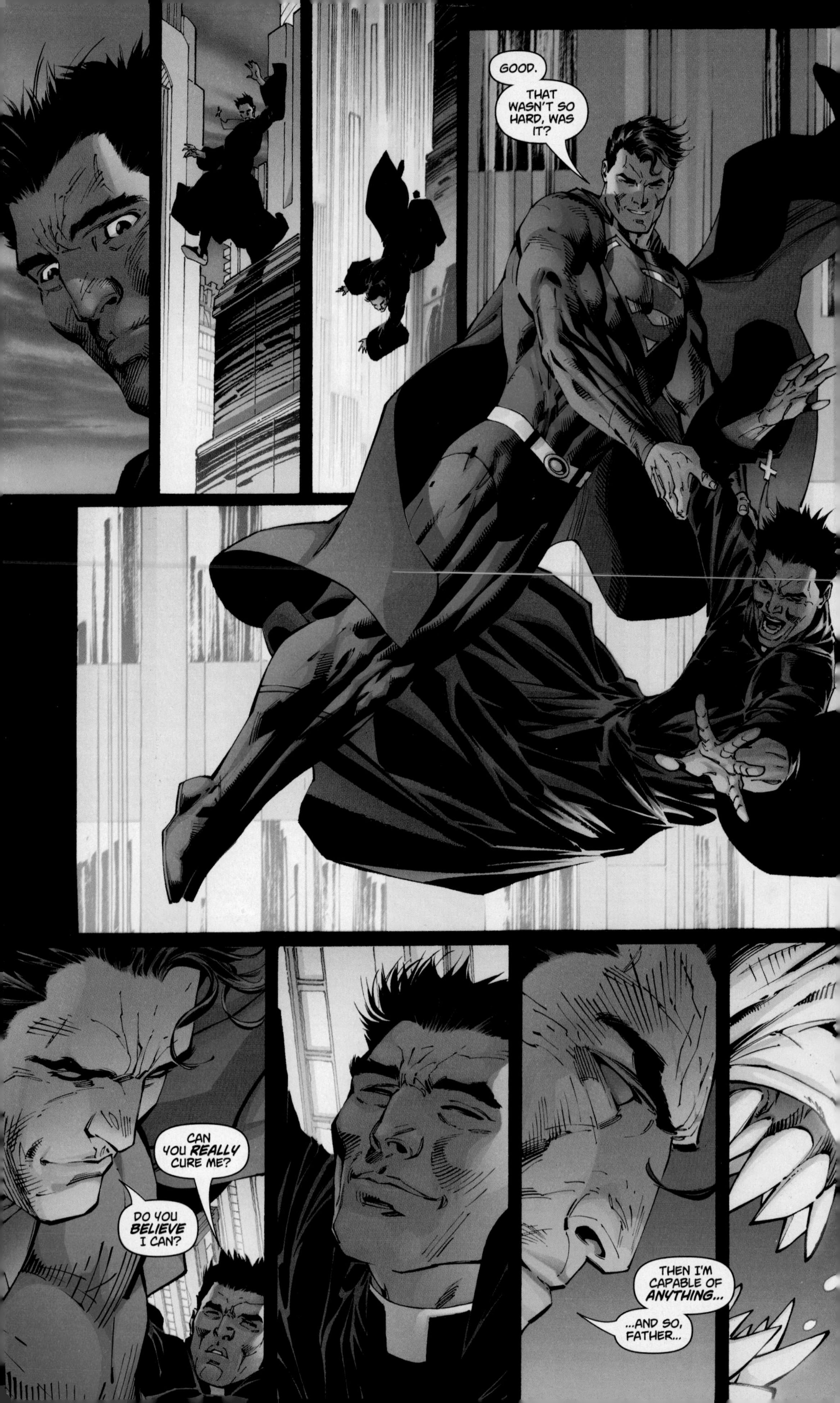

GOOD.
THAT WASN'T SO HARD, WAS IT?
CAN YOU REALLY CURE ME?
DO YOU BELIEVE I CAN?
THEN I'M CAPABLE OF ANYTHING...
...AND SO, FATHER...

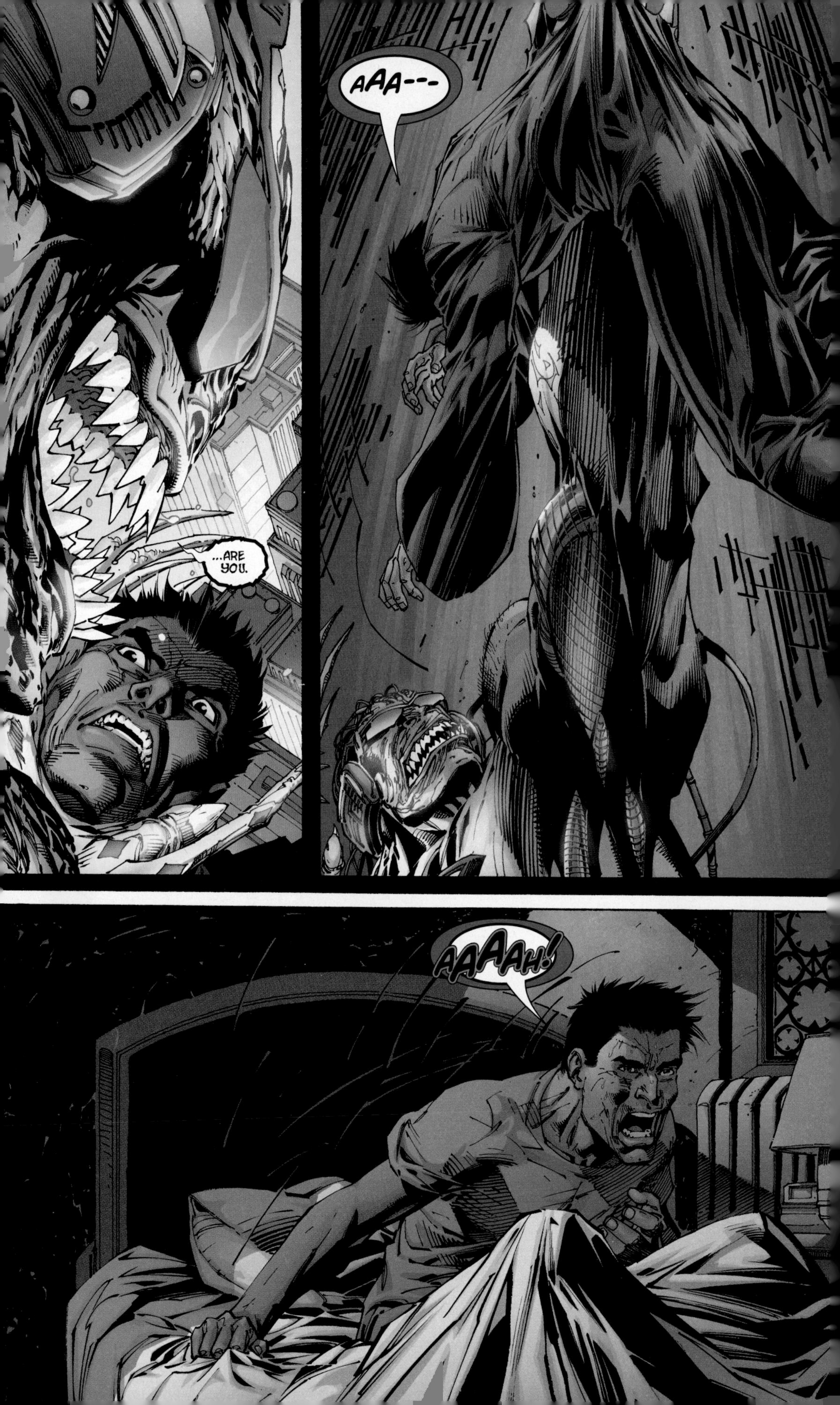

...ARE YOU.
AAA---
AAAAH!

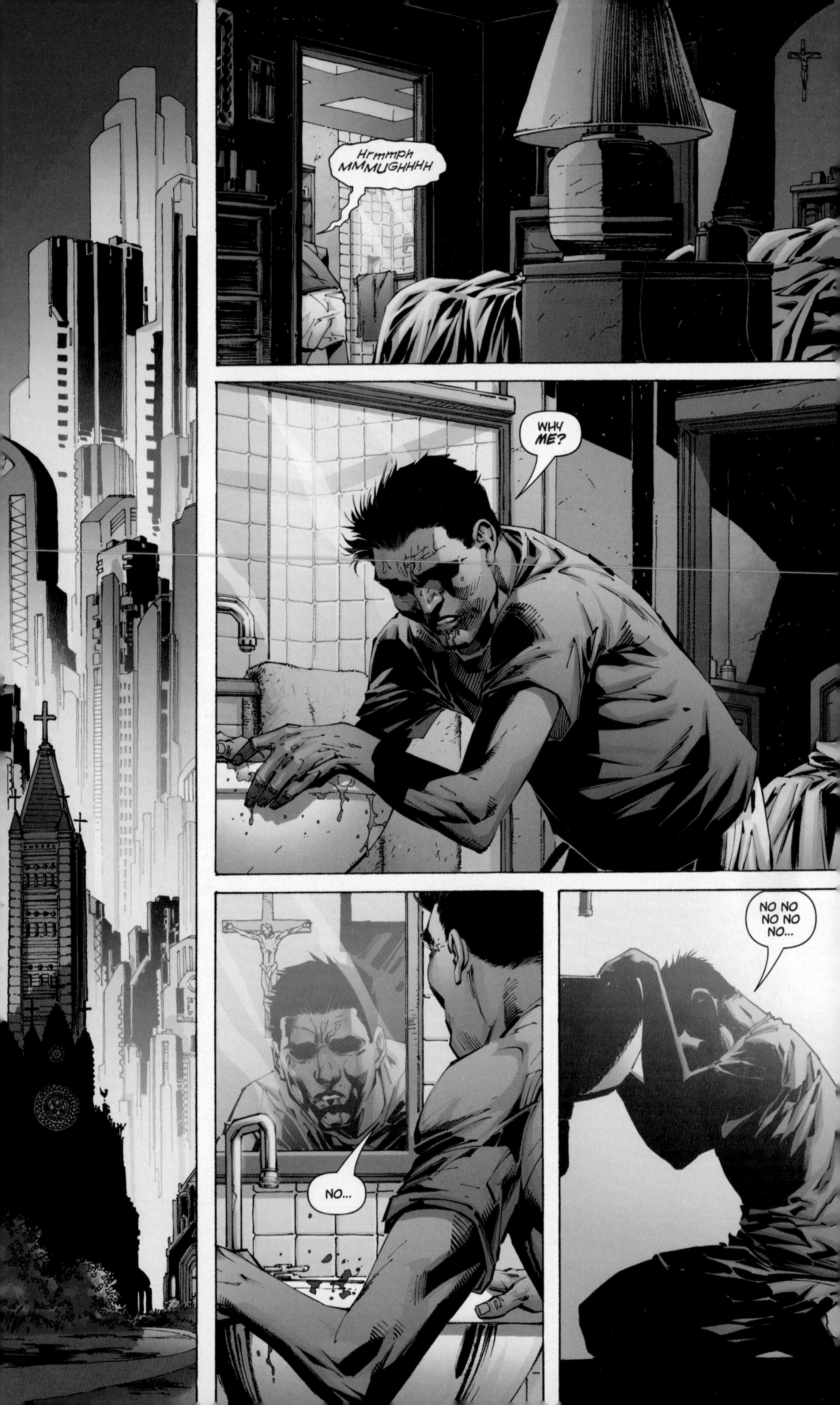

Hrmmph MMMUGHHHH
WHY ME?
NO...
NO NO NO NO NO...

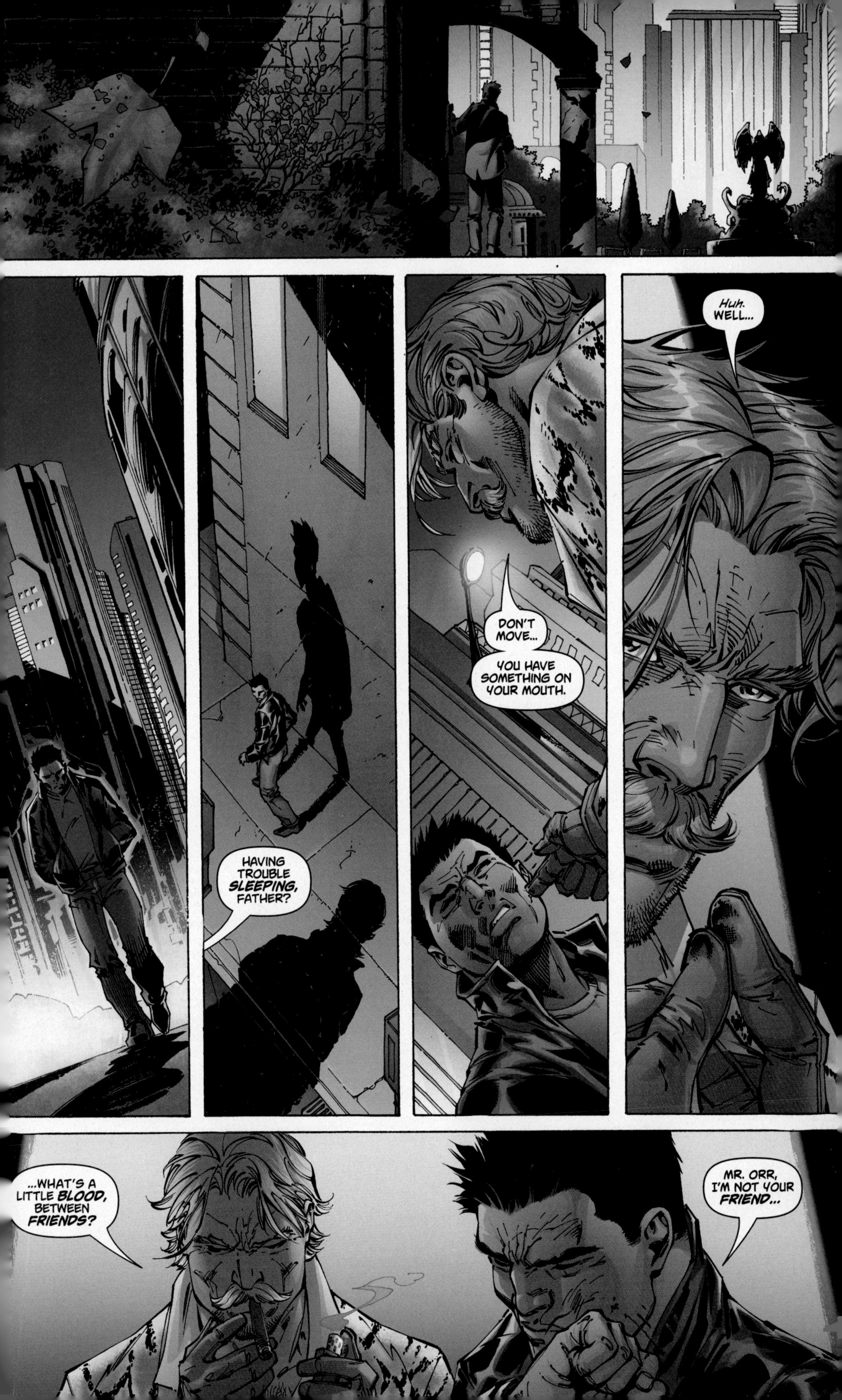
HAVING TROUBLE SLEEPING, FATHER?
DON'T MOVE...
YOU HAVE SOMETHING ON YOUR MOUTH.
Huh. WELL...
...WHAT'S A LITTLE BLOOD, BETWEEN FRIENDS?
MR. ORR, I'M NOT YOUR FRIEND...

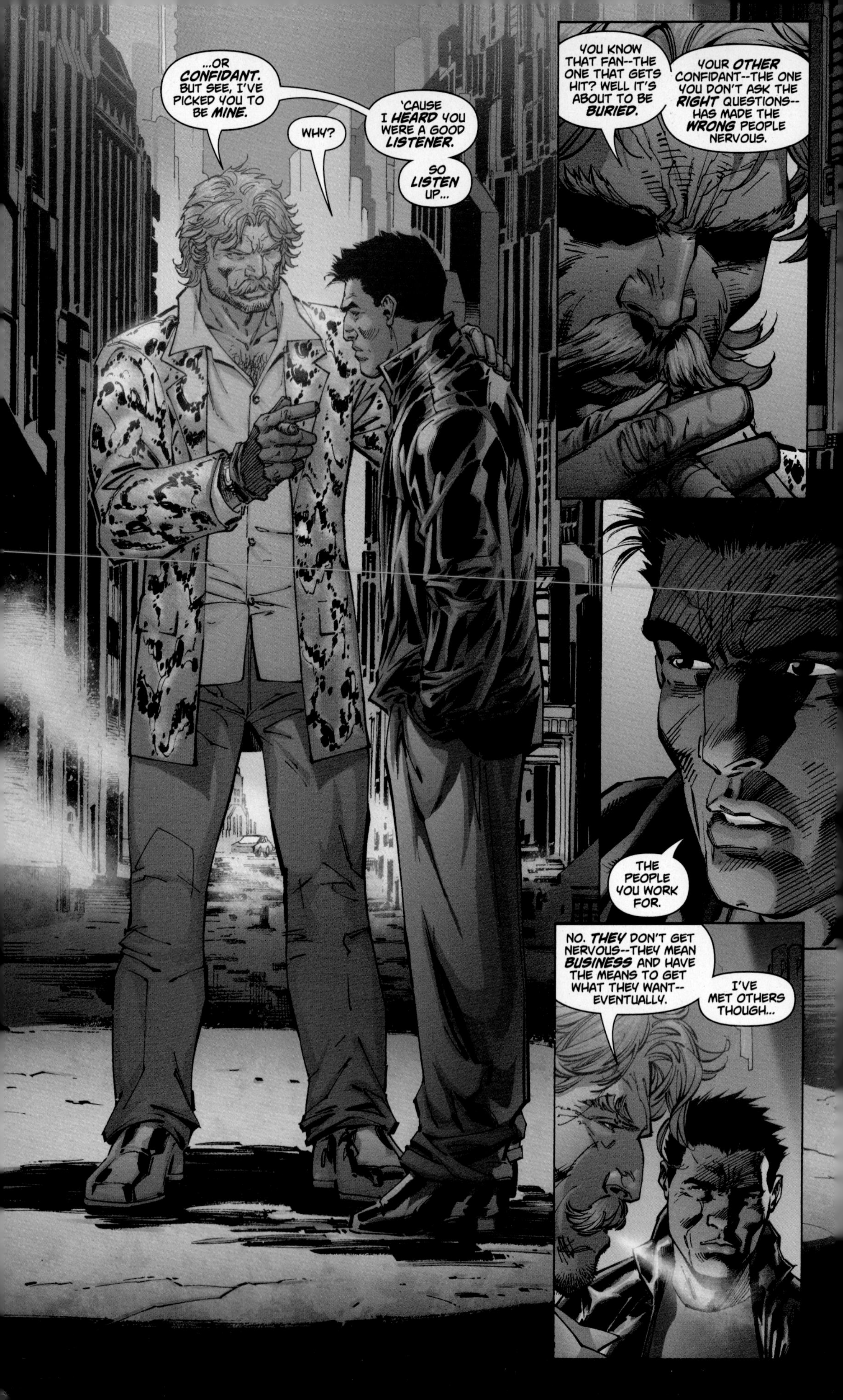
...OR CONFIDANT. BUT SEE, I'VE PICKED YOU TO BE MINE.
WHY?
'CAUSE I HEARD YOU WERE A GOOD LISTENER.
SO LISTEN UP...
YOU KNOW THAT FAN--THE ONE THAT GETS HIT? WELL IT'S ABOUT TO BE BURIED.
YOUR OTHER CONFIDANT--THE ONE YOU DON'T ASK THE RIGHT QUESTIONS--HAS MADE THE WRONG PEOPLE NERVOUS.
THE PEOPLE YOU WORK FOR.
NO. THEY DON'T GET NERVOUS--THEY MEAN BUSINESS AND HAVE THE MEANS TO GET WHAT THEY WANT--EVENTUALLY.
I'VE MET OTHERS THOUGH...

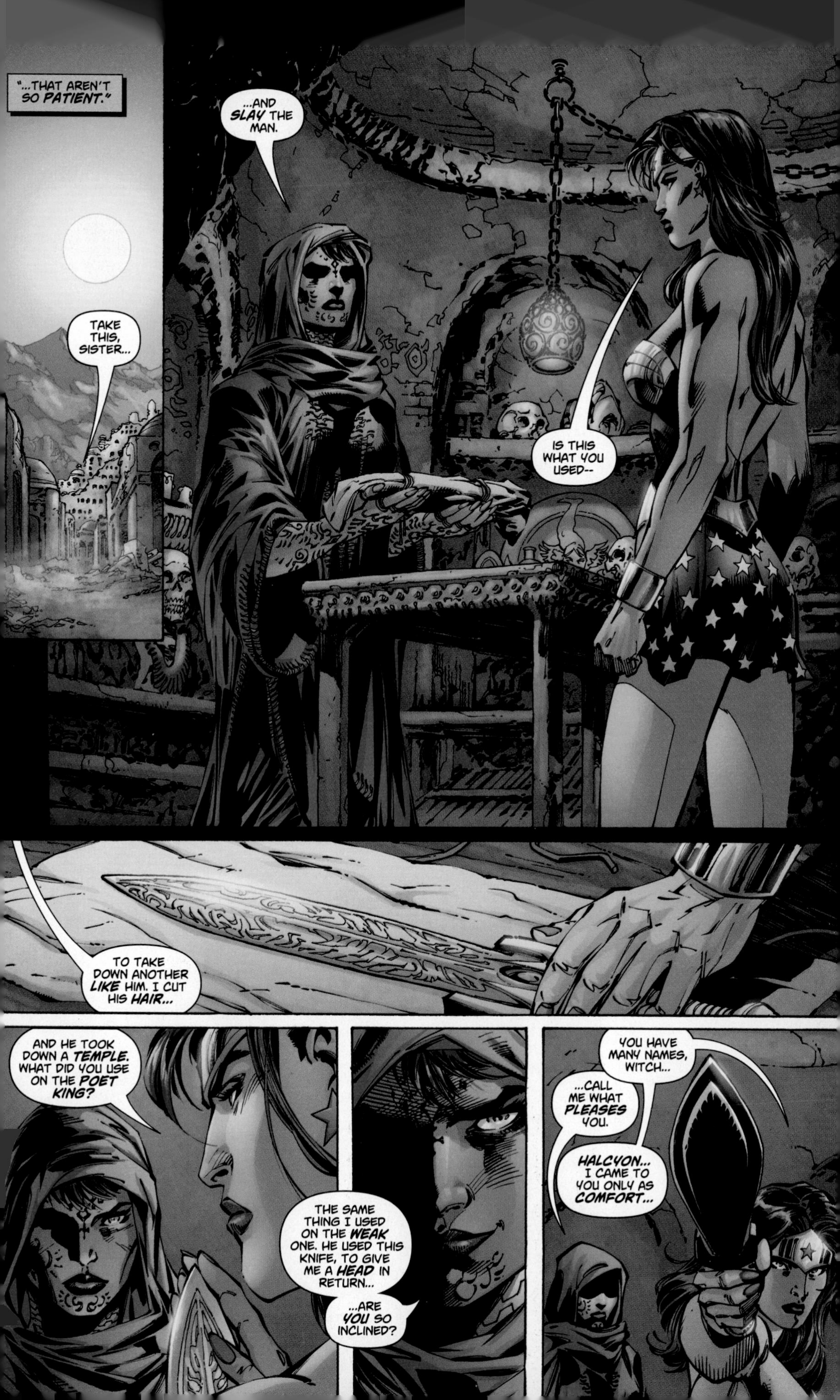
"...THAT AREN'T SO PATIENT."
TAKE THIS, SISTER...
...AND SLAY THE MAN.
IS THIS WHAT YOU USED--
TO TAKE DOWN ANOTHER LIKE HIM. I CUT HIS HAIR...
AND HE TOOK DOWN A TEMPLE. WHAT DID YOU USE ON THE POET KING?
THE SAME THING I USED ON THE WEAK ONE. HE USED THIS KNIFE, TO GIVE ME A HEAD IN RETURN...
...ARE YOU SO INCLINED?
YOU HAVE MANY NAMES, WITCH...
...CALL ME WHAT PLEASES YOU.
HALCYON... I CAME TO YOU ONLY AS COMFORT...

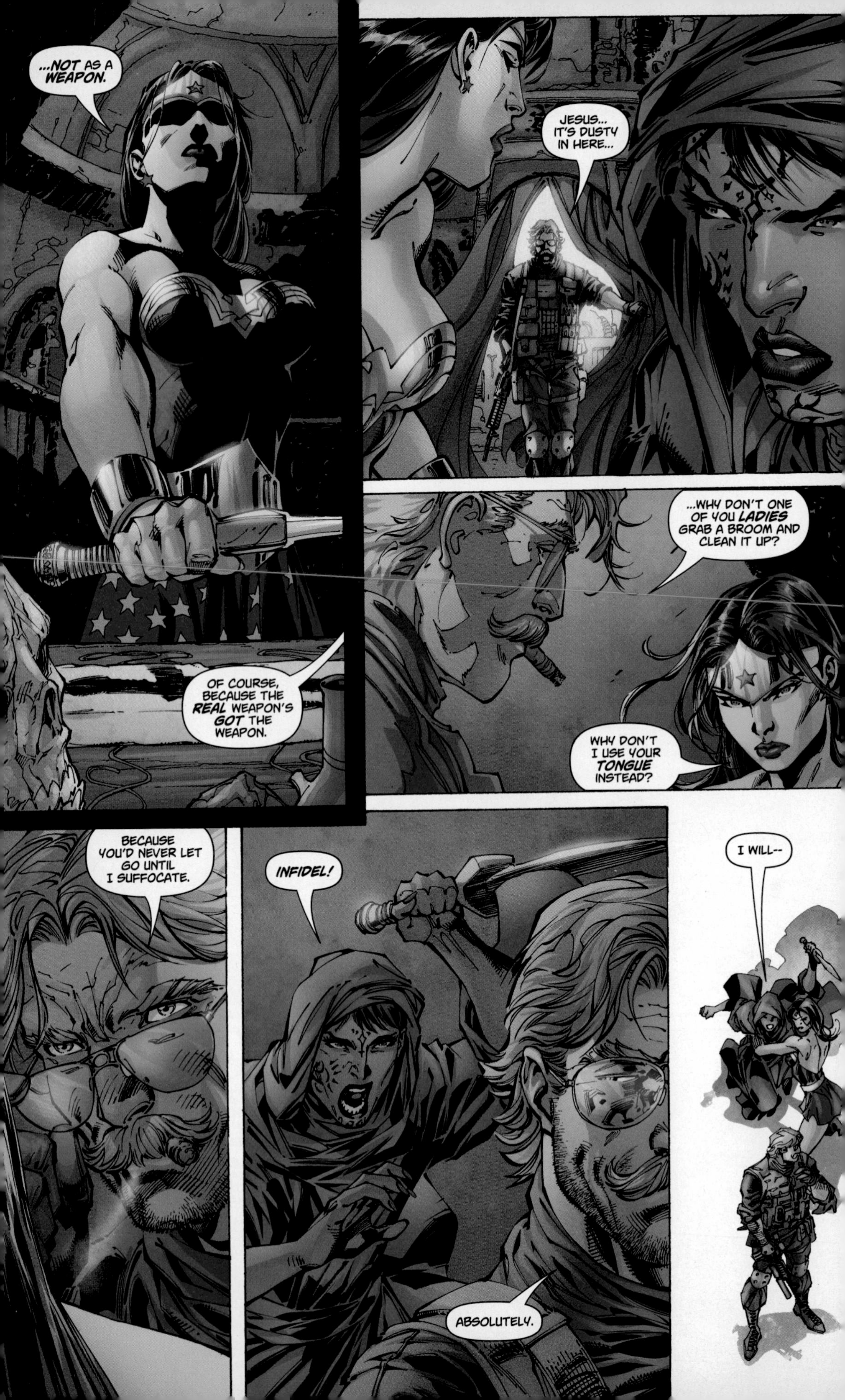
...NOT AS A WEAPON.
OF COURSE, BECAUSE THE REAL WEAPON'S GOT THE WEAPON.
JESUS... IT'S DUSTY IN HERE...
...WHY DON'T ONE OF YOU LADIES GRAB A BROOM AND CLEAN IT UP?
WHY DON'T I USE YOUR TONGUE INSTEAD?
BECAUSE YOU'D NEVER LET GO UNTIL I SUFFOCATE.
INFIDEL!
ABSOLUTELY.
I WILL--

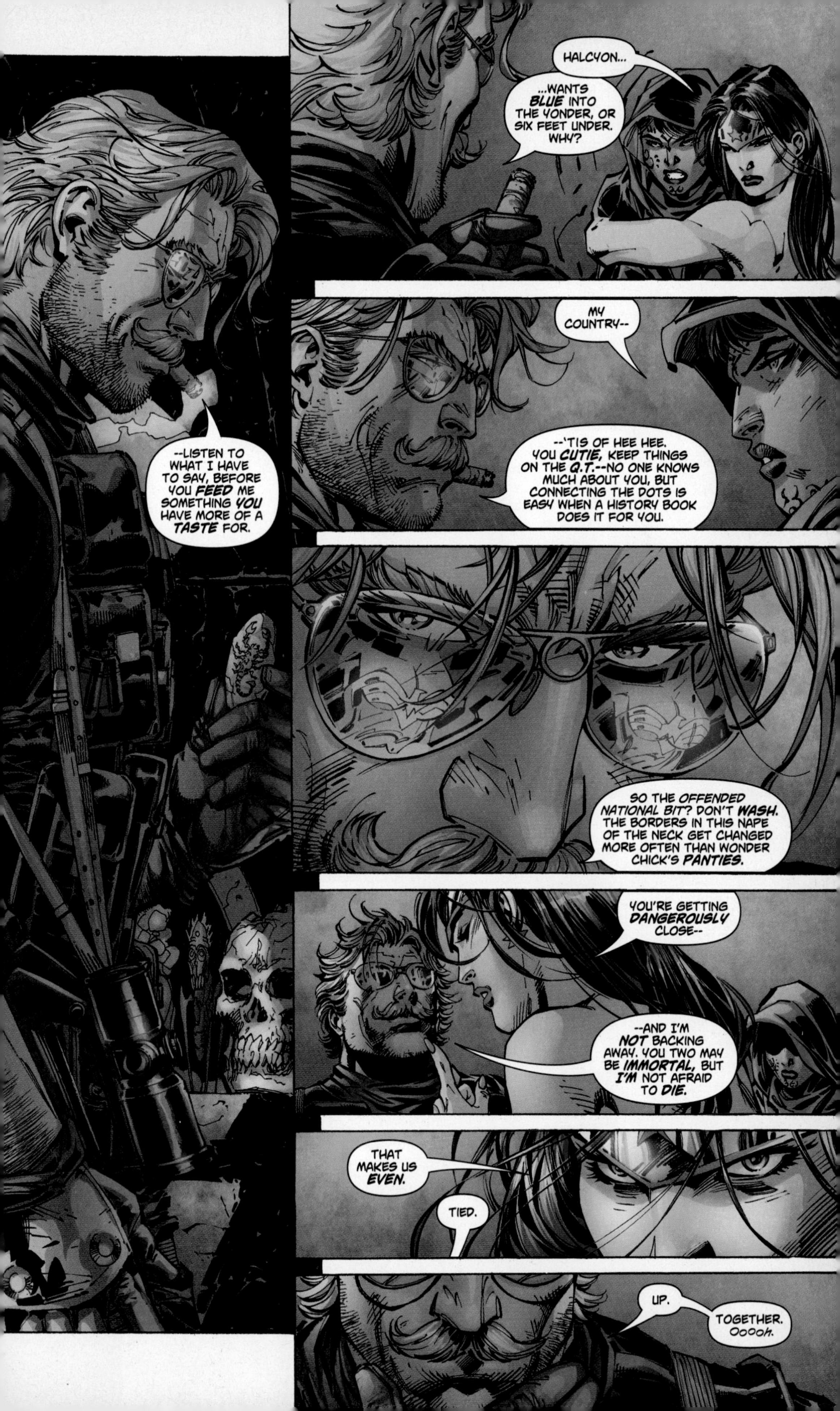
--LISTEN TO WHAT I HAVE TO SAY, BEFORE YOU FEED ME SOMETHING YOU HAVE MORE OF A TASTE FOR.
HALCYON...
...WANTS BLUE INTO THE YONDER, OR SIX FEET UNDER. WHY?
MY COUNTRY--
--'TIS OF HEE HEE. YOU CUTIE, KEEP THINGS ON THE Q.T.--NO ONE KNOWS MUCH ABOUT YOU, BUT CONNECTING THE DOTS IS EASY WHEN A HISTORY BOOK DOES IT FOR YOU.
SO THE OFFENDED NATIONAL BIT? DON'T WASH. THE BORDERS IN THIS NAPE OF THE NECK GET CHANGED MORE OFTEN THAN WONDER CHICK'S PANTIES.
YOU'RE GETTING DANGEROUSLY CLOSE--
--AND I'M NOT BACKING AWAY. YOU TWO MAY BE IMMORTAL, BUT I'M NOT AFRAID TO DIE.
THAT MAKES US EVEN.
TIED.
UP.
TOGETHER. Ooooh.

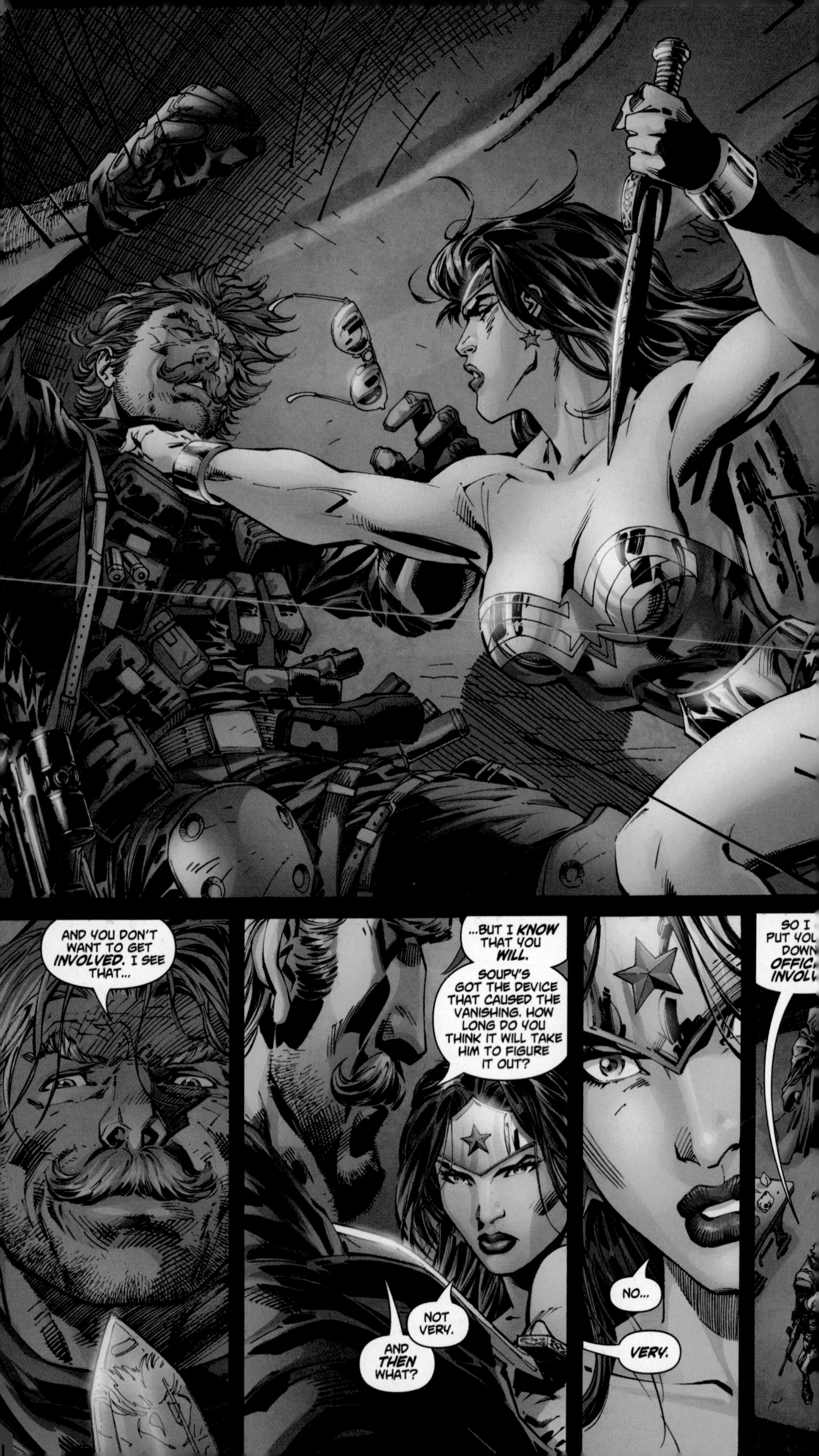

AND YOU DON'T WANT TO GET INVOLVED. I SEE THAT...
...BUT I KNOW THAT YOU WILL.
SOUPY'S GOT THE DEVICE THAT CAUSED THE VANISHING. HOW LONG DO YOU THINK IT WILL TAKE HIM TO FIGURE IT OUT?
NOT VERY.
AND THEN WHAT?
NO...
VERY.
SO I
PUT YOU
DOWN
OFFIC
INVOLV

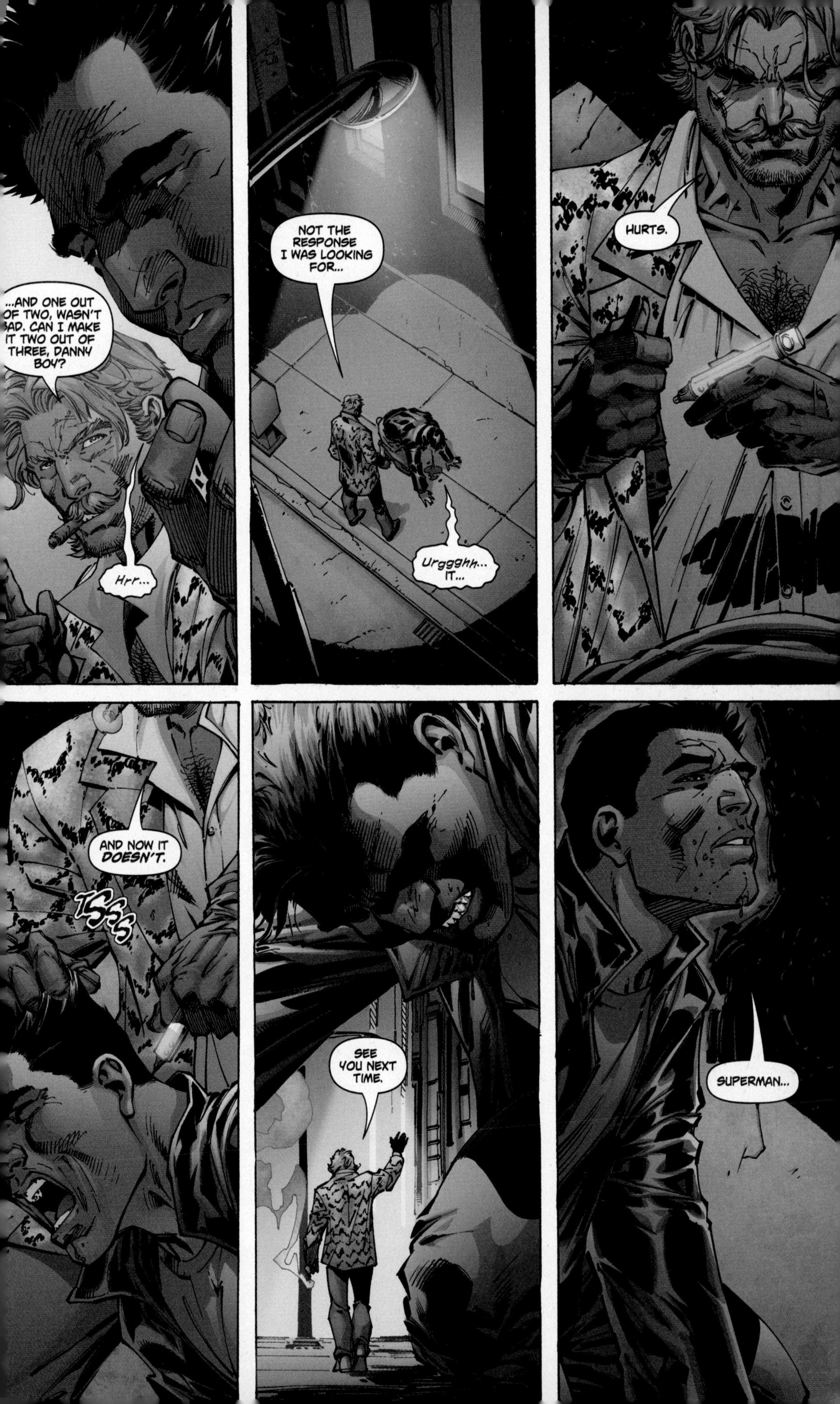
...AND ONE OUT OF TWO, WASN'T BAD. CAN I MAKE IT TWO OUT OF THREE, DANNY BOY?
Hrr...
NOT THE RESPONSE I WAS LOOKING FOR...
Urggghh... IT...
HURTS.
AND NOW IT DOESN'T.
TSSS
SEE YOU NEXT TIME.
SUPERMAN...

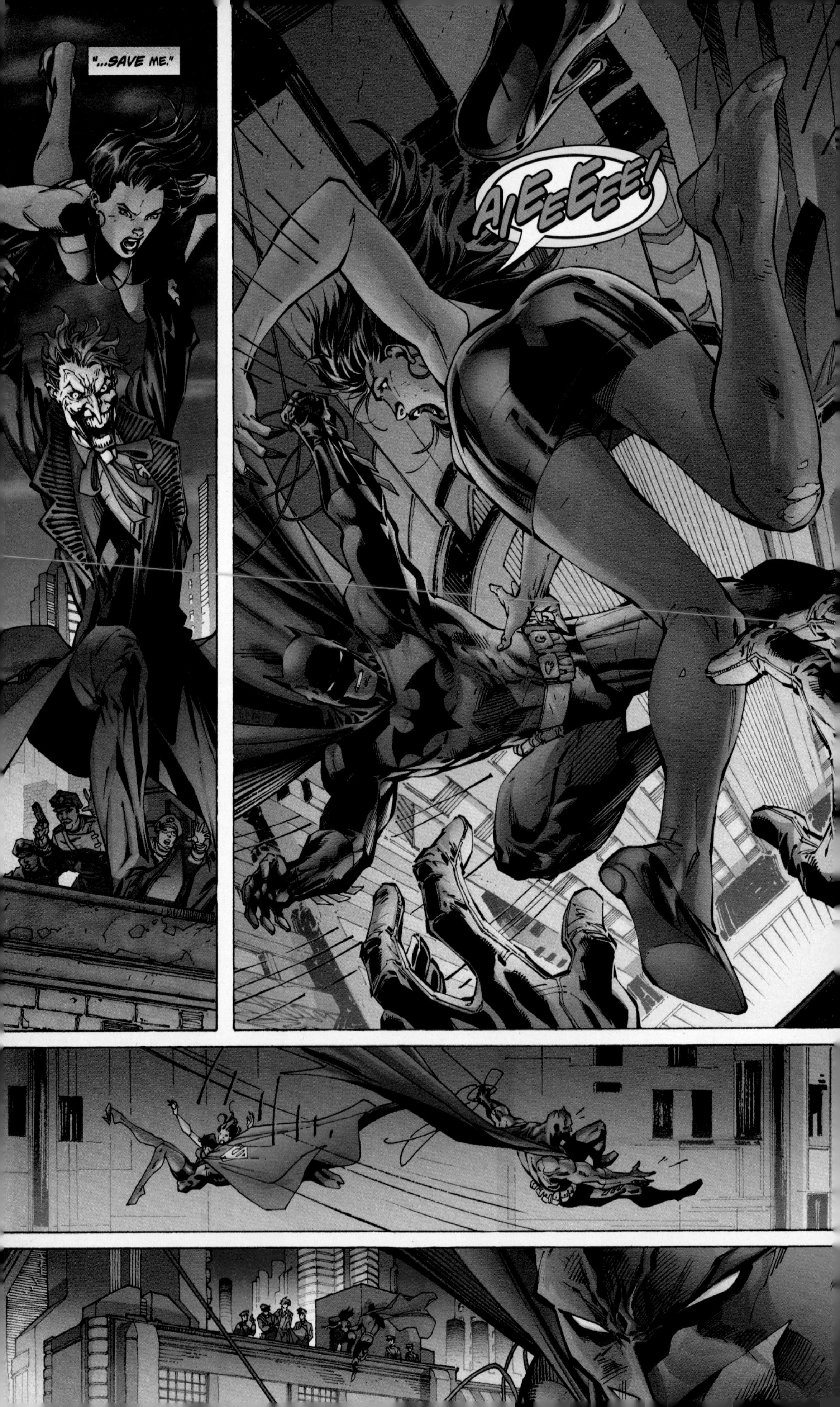
"...SAVE ME."
AIEEEEEE!

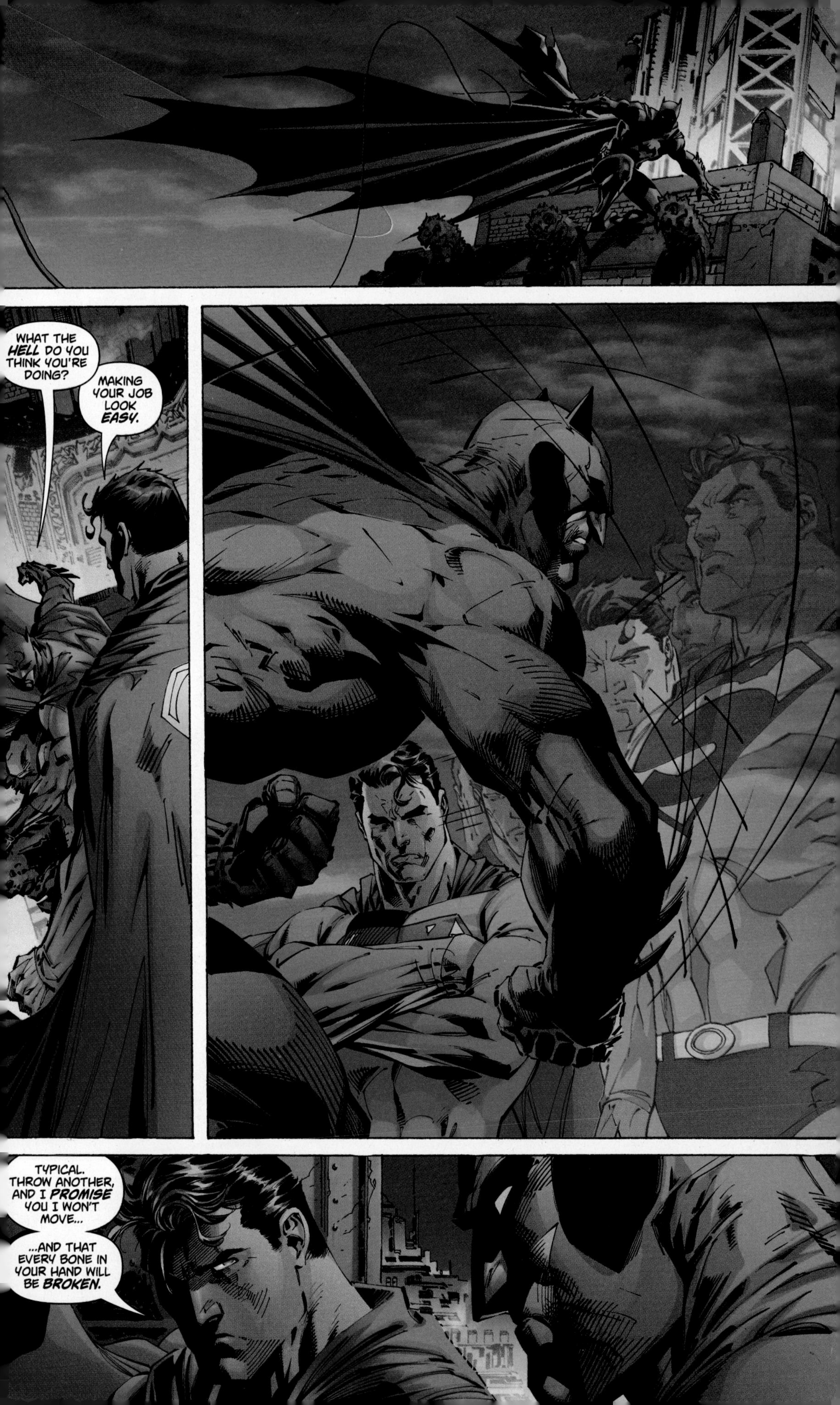

WHAT THE HELL DO YOU THINK YOU'RE DOING?
MAKING YOUR JOB LOOK EASY.
TYPICAL. THROW ANOTHER, AND I PROMISE YOU I WON'T MOVE...
...AND THAT EVERY BONE IN YOUR HAND WILL BE BROKEN.

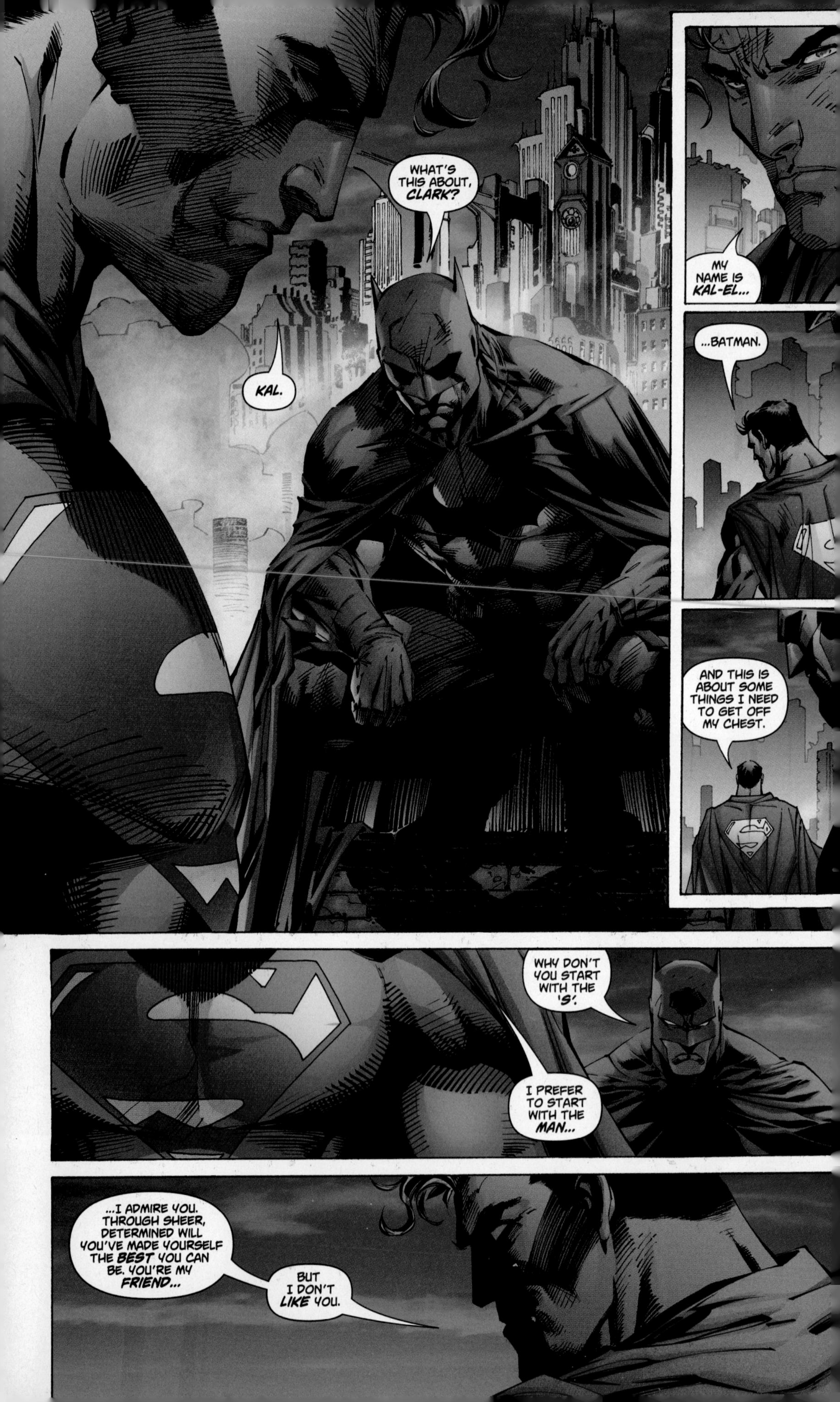
WHAT'S THIS ABOUT, CLARK?
KAL.
MY NAME IS KAL-EL...
...BATMAN.
AND THIS IS ABOUT SOME THINGS I NEED TO GET OFF MY CHEST.
WHY DON'T YOU START WITH THE 'S'.
I PREFER TO START WITH THE MAN...
...I ADMIRE YOU. THROUGH SHEER, DETERMINED WILL YOU'VE MADE YOURSELF THE BEST YOU CAN BE. YOU'RE MY FRIEND...
BUT I DON'T LIKE YOU.

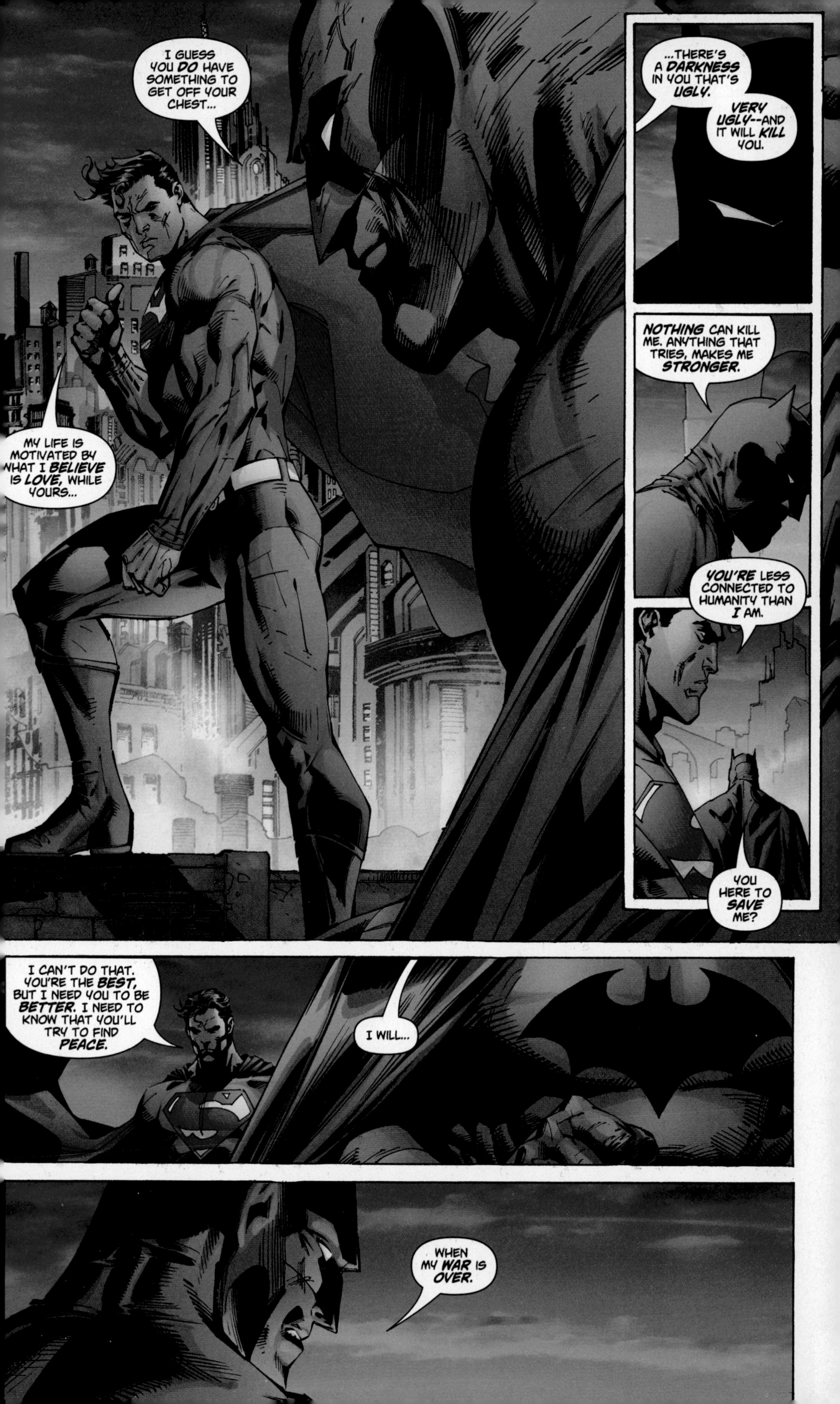

I GUESS YOU **DO** HAVE SOMETHING TO GET OFF YOUR CHEST...
...THERE'S A **DARKNESS** IN YOU THAT'S **UGLY.**
VERY UGLY--AND IT WILL **KILL** YOU.
MY LIFE IS MOTIVATED BY WHAT I **BELIEVE** IS **LOVE**, WHILE YOURS...
NOTHING CAN KILL ME. ANYTHING THAT TRIES, MAKES ME **STRONGER.**
YOU'RE LESS CONNECTED TO HUMANITY THAN **I** AM.
YOU HERE TO **SAVE** ME?
I CAN'T DO THAT. YOU'RE THE **BEST,** BUT I NEED YOU TO BE **BETTER.** I NEED TO KNOW THAT YOU'LL TRY TO FIND **PEACE.**
I WILL...
WHEN MY **WAR** IS **OVER.**

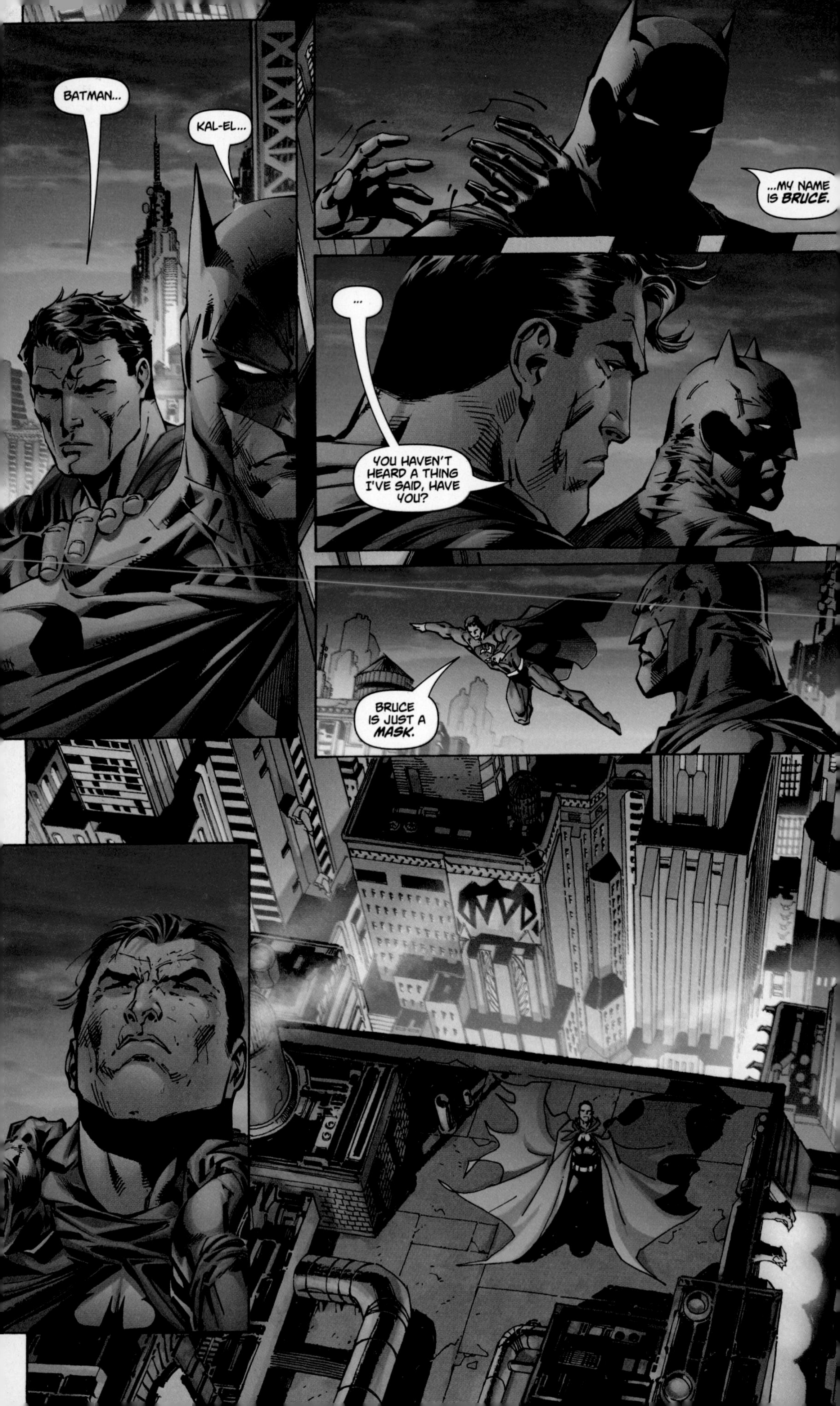

BATMAN...
KAL-EL...
...MY NAME IS BRUCE.
...
YOU HAVEN'T HEARD A THING I'VE SAID, HAVE YOU?
BRUCE IS JUST A MASK.

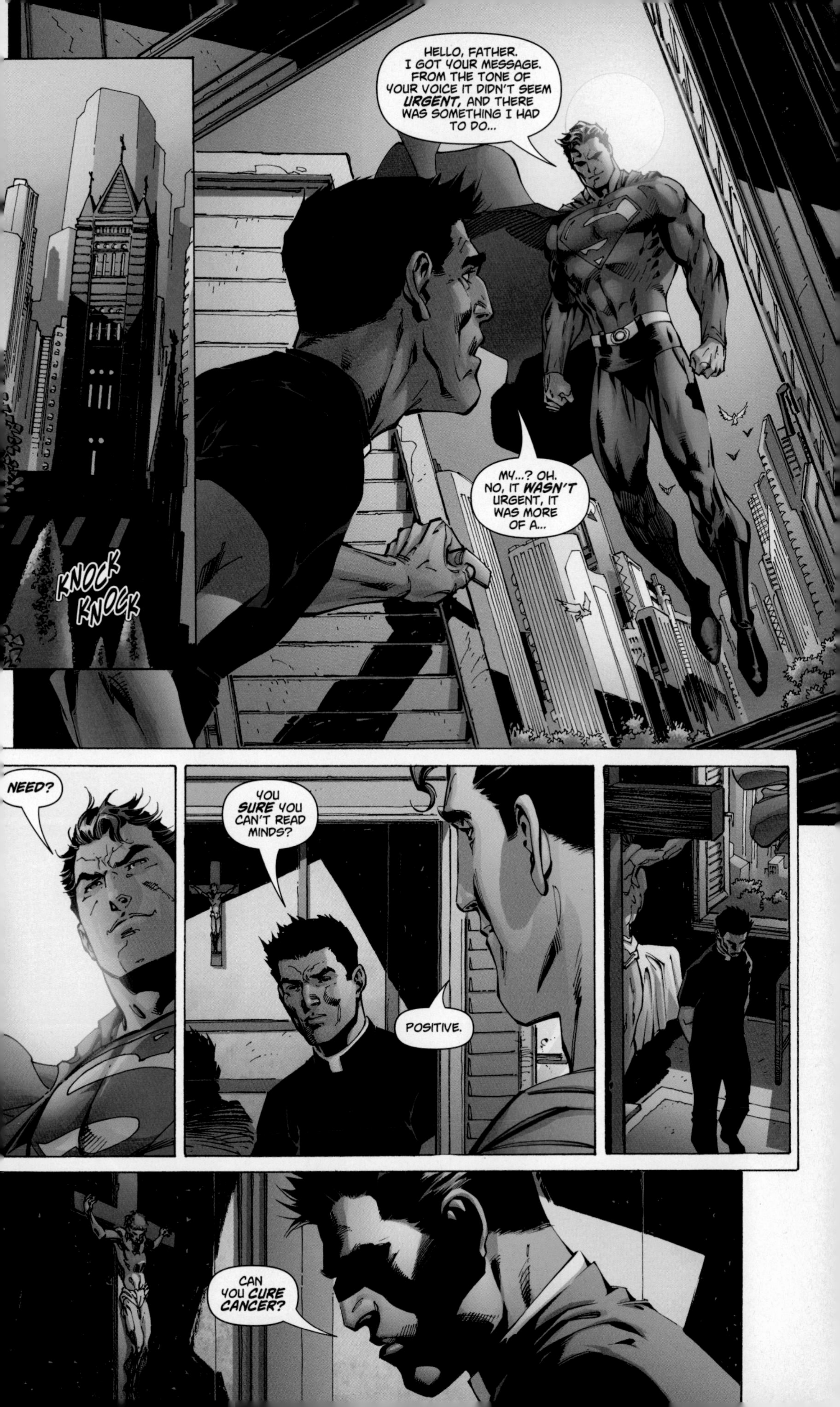
KNOCK KNOCK
HELLO, FATHER. I GOT YOUR MESSAGE. FROM THE TONE OF YOUR VOICE IT DIDN'T SEEM URGENT, AND THERE WAS SOMETHING I HAD TO DO...
MY...? OH. NO, IT WASN'T URGENT, IT WAS MORE OF A...
NEED?
YOU SURE YOU CAN'T READ MINDS?
POSITIVE.
CAN YOU CURE CANCER?

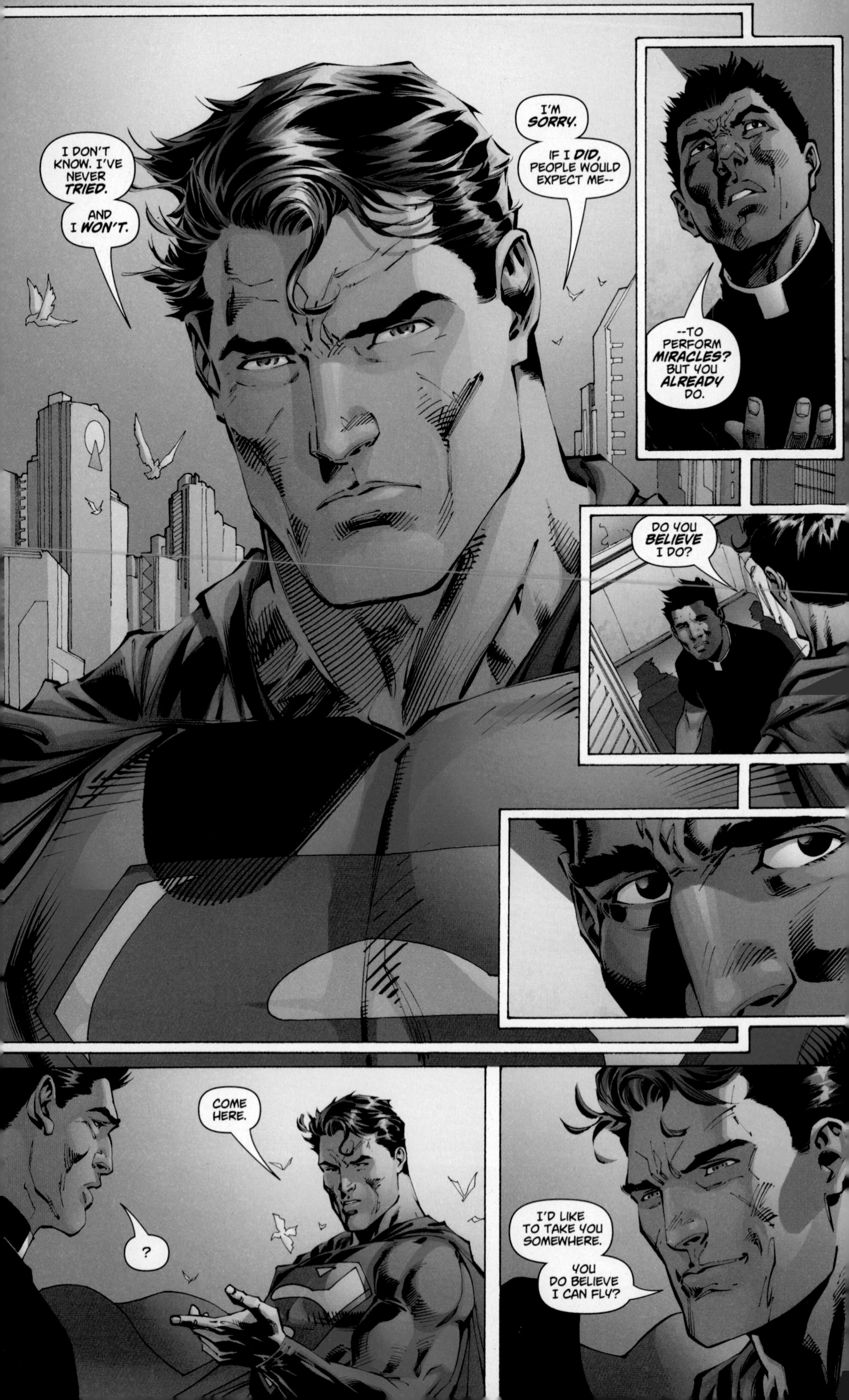
I DON'T KNOW. I'VE NEVER TRIED.
AND I WON'T.
I'M SORRY.
IF I DID, PEOPLE WOULD EXPECT ME--
--TO PERFORM MIRACLES? BUT YOU ALREADY DO.
DO YOU BELIEVE I DO?
COME HERE.
?
I'D LIKE TO TAKE YOU SOMEWHERE.
YOU DO BELIEVE I CAN FLY?

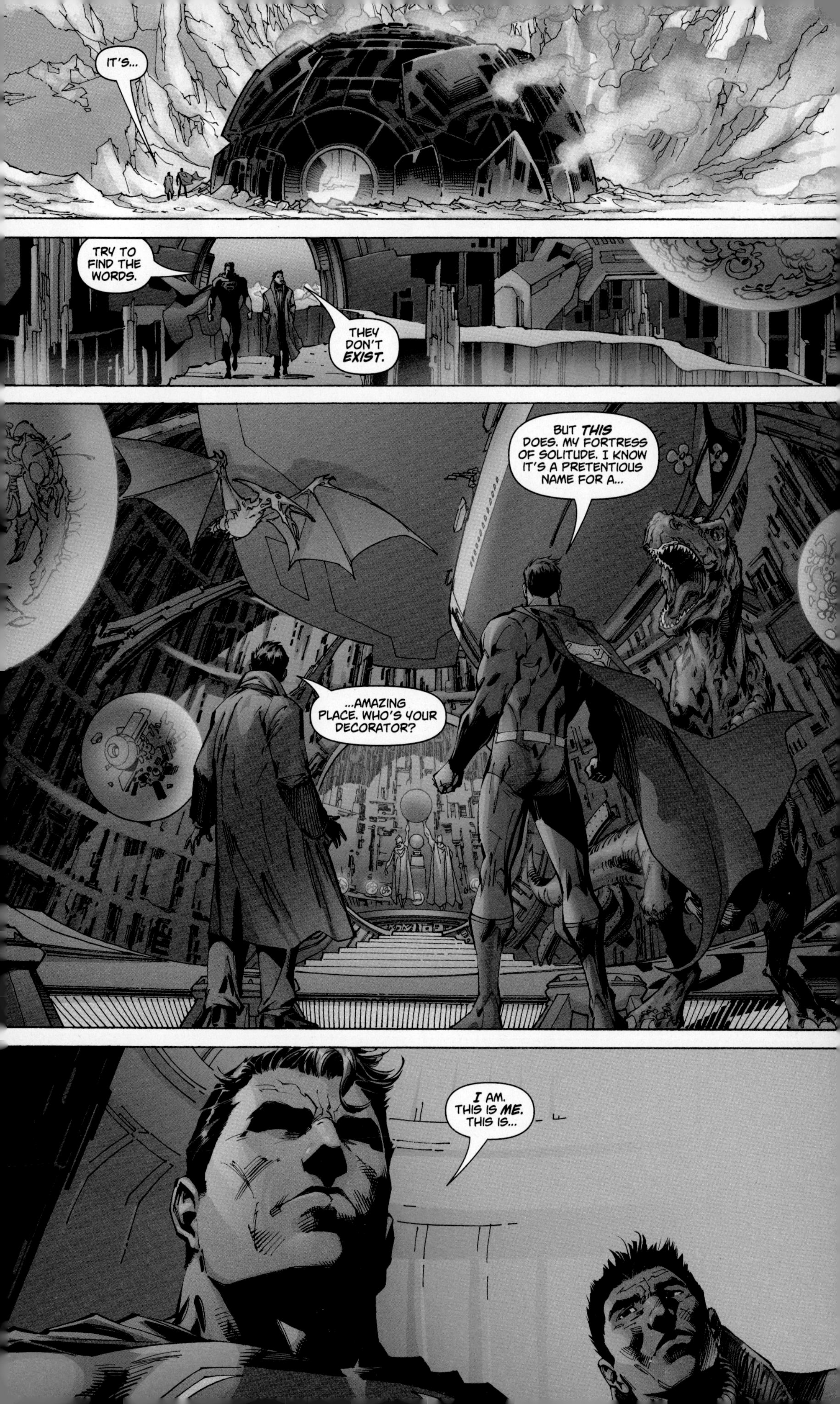
IT'S...
TRY TO FIND THE WORDS.
THEY DON'T EXIST.
BUT THIS DOES. MY FORTRESS OF SOLITUDE. I KNOW IT'S A PRETENTIOUS NAME FOR A...
...AMAZING PLACE. WHO'S YOUR DECORATOR?
I AM. THIS IS ME. THIS IS...

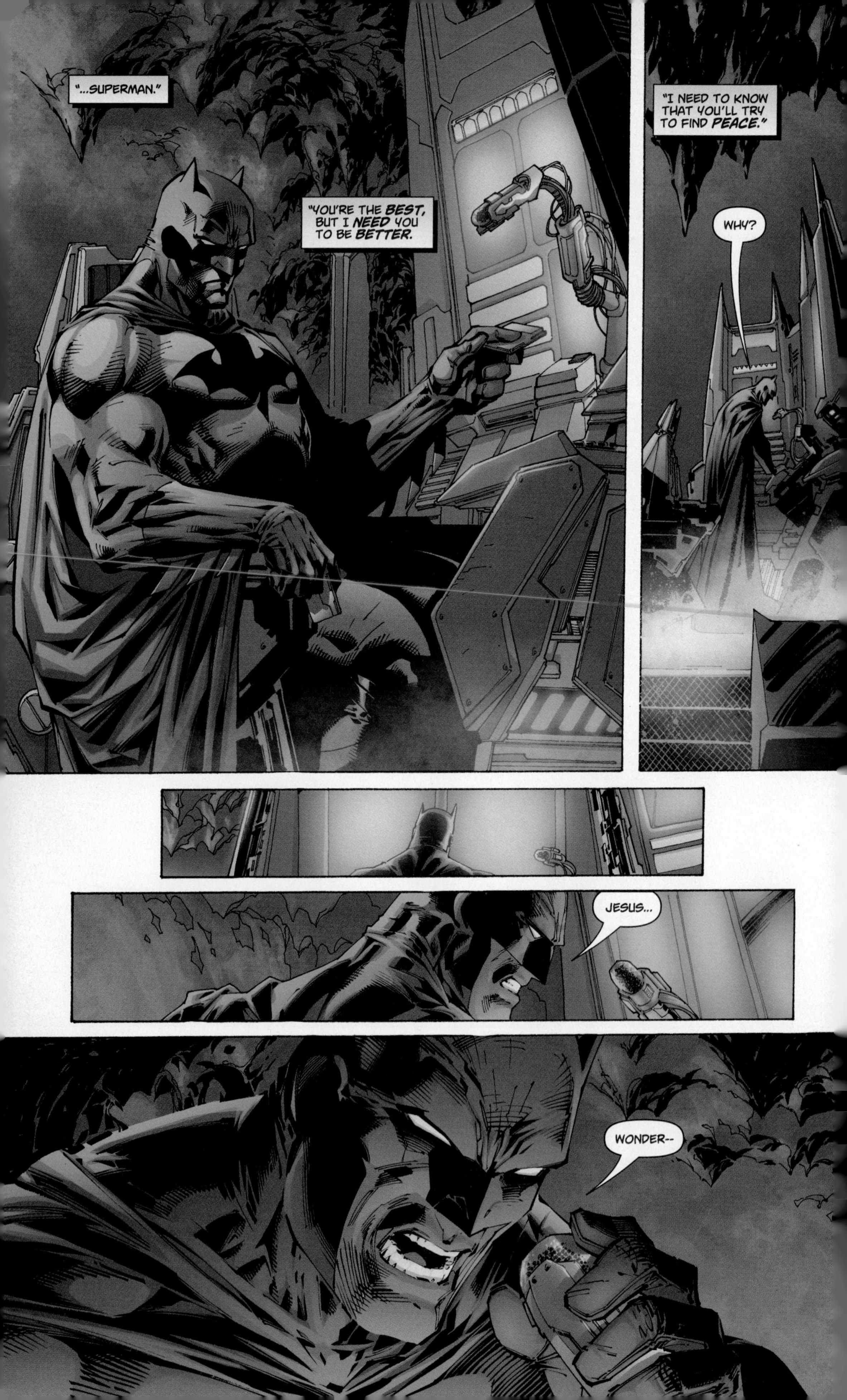
"...SUPERMAN."
"YOU'RE THE BEST, BUT I NEED YOU TO BE BETTER.
"I NEED TO KNOW THAT YOU'LL TRY TO FIND PEACE."
WHY?
JESUS...
WONDER--

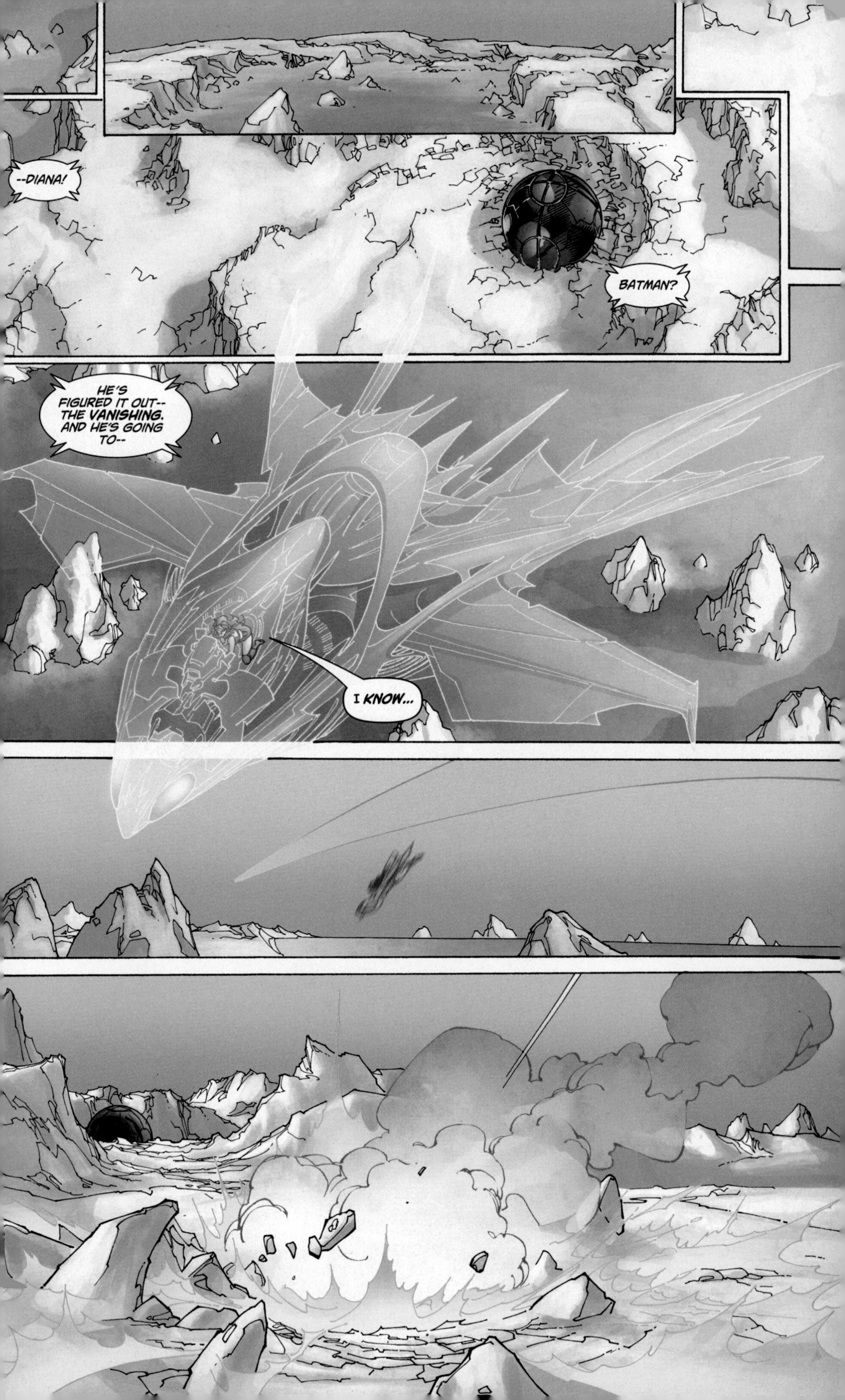
--DIANA!
BATMAN?
HE'S FIGURED IT OUT-- THE VANISHING. AND HE'S GOING TO--
I KNOW...

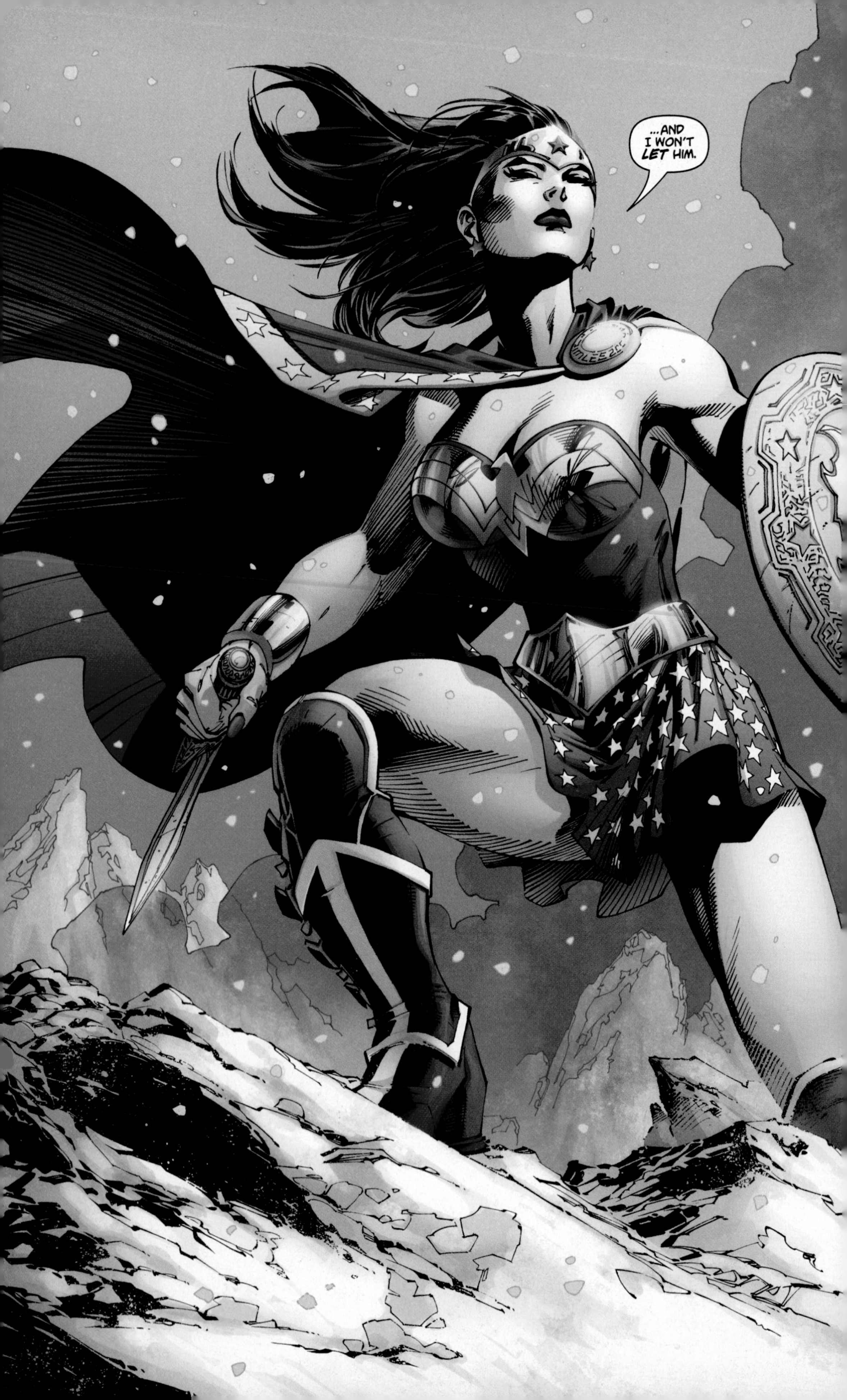
...AND I WON'T LET HIM.

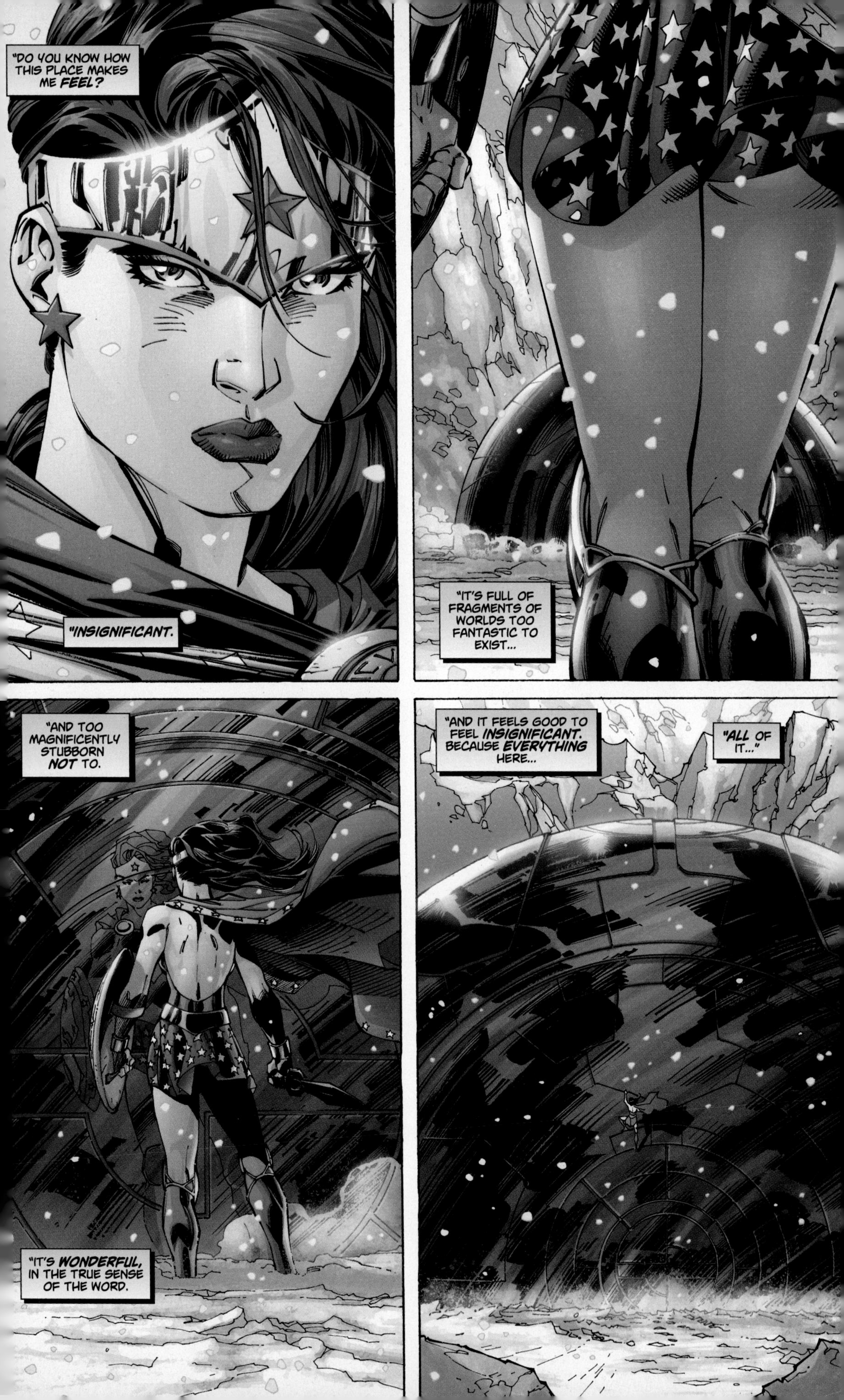
"DO YOU KNOW HOW THIS PLACE MAKES ME FEEL?
"INSIGNIFICANT.
"IT'S FULL OF FRAGMENTS OF WORLDS TOO FANTASTIC TO EXIST...
"AND TOO MAGNIFICENTLY STUBBORN NOT TO.
"IT'S WONDERFUL, IN THE TRUE SENSE OF THE WORD.
"AND IT FEELS GOOD TO FEEL INSIGNIFICANT. BECAUSE EVERYTHING HERE...
"ALL OF IT..."

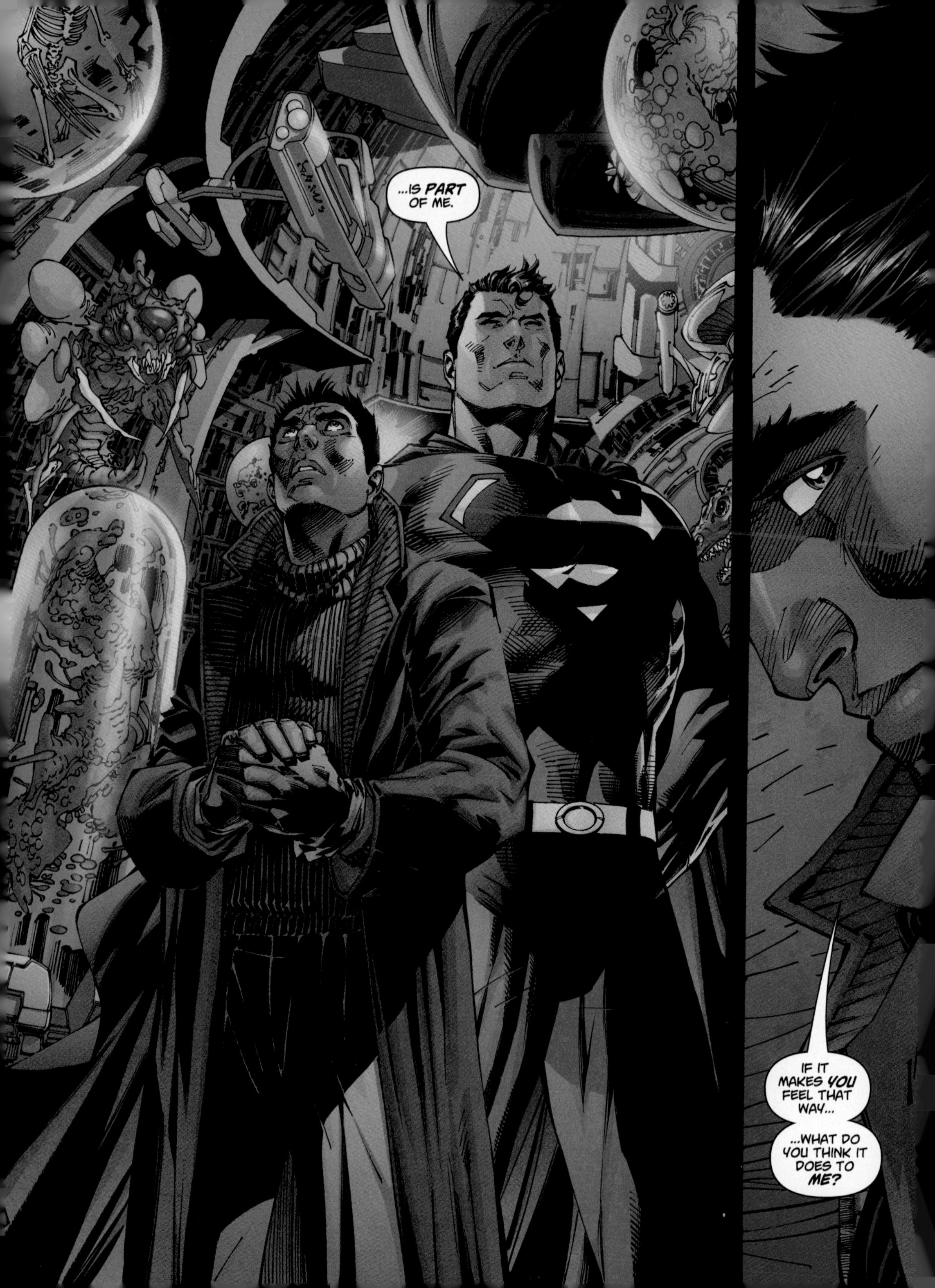
...IS PART OF ME.
IF IT MAKES YOU FEEL THAT WAY...
...WHAT DO YOU THINK IT DOES TO ME?

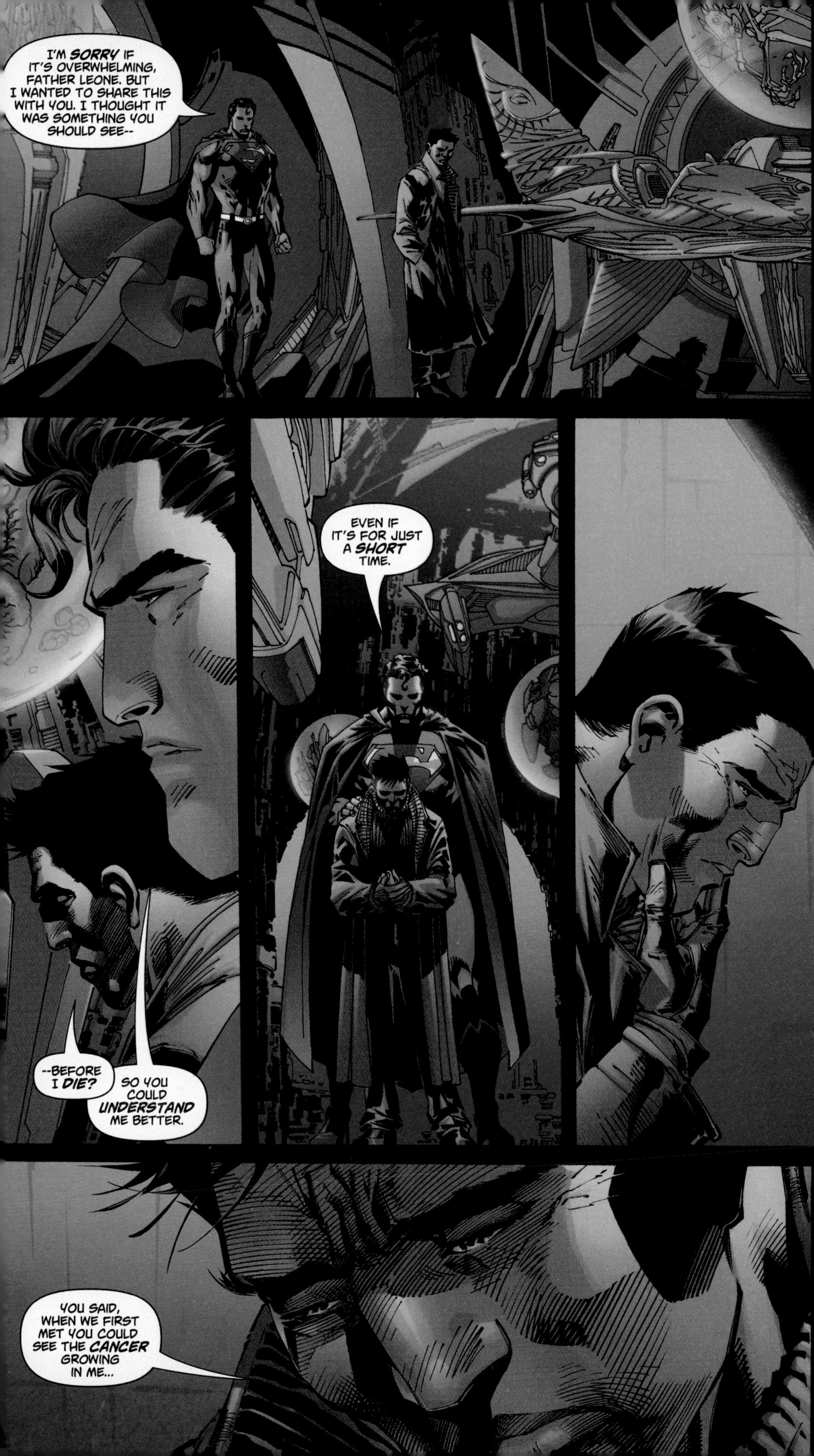
I'M SORRY IF IT'S OVERWHELMING, FATHER LEONE. BUT I WANTED TO SHARE THIS WITH YOU. I THOUGHT IT WAS SOMETHING YOU SHOULD SEE--
SO YOU COULD UNDERSTAND ME BETTER.
--BEFORE I DIE?
EVEN IF IT'S FOR JUST A SHORT TIME.
YOU SAID, WHEN WE FIRST MET YOU COULD SEE THE CANCER GROWING IN ME...

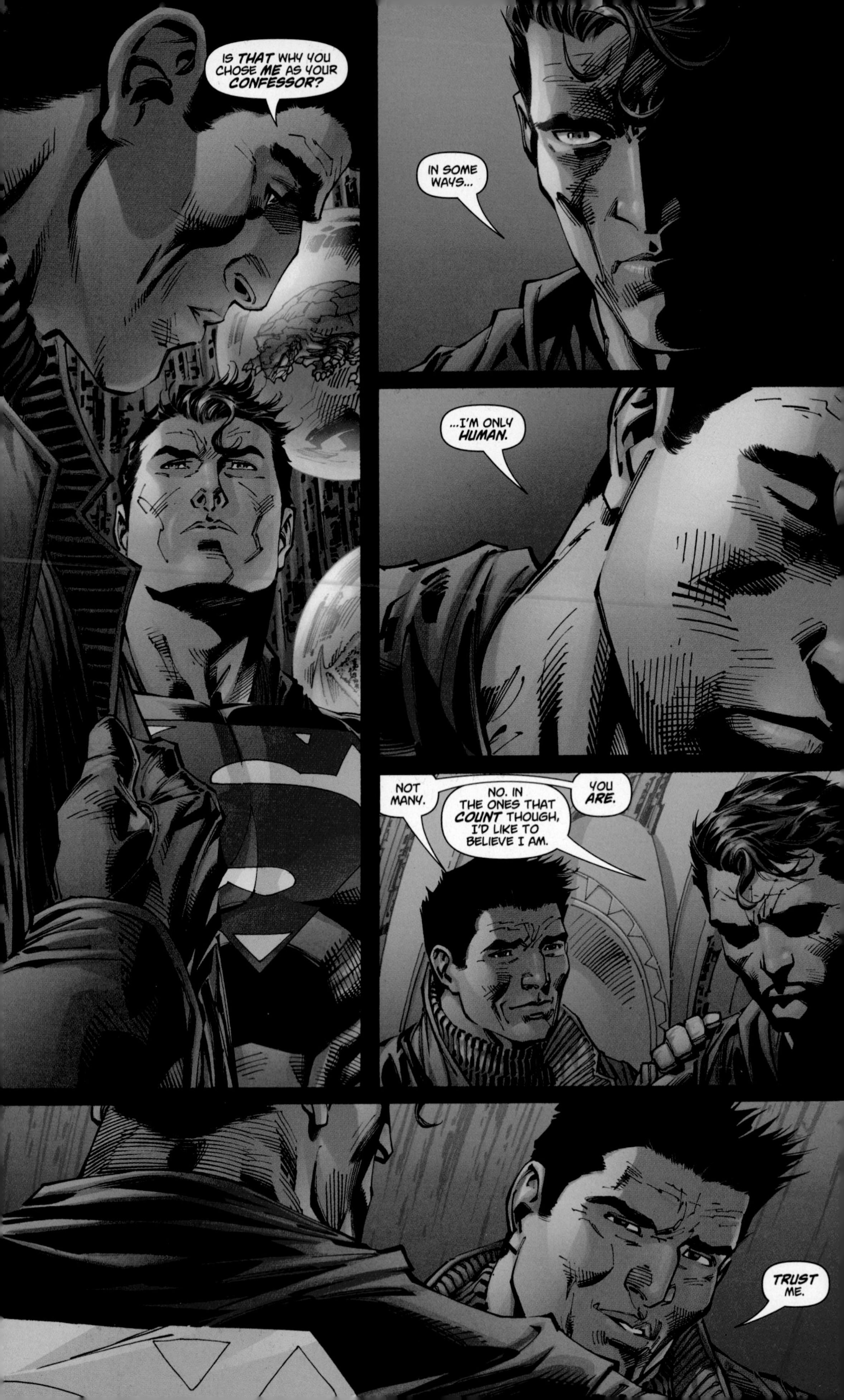

IS THAT WHY YOU CHOSE ME AS YOUR CONFESSOR?
IN SOME WAYS...
...I'M ONLY HUMAN.
NOT MANY.
NO. IN THE ONES THAT COUNT THOUGH, I'D LIKE TO BELIEVE I AM.
YOU ARE.
TRUST ME.

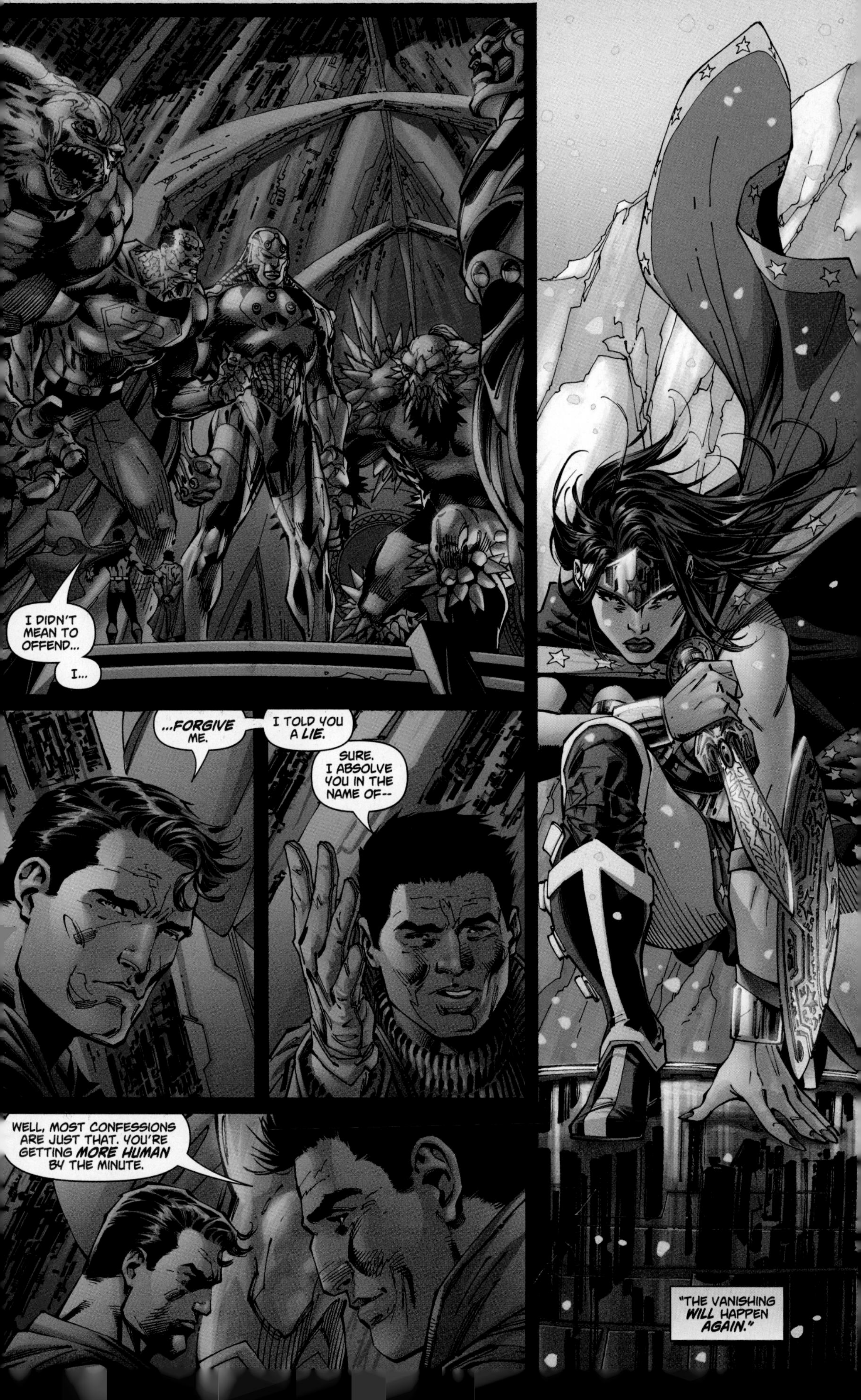

I DIDN'T MEAN TO OFFEND...
I...
...FORGIVE ME.
I TOLD YOU A LIE.
SURE. I ABSOLVE YOU IN THE NAME OF--
WELL, MOST CONFESSIONS ARE JUST THAT. YOU'RE GETTING MORE HUMAN BY THE MINUTE.
"THE VANISHING WILL HAPPEN AGAIN."

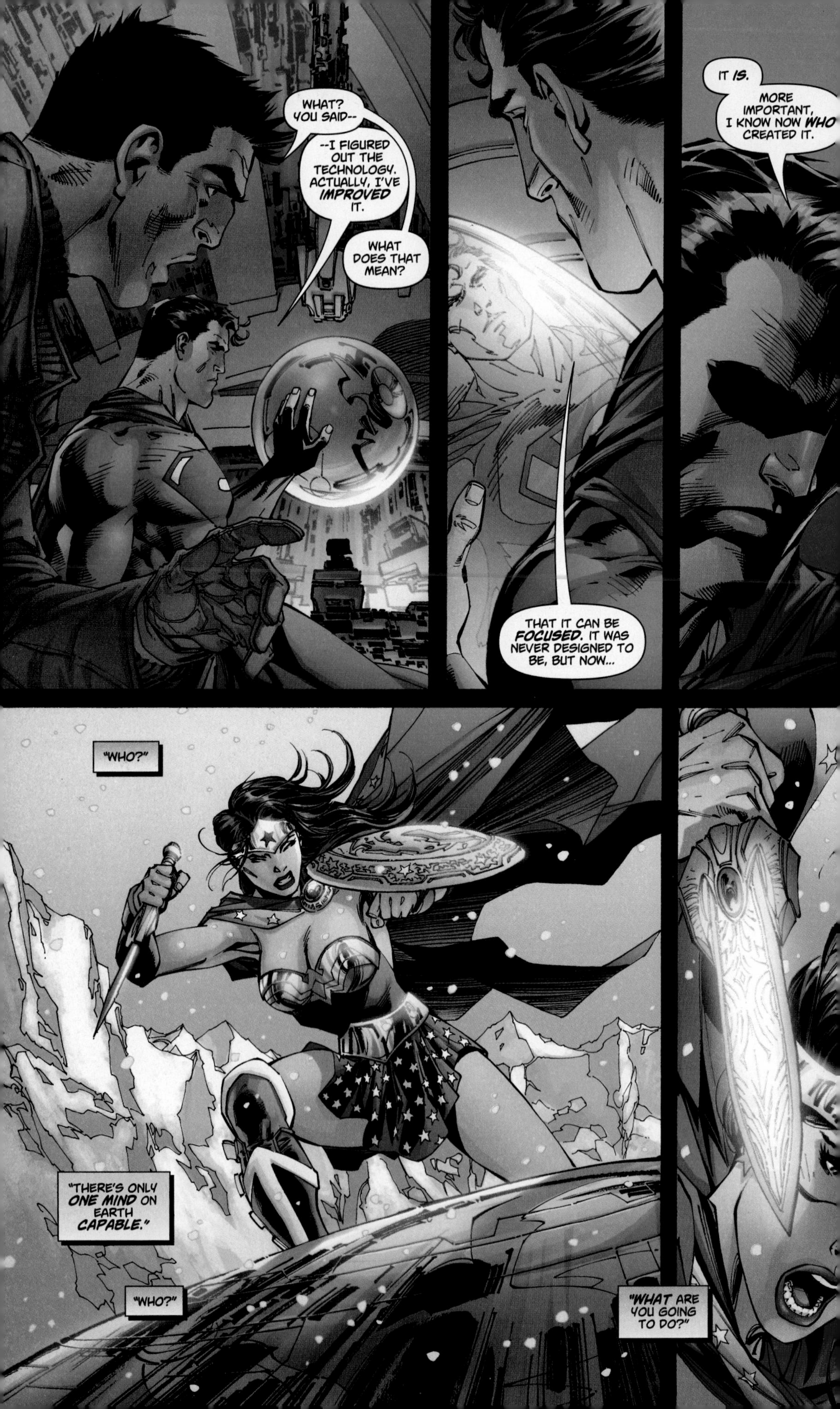

WHAT? YOU SAID--
--I FIGURED OUT THE TECHNOLOGY. ACTUALLY, I'VE IMPROVED IT.
WHAT DOES THAT MEAN?
THAT IT CAN BE FOCUSED. IT WAS NEVER DESIGNED TO BE, BUT NOW...
IT IS.
MORE IMPORTANT, I KNOW NOW WHO CREATED IT.
"WHO?"
"THERE'S ONLY ONE MIND ON EARTH CAPABLE."
"WHO?"
"WHAT ARE YOU GOING TO DO?"

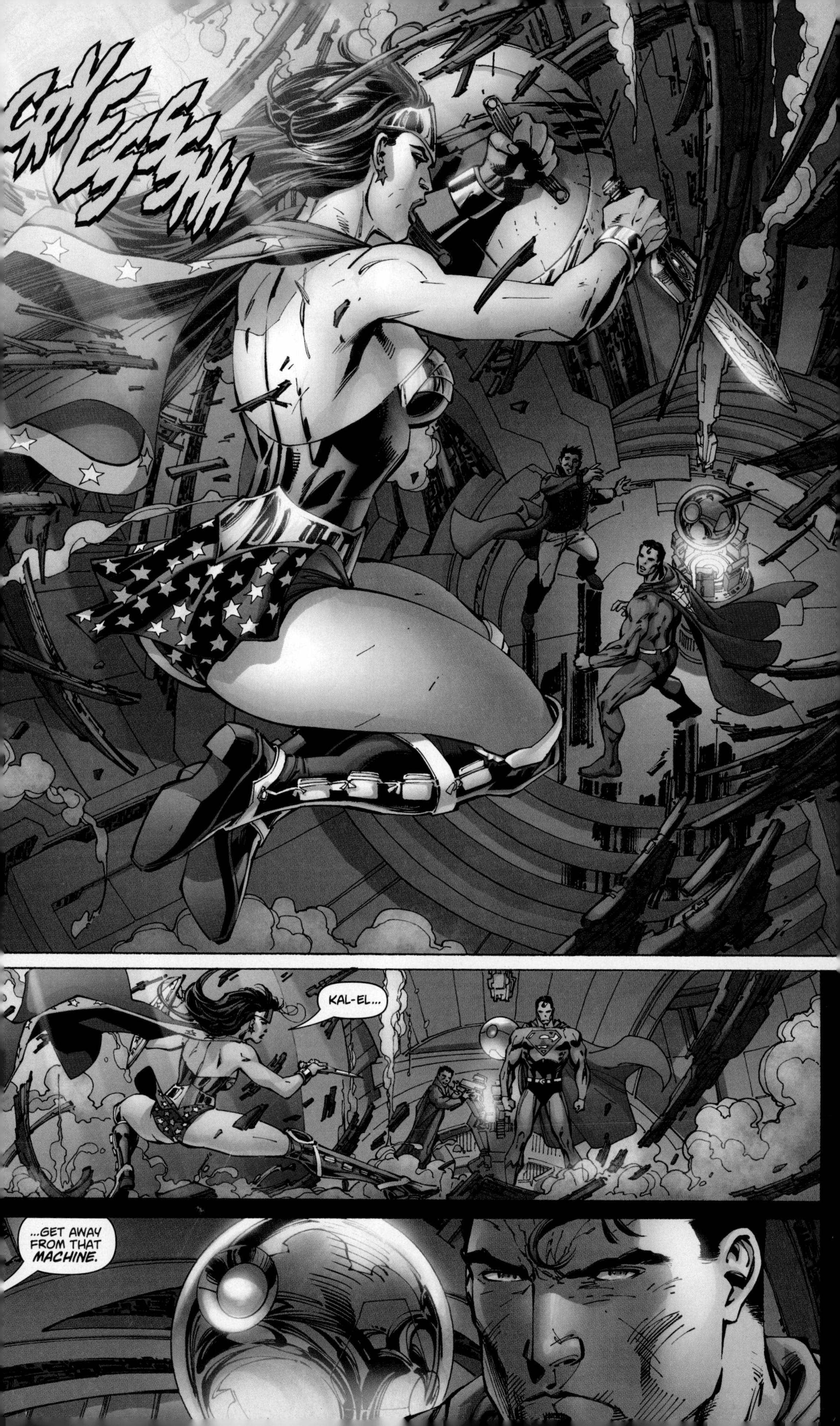
KAL-EL...
...GET AWAY FROM THAT *MACHINE*.

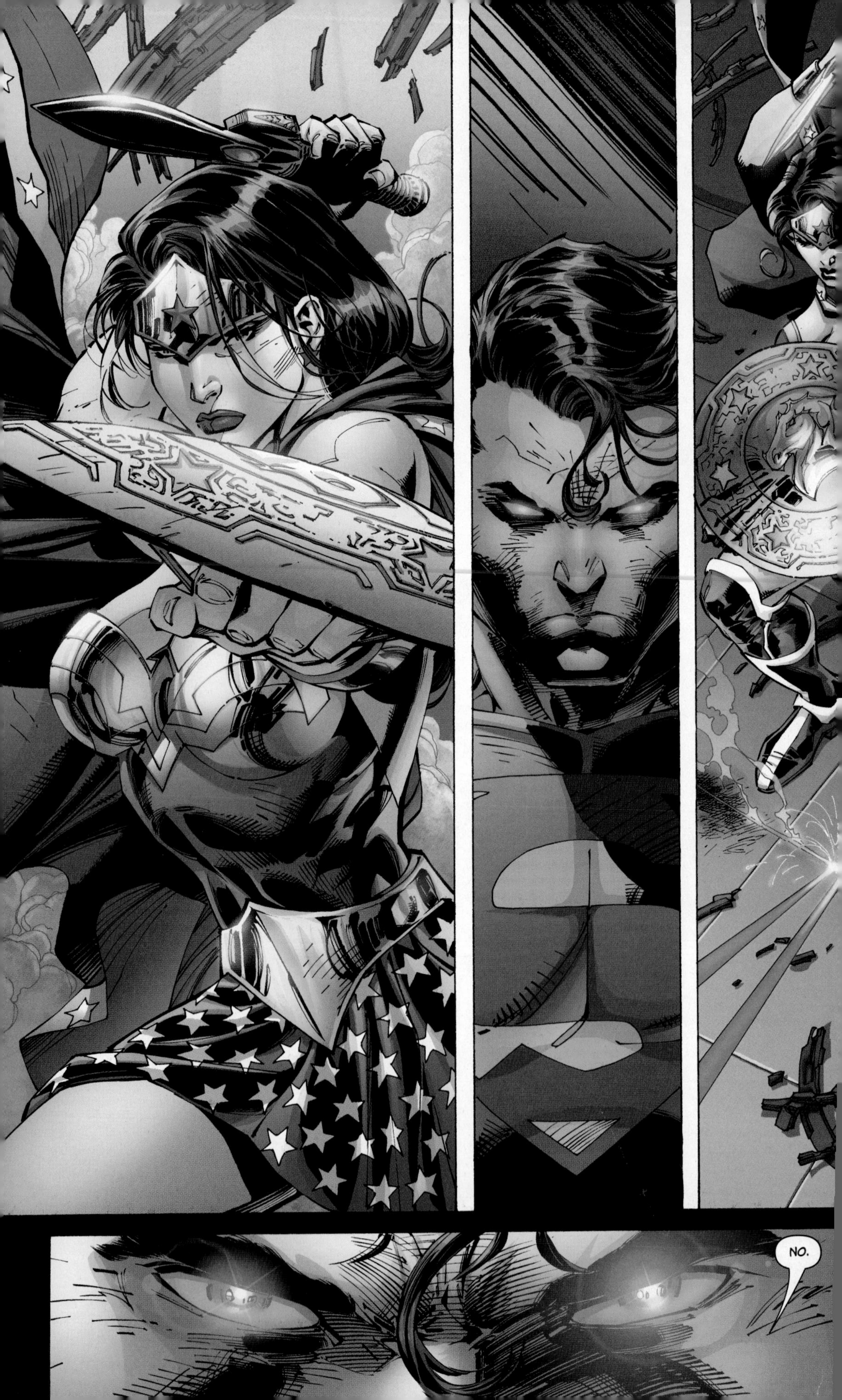
NO.

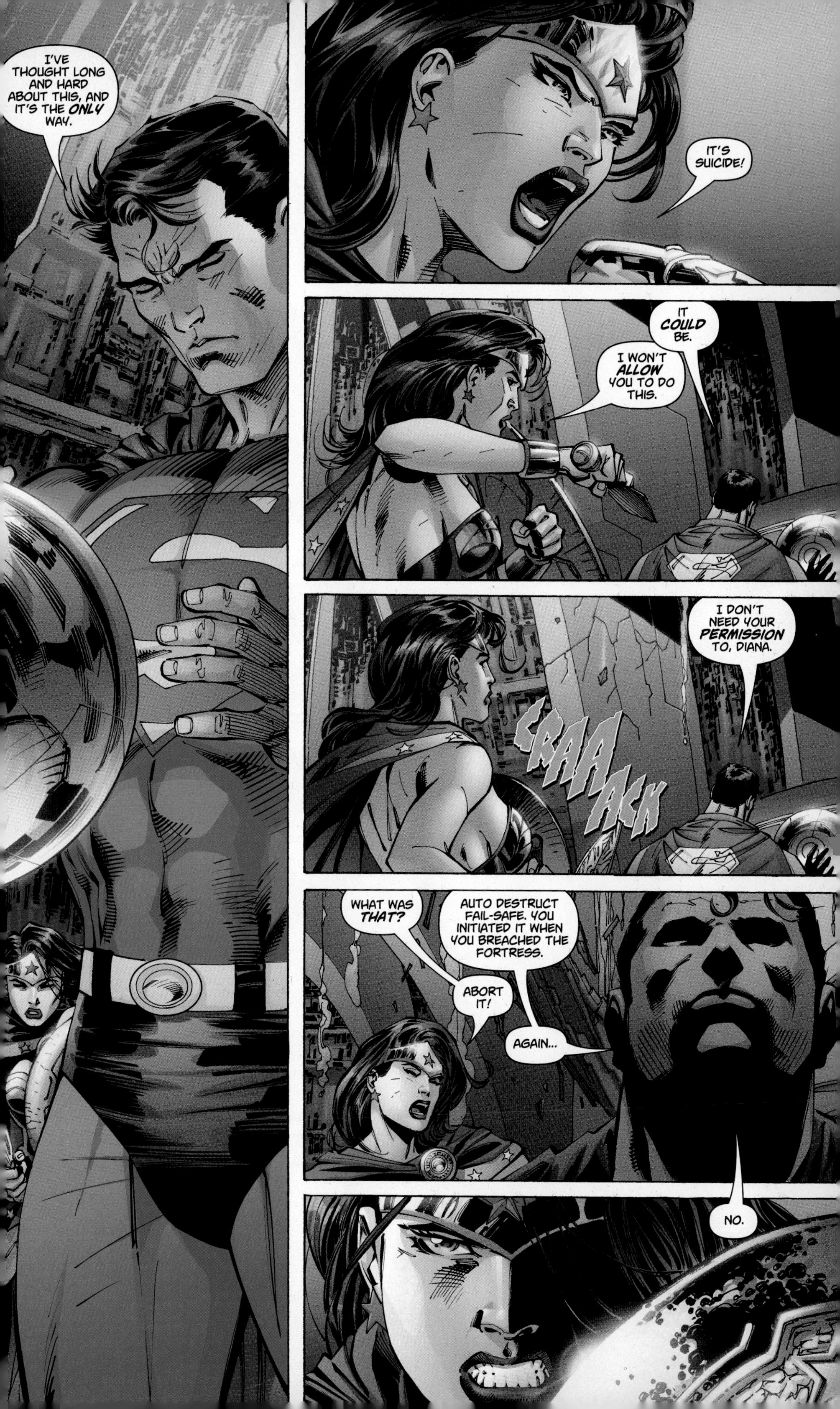
I'VE THOUGHT LONG AND HARD ABOUT THIS, AND IT'S THE ONLY WAY.
IT'S SUICIDE!
IT COULD BE.
I WON'T ALLOW YOU TO DO THIS.
I DON'T NEED YOUR PERMISSION TO, DIANA.
CRAAACK
WHAT WAS THAT?
AUTO DESTRUCT FAIL-SAFE. YOU INITIATED IT WHEN YOU BREACHED THE FORTRESS.
ABORT IT!
AGAIN...
NO.

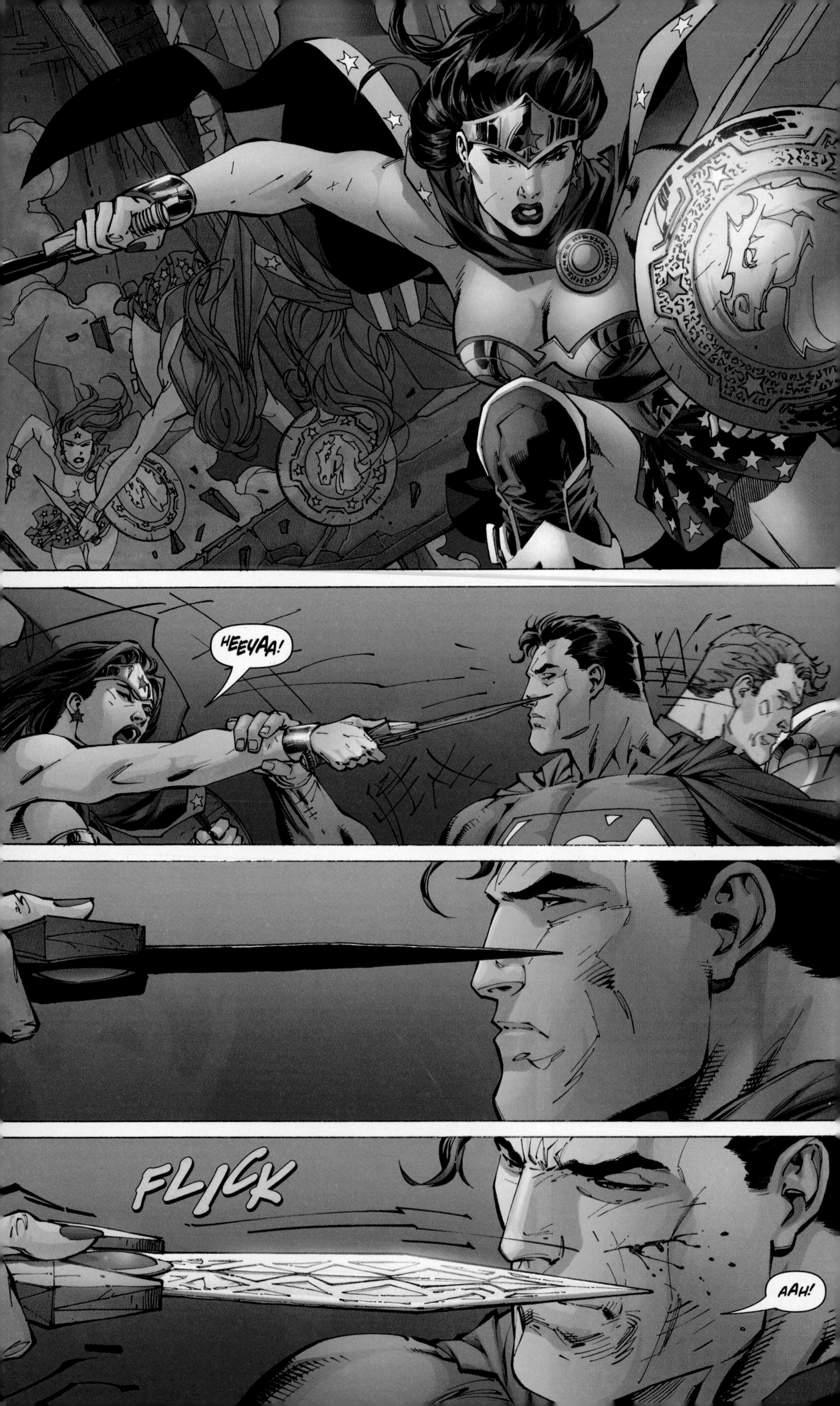
HEEYAA!
FLICK
AAH!

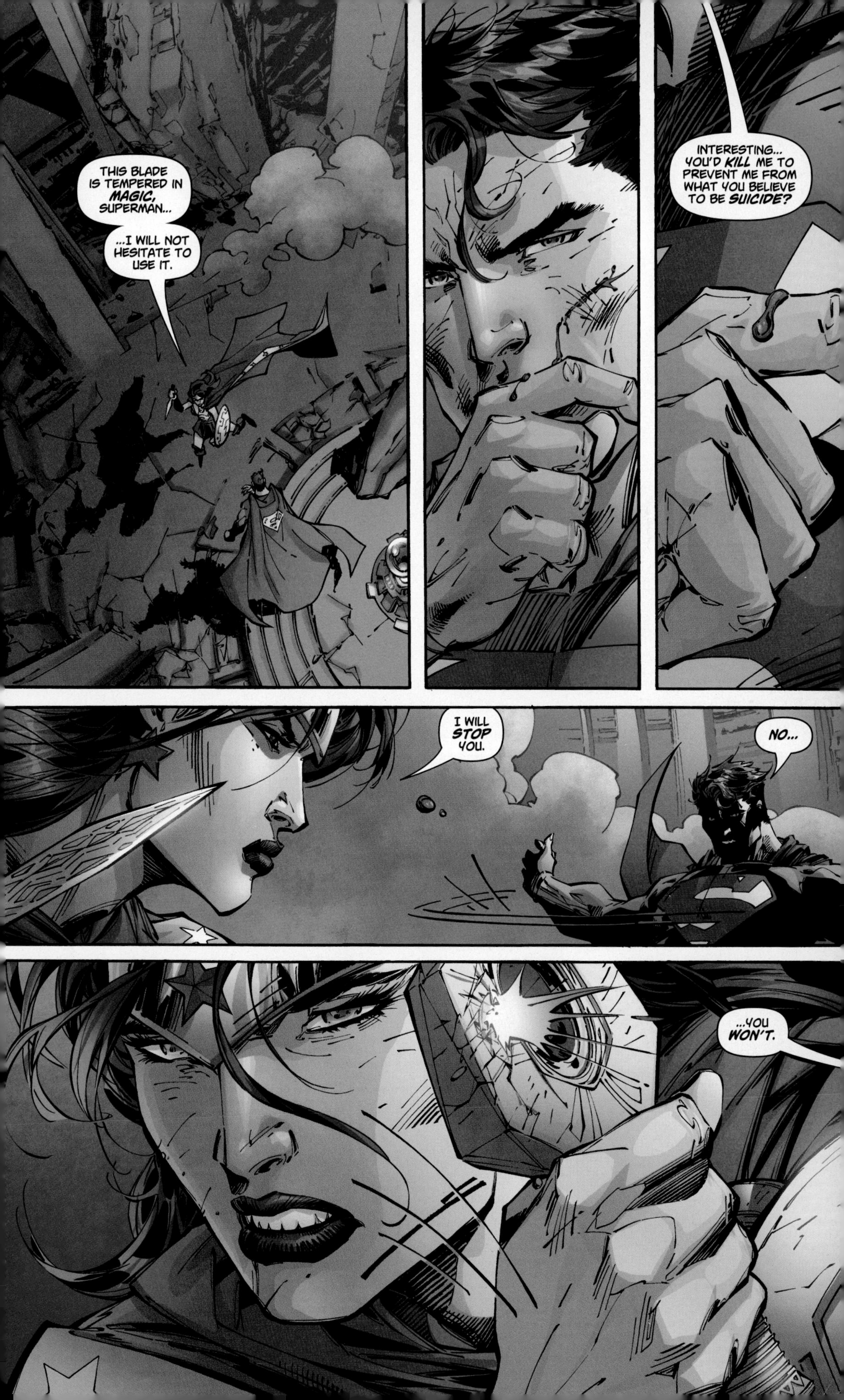
THIS BLADE IS TEMPERED IN MAGIC, SUPERMAN...
...I WILL NOT HESITATE TO USE IT.
INTERESTING... YOU'D KILL ME TO PREVENT ME FROM WHAT YOU BELIEVE TO BE SUICIDE?
I WILL STOP YOU.
NO...
...YOU WON'T.

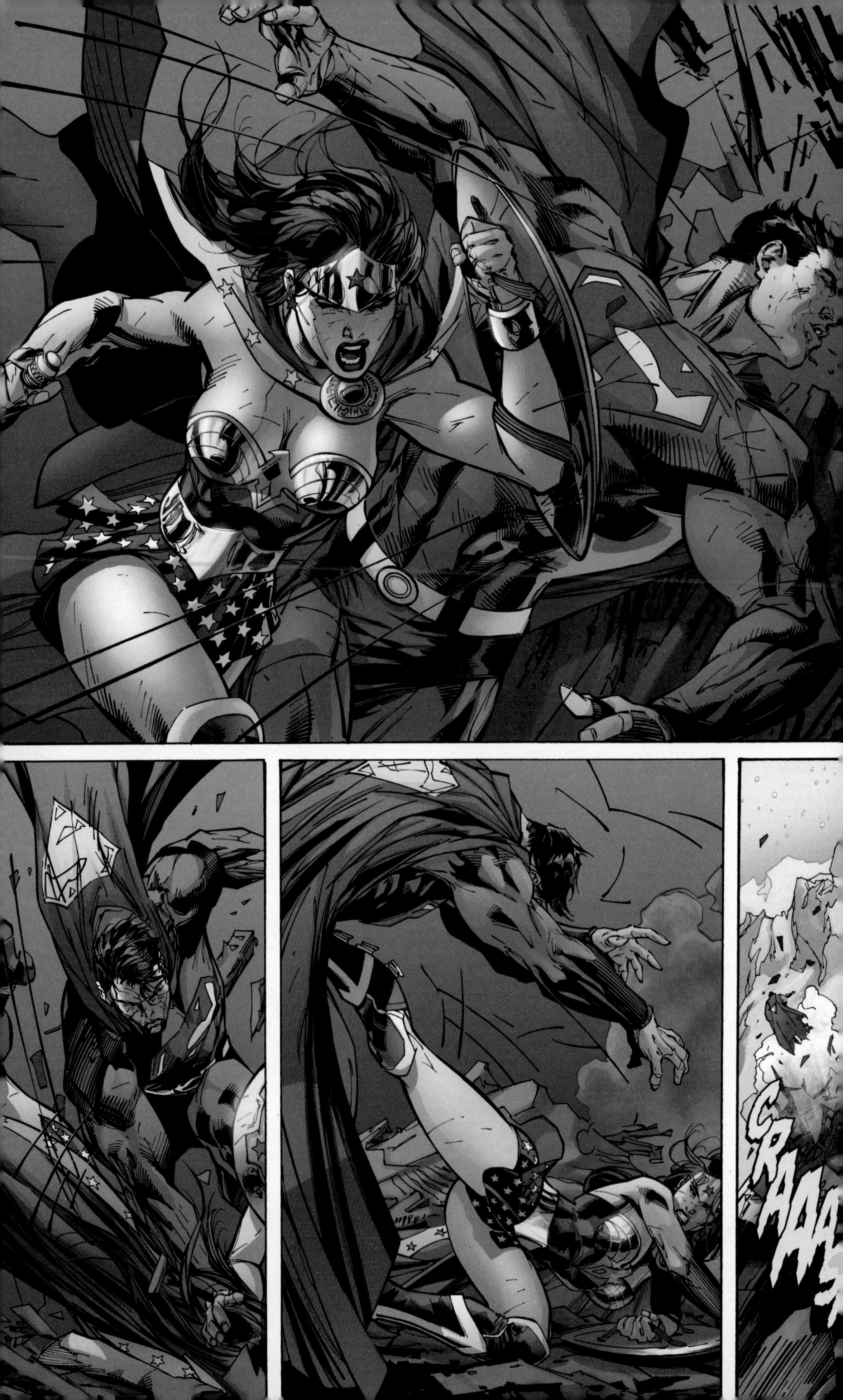
CRAAA

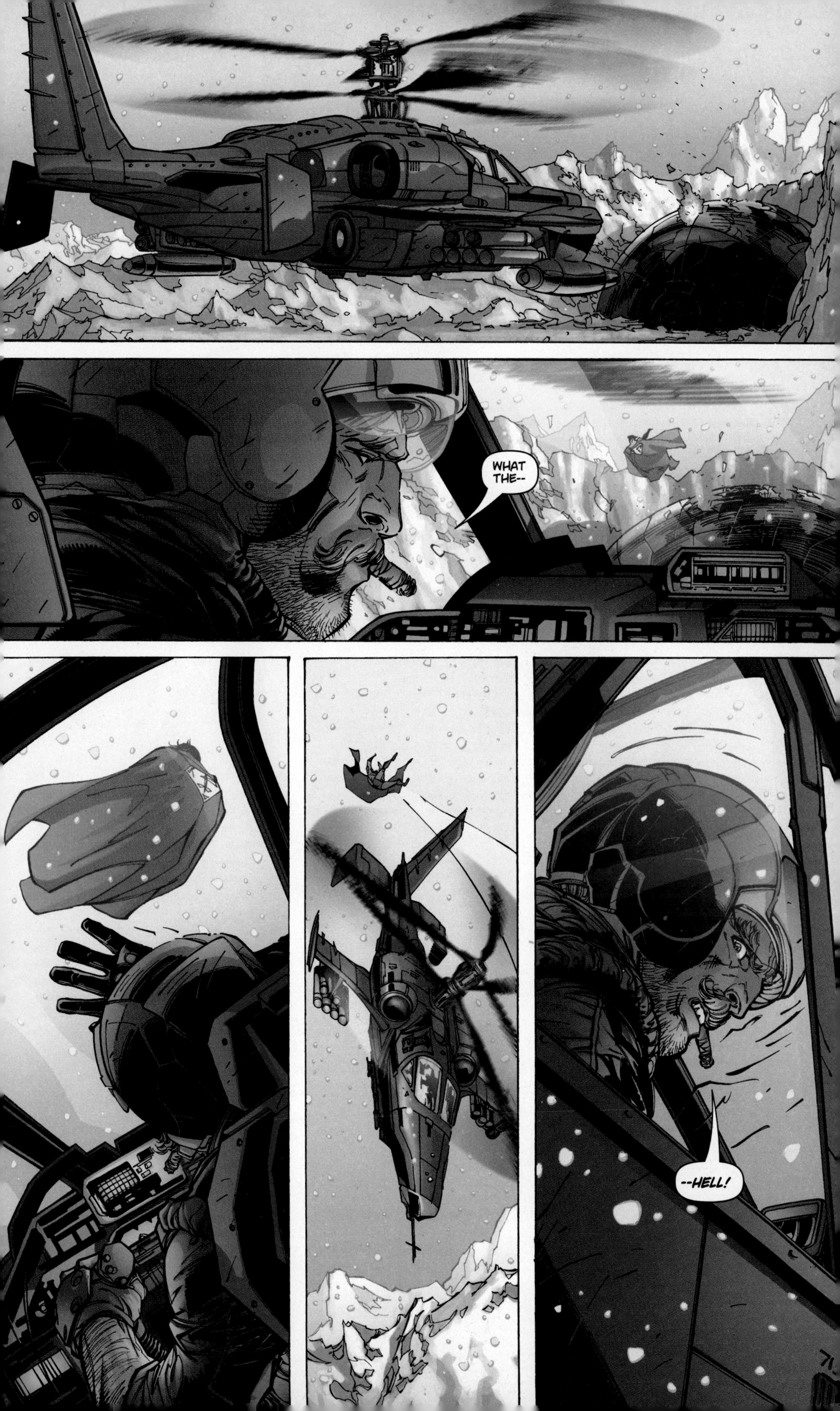
WHAT THE--
--HELL!

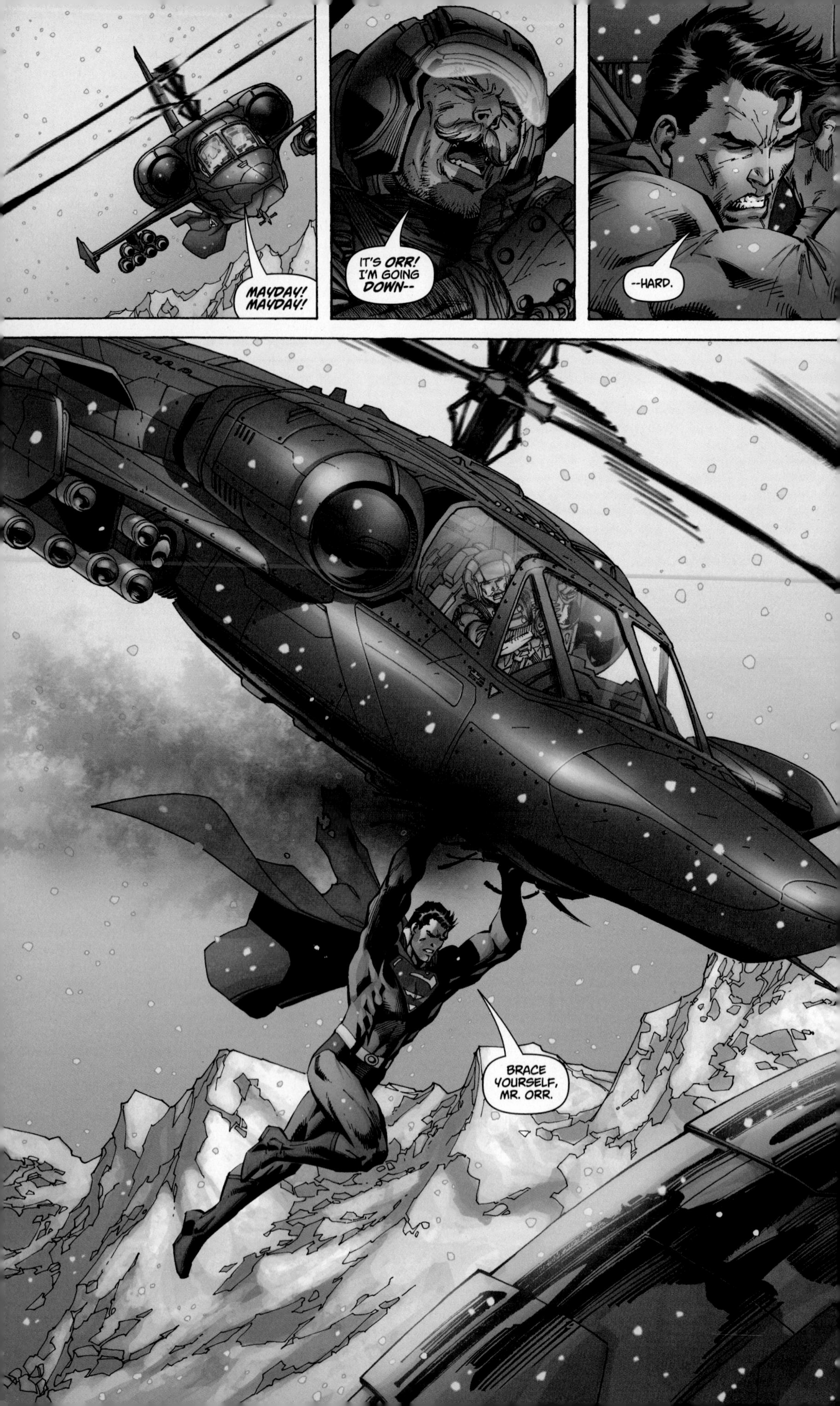
MAYDAY! MAYDAY!
IT'S ORR! I'M GOING DOWN--
--HARD.
BRACE YOURSELF, MR. ORR.

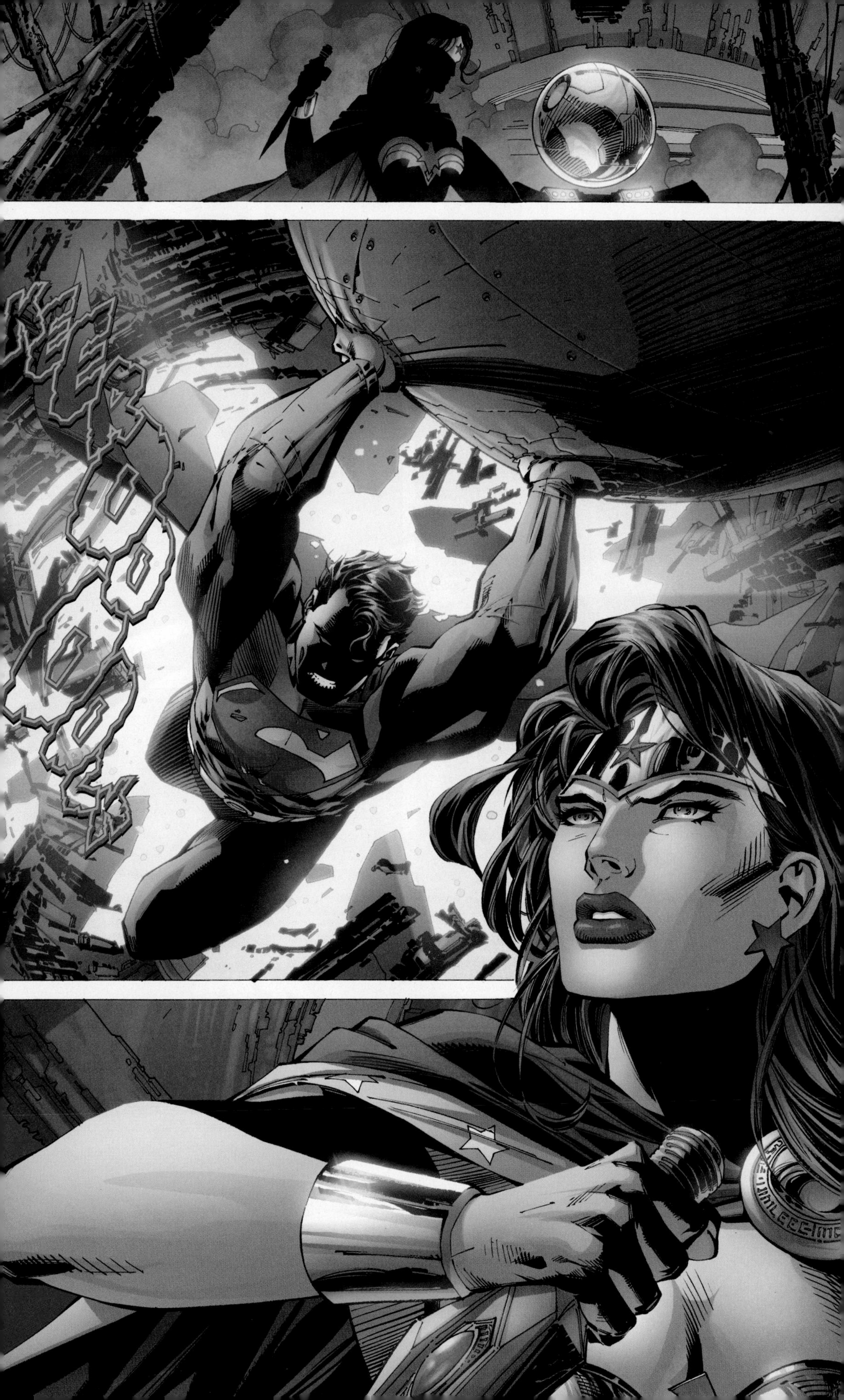

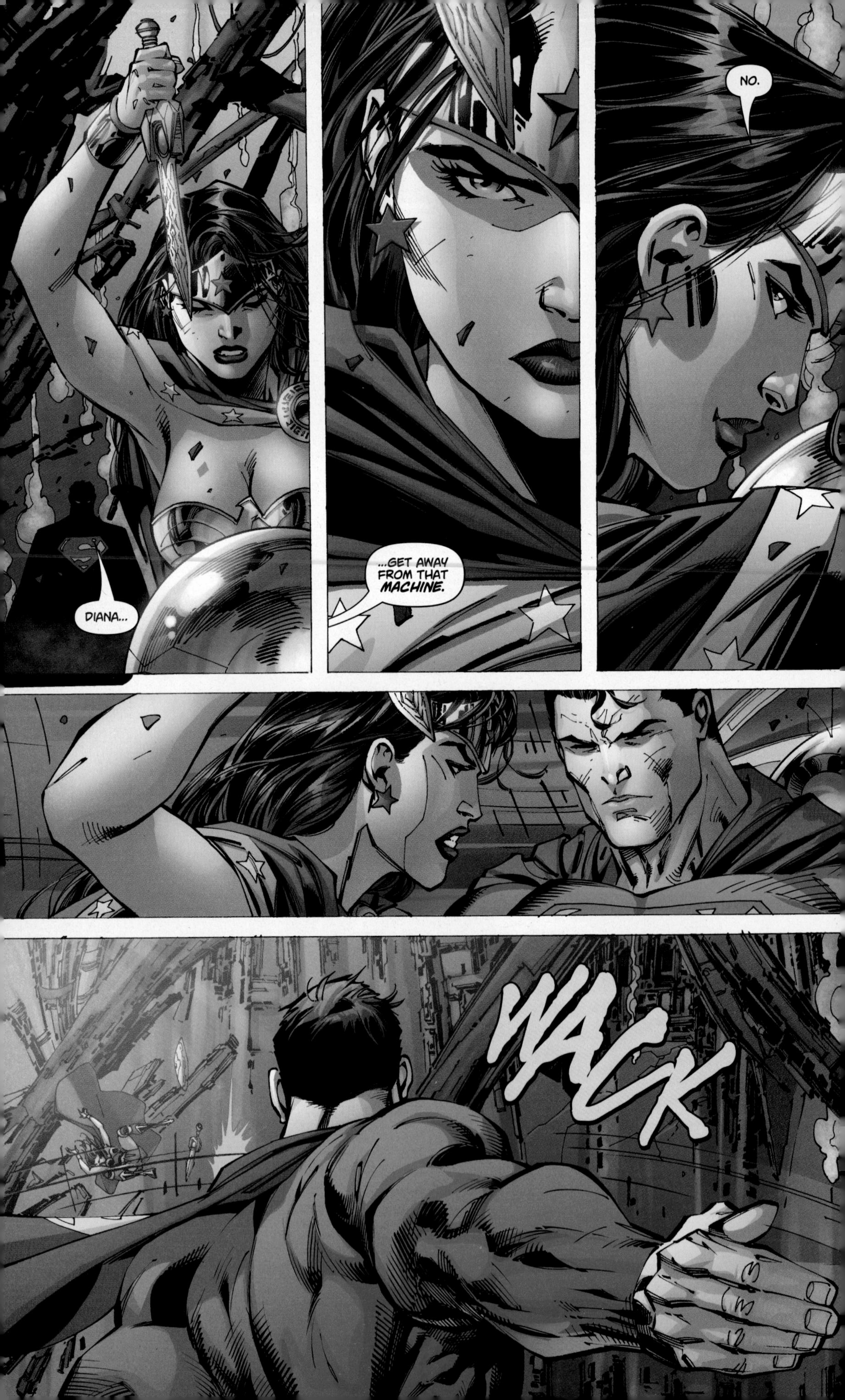
DIANA...
...GET AWAY FROM THAT MACHINE.
NO.
WACK

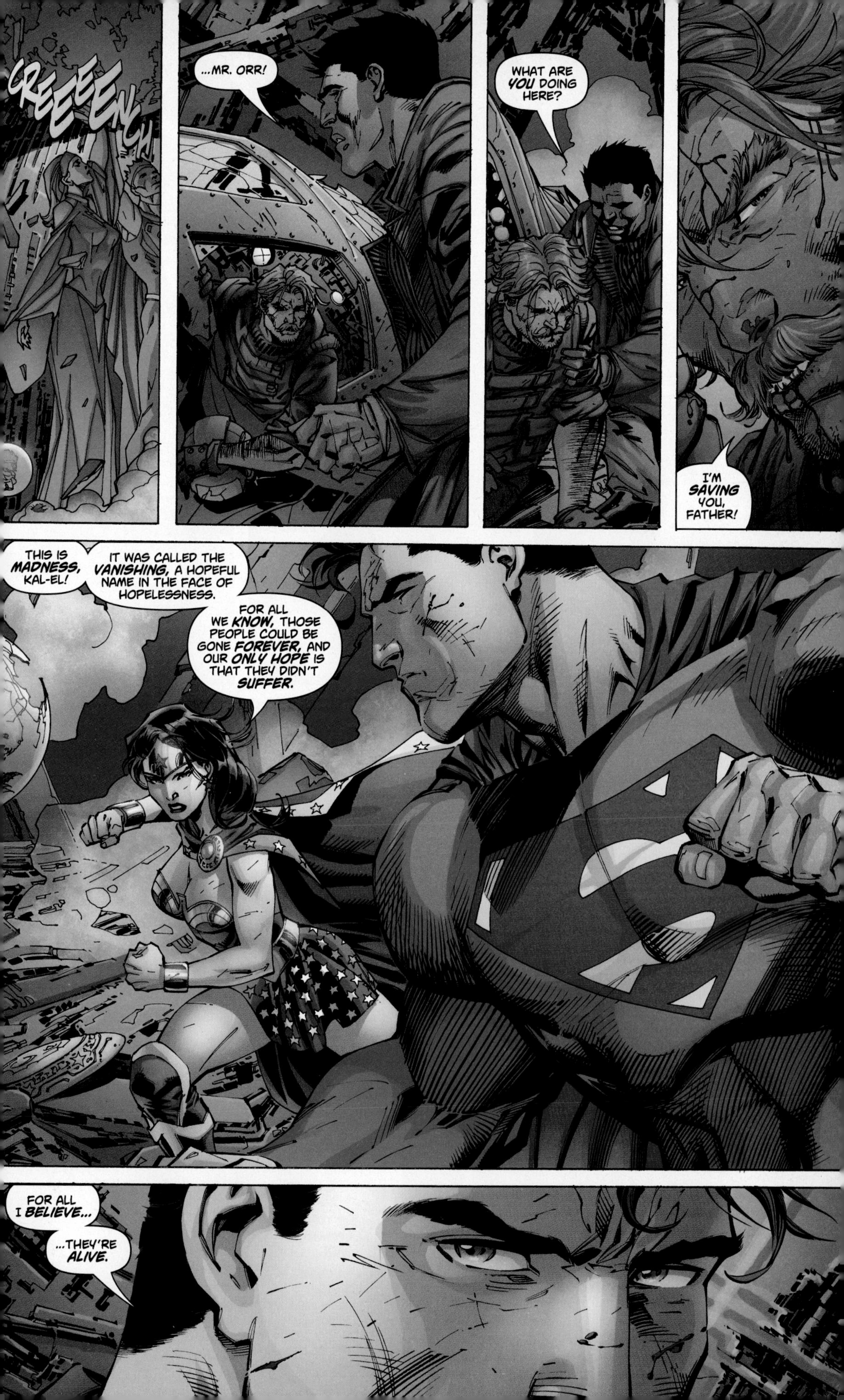

CREEEENCH
...MR. ORR!
WHAT ARE YOU DOING HERE?
I'M SAVING YOU, FATHER!
THIS IS MADNESS, KAL-EL!
IT WAS CALLED THE VANISHING, A HOPEFUL NAME IN THE FACE OF HOPELESSNESS.
FOR ALL WE KNOW, THOSE PEOPLE COULD BE GONE FOREVER, AND OUR ONLY HOPE IS THAT THEY DIDN'T SUFFER.
FOR ALL I BELIEVE...
...THEY'RE ALIVE.

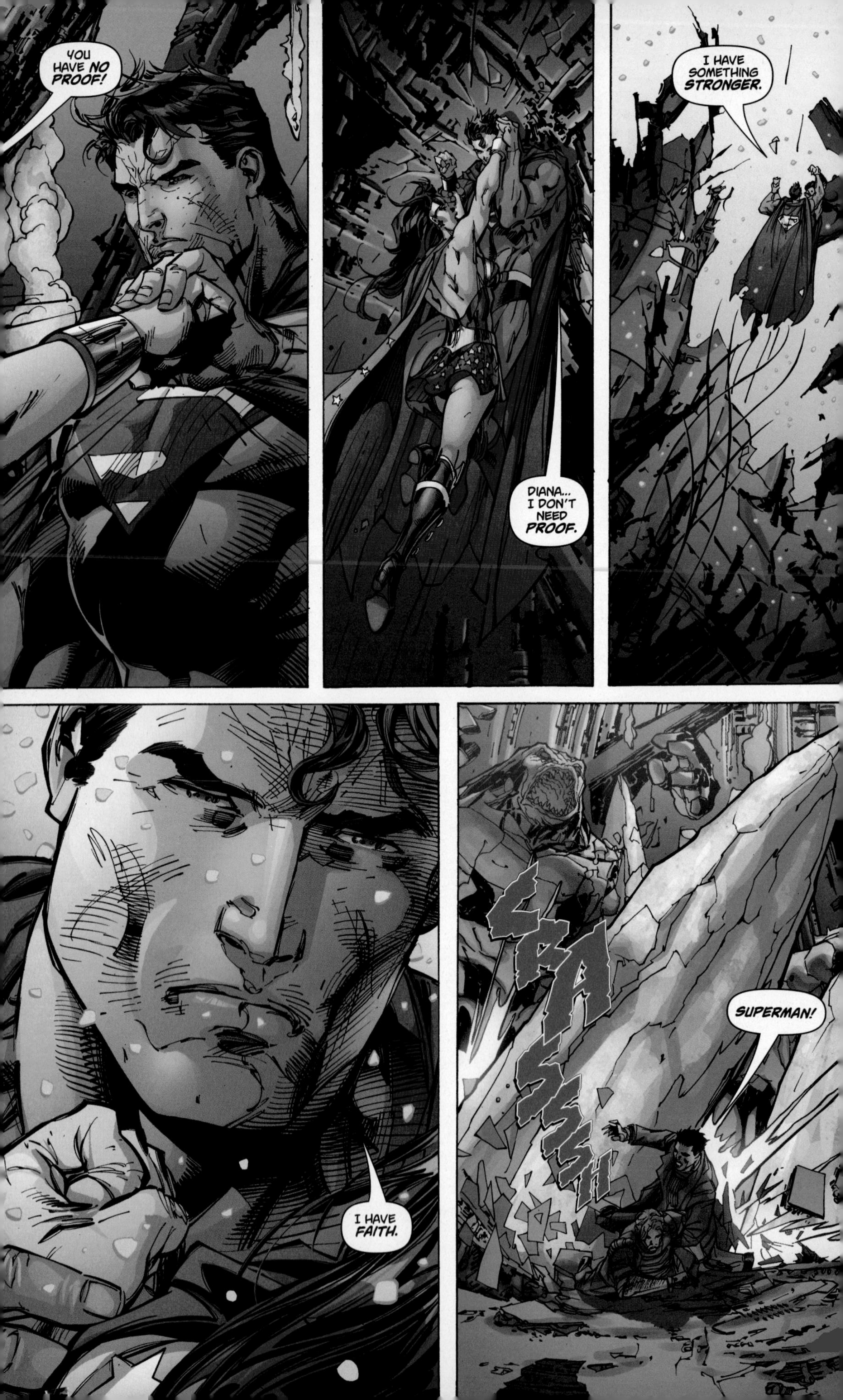
YOU HAVE NO PROOF!
DIANA... I DON'T NEED PROOF.
I HAVE SOMETHING STRONGER.
I HAVE FAITH.
CRASSSH
SUPERMAN!

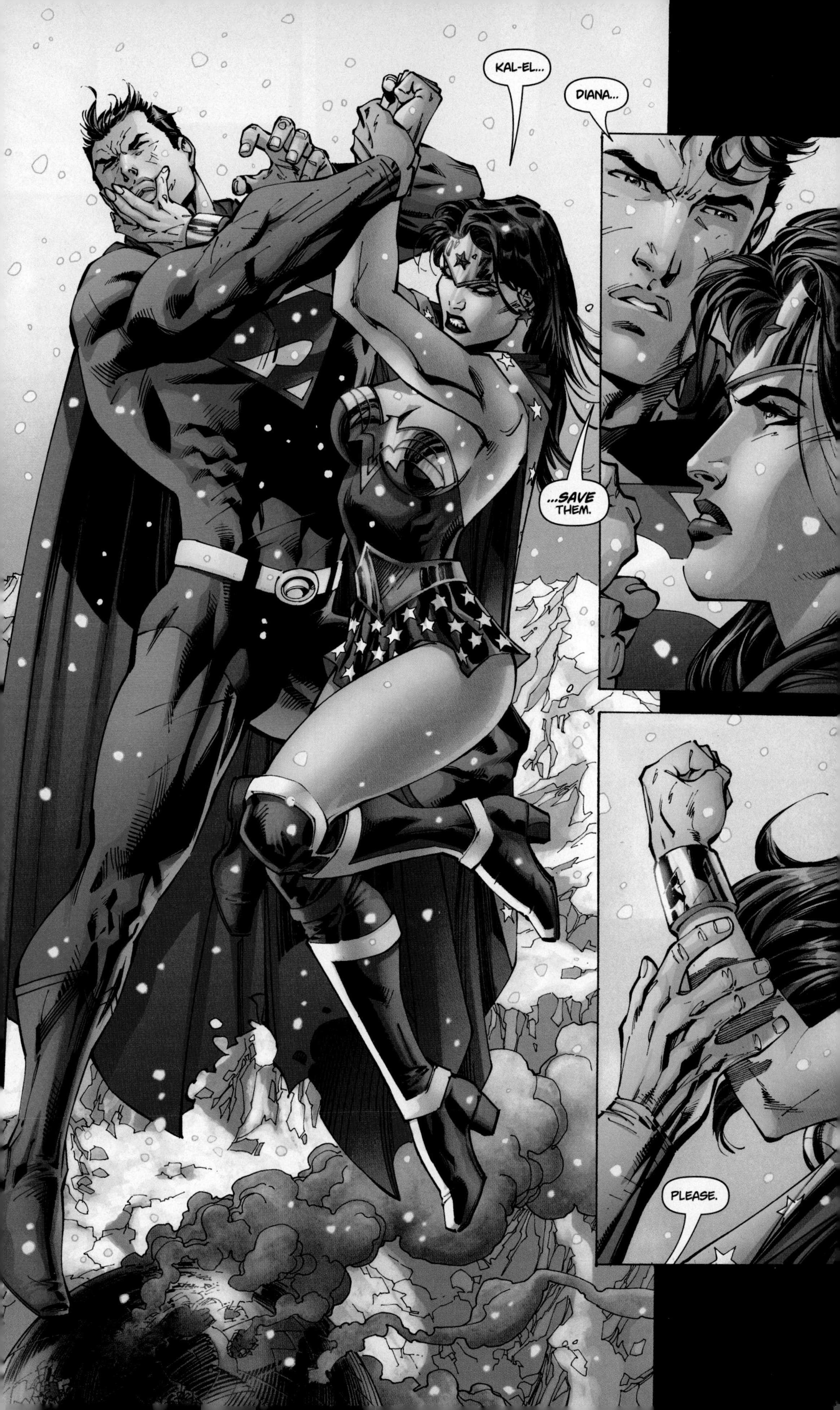

KAL-EL...
DIANA...
...SAVE THEM.
PLEASE.

I WAS A BABY WHEN HE BUILT A ROCKET SHIP THAT SENT ME TO THIS WORLD WHEN HIS WAS DOOMED TO BE *DESTROYED.*

HE CHOSE TO *SAVE ME,* WHEN HE *COULDN'T SAVE* ANY OTHERS.

MY FATHER WAS THE GREATEST SCIENTIST ON THE PLANET KRYPTON.

AN *INTELLIGENT* MAN.

HE SAVED *ME.*

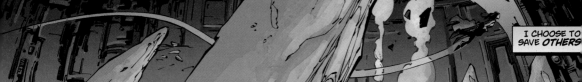

I CHOOSE TO SAVE *OTHERS.*

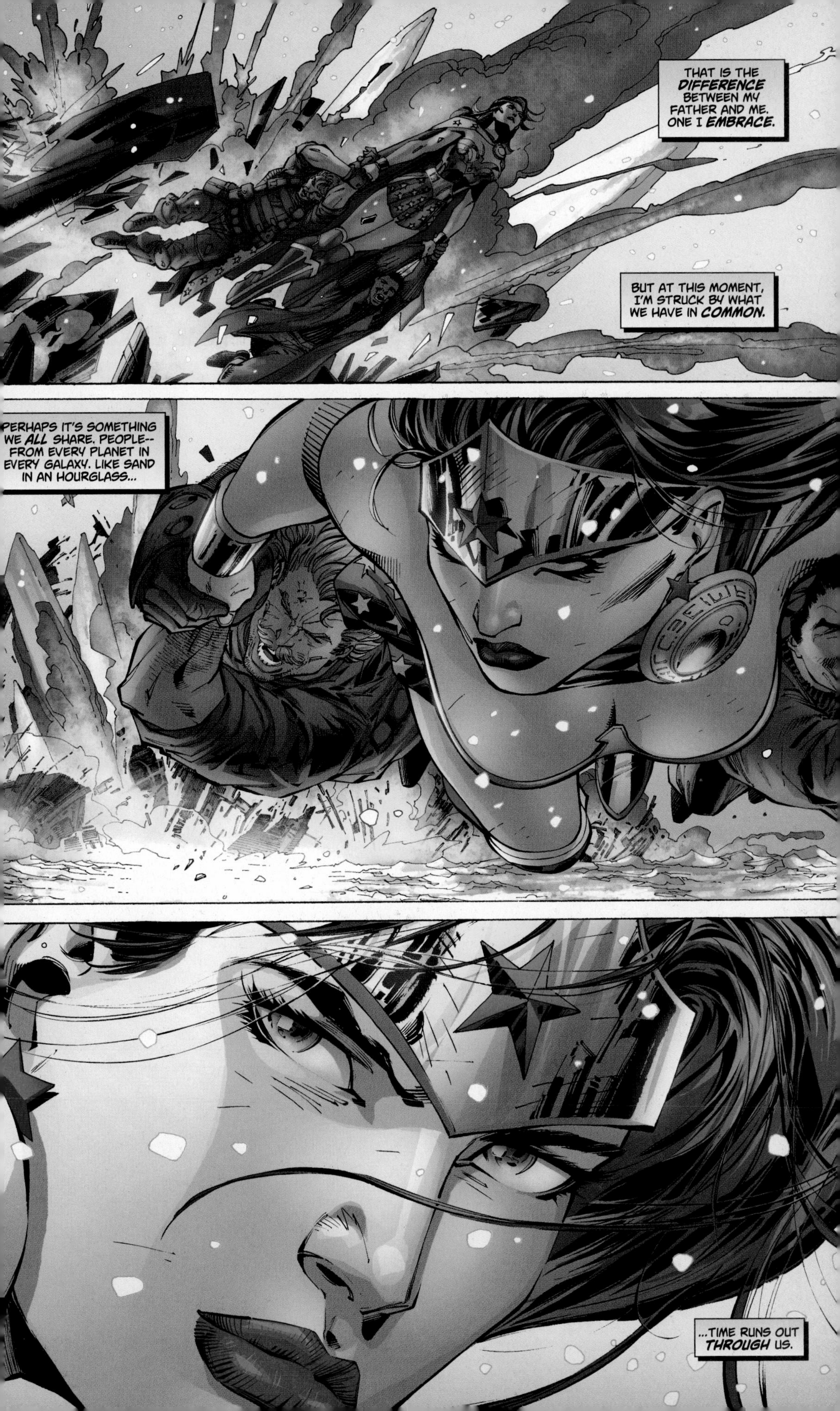
THAT IS THE DIFFERENCE BETWEEN MY FATHER AND ME. ONE I EMBRACE.
BUT AT THIS MOMENT, I'M STRUCK BY WHAT WE HAVE IN COMMON.
PERHAPS IT'S SOMETHING WE ALL SHARE. PEOPLE-- FROM EVERY PLANET IN EVERY GALAXY. LIKE SAND IN AN HOURGLASS...
...TIME RUNS OUT THROUGH US.

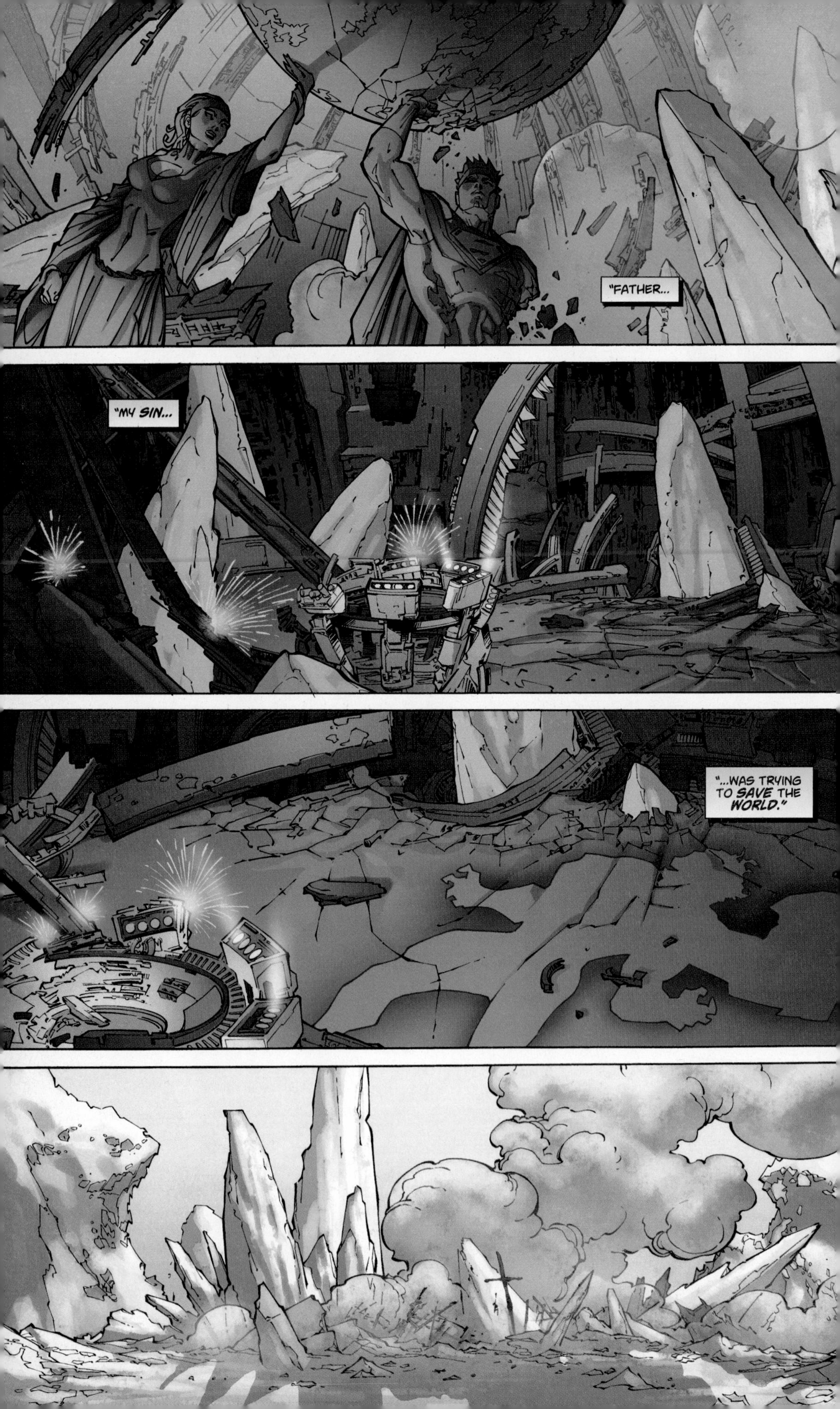
"FATHER...
"MY SIN...
"...WAS TRYING TO SAVE THE WORLD."

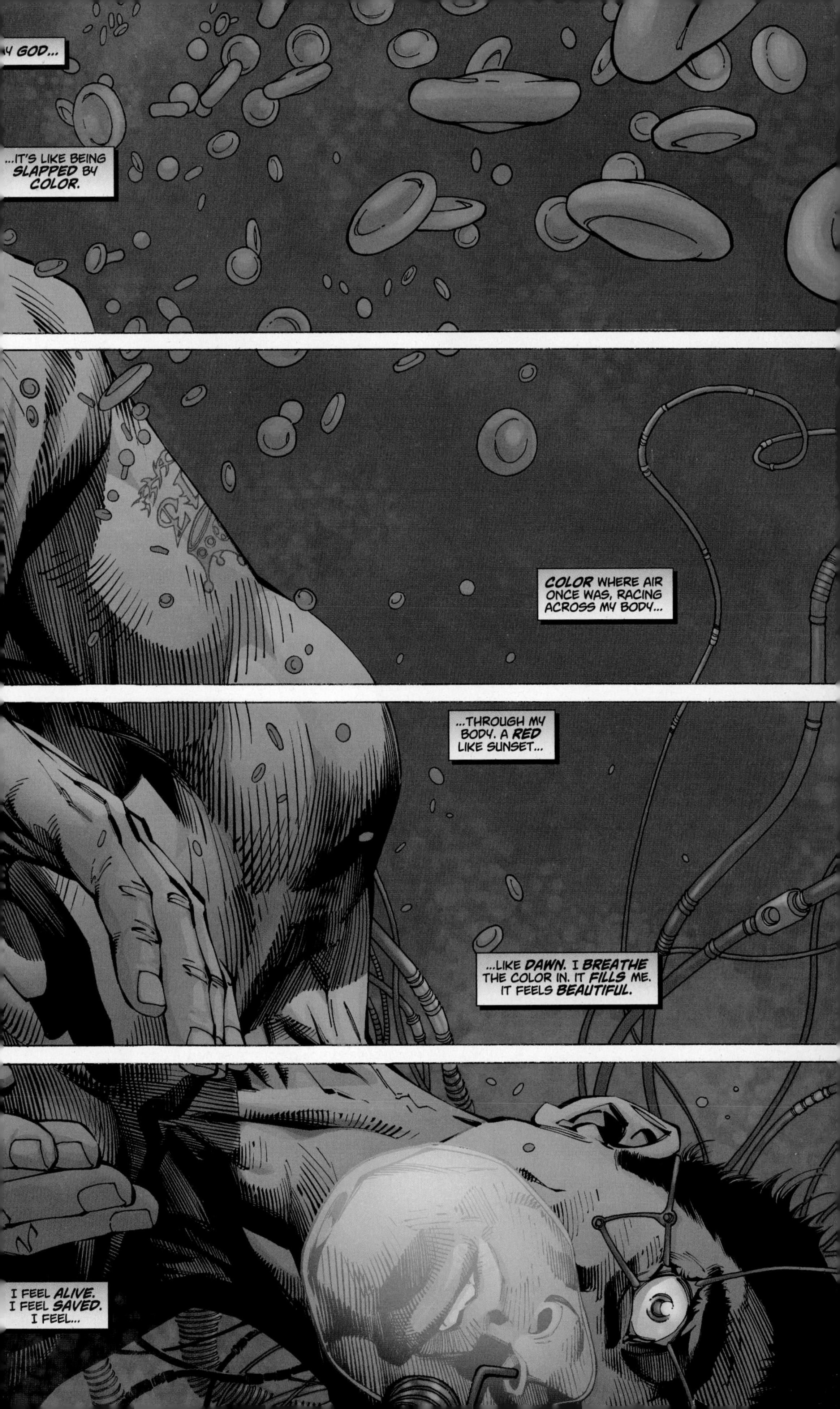
Y GOD...
...IT'S LIKE BEING SLAPPED BY COLOR.
COLOR WHERE AIR ONCE WAS, RACING ACROSS MY BODY...
...THROUGH MY BODY. A RED LIKE SUNSET...
...LIKE DAWN. I BREATHE THE COLOR IN. IT FILLS ME. IT FEELS BEAUTIFUL.
I FEEL ALIVE. I FEEL SAVED. I FEEL...

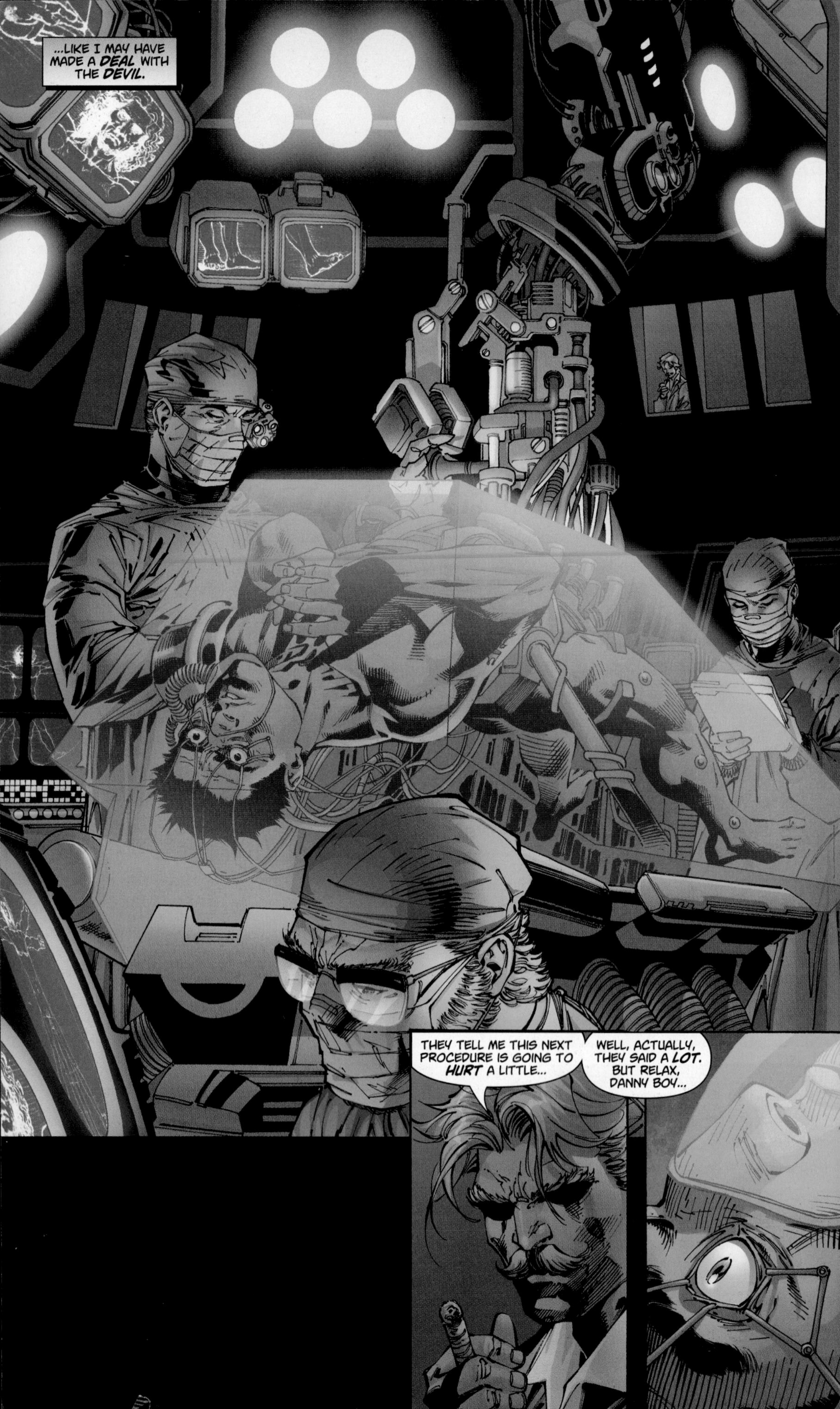
...LIKE I MAY HAVE MADE A DEAL WITH THE DEVIL.
THEY TELL ME THIS NEXT PROCEDURE IS GOING TO HURT A LITTLE...
WELL, ACTUALLY, THEY SAID A LOT. BUT RELAX, DANNY BOY...

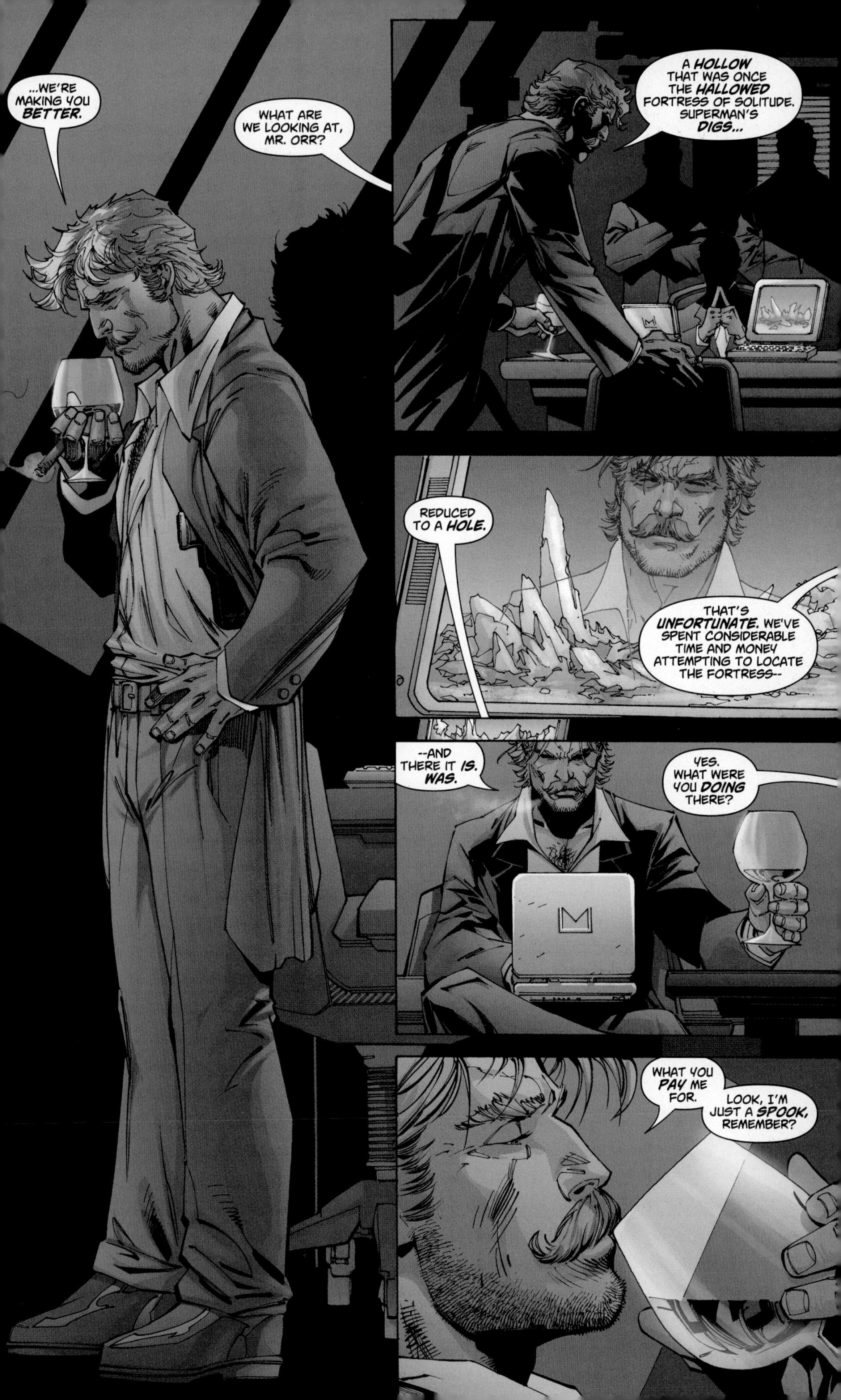
...WE'RE MAKING YOU BETTER.
WHAT ARE WE LOOKING AT, MR. ORR?
A HOLLOW THAT WAS ONCE THE HALLOWED FORTRESS OF SOLITUDE. SUPERMAN'S DIGS...
REDUCED TO A HOLE.
THAT'S UNFORTUNATE. WE'VE SPENT CONSIDERABLE TIME AND MONEY ATTEMPTING TO LOCATE THE FORTRESS--
--AND THERE IT IS. WAS.
YES. WHAT WERE YOU DOING THERE?
WHAT YOU PAY ME FOR.
LOOK, I'M JUST A SPOOK, REMEMBER?

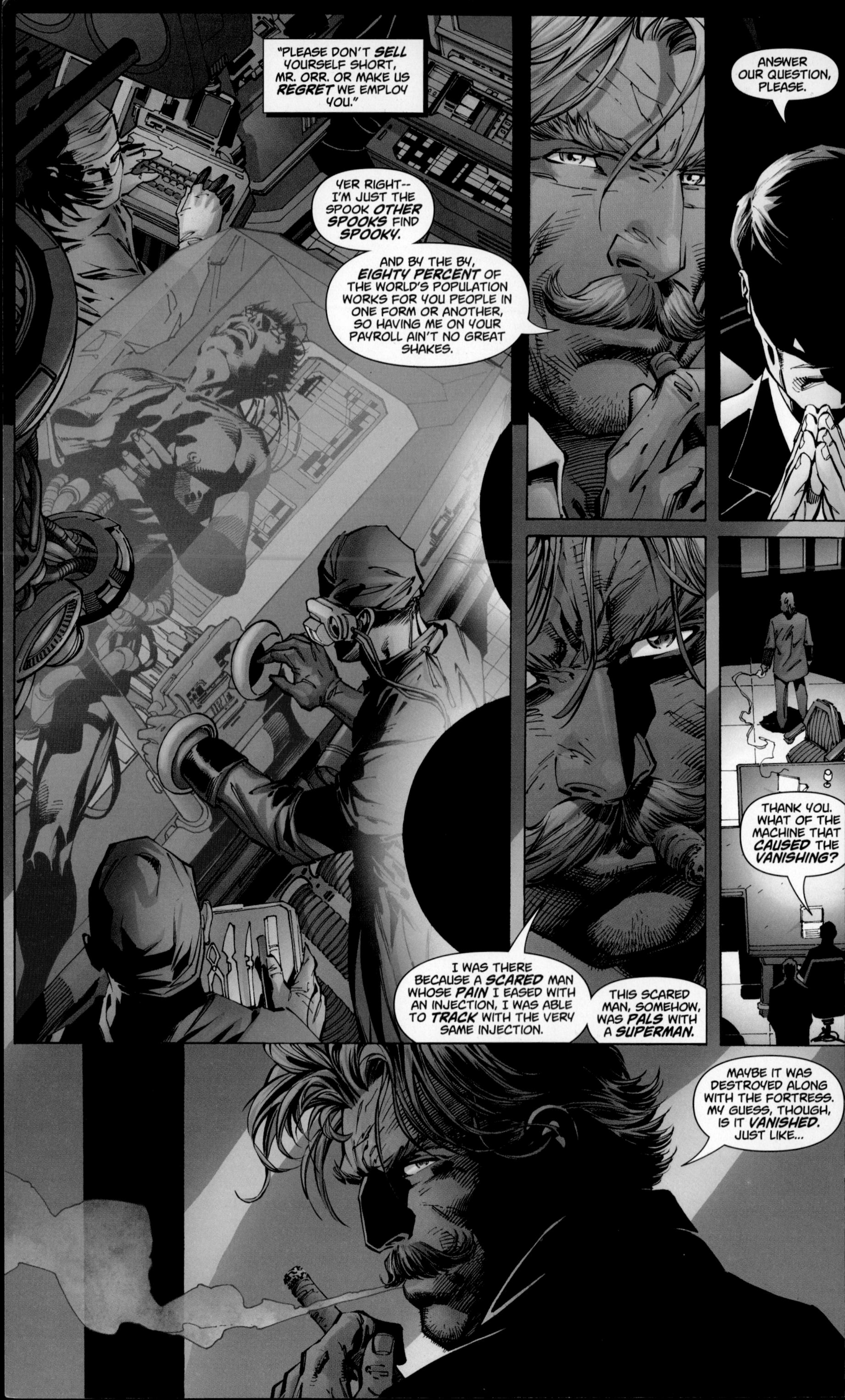
"PLEASE DON'T SELL YOURSELF SHORT, MR. ORR. OR MAKE US REGRET WE EMPLOY YOU."
YER RIGHT-- I'M JUST THE SPOOK OTHER SPOOKS FIND SPOOKY.
AND BY THE BY, EIGHTY PERCENT OF THE WORLD'S POPULATION WORKS FOR YOU PEOPLE IN ONE FORM OR ANOTHER, SO HAVING ME ON YOUR PAYROLL AIN'T NO GREAT SHAKES.
ANSWER OUR QUESTION, PLEASE.
I WAS THERE BECAUSE A SCARED MAN WHOSE PAIN I EASED WITH AN INJECTION, I WAS ABLE TO TRACK WITH THE VERY SAME INJECTION.
THIS SCARED MAN, SOMEHOW, WAS PALS WITH A SUPERMAN.
THANK YOU. WHAT OF THE MACHINE THAT CAUSED THE VANISHING?
MAYBE IT WAS DESTROYED ALONG WITH THE FORTRESS. MY GUESS, THOUGH, IS IT VANISHED. JUST LIKE...

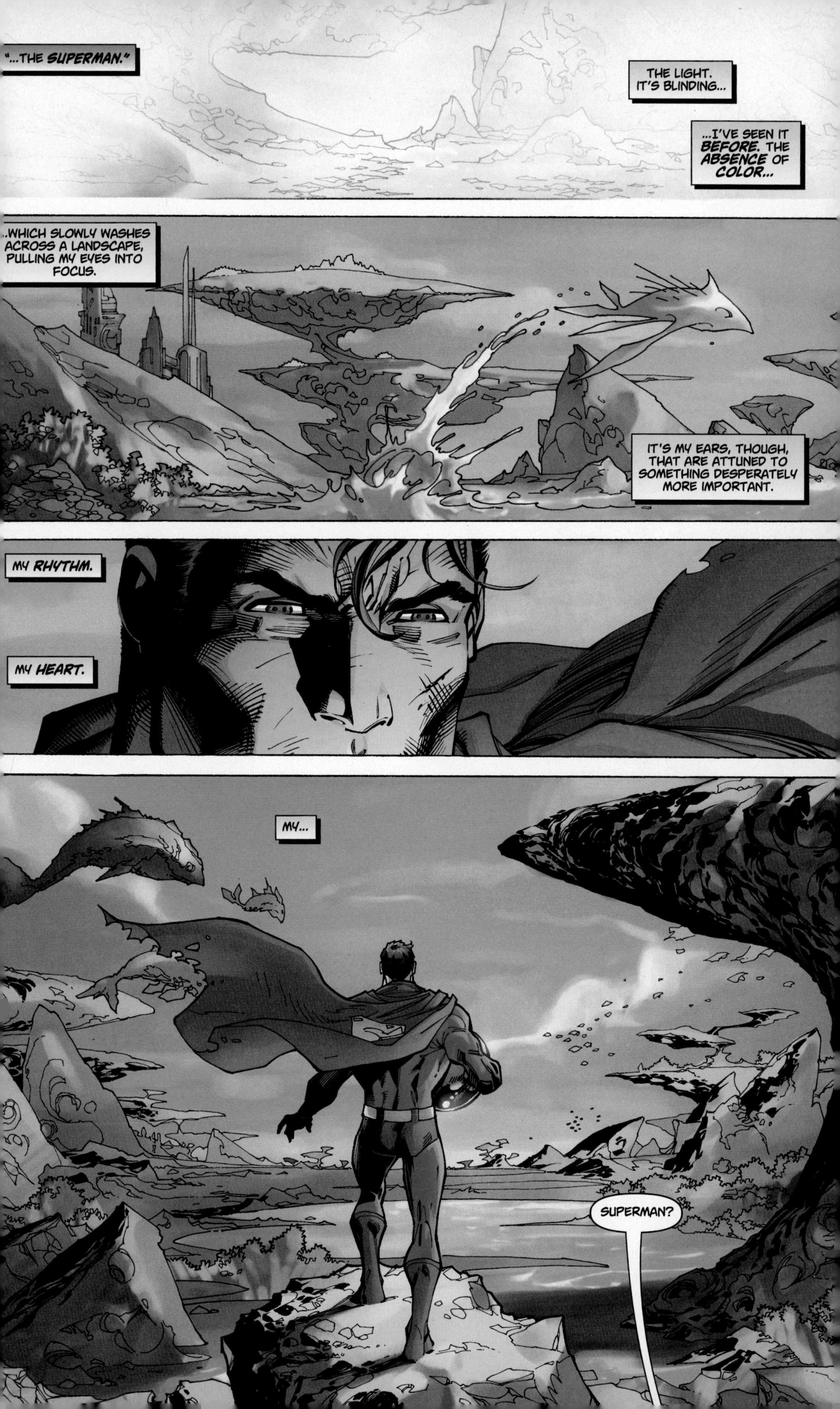
"...THE SUPERMAN."
THE LIGHT. IT'S BLINDING...
...I'VE SEEN IT BEFORE. THE ABSENCE OF COLOR...
..WHICH SLOWLY WASHES ACROSS A LANDSCAPE, PULLING MY EYES INTO FOCUS.
IT'S MY EARS, THOUGH, THAT ARE ATTUNED TO SOMETHING DESPERATELY MORE IMPORTANT.
MY RHYTHM.
MY HEART.
MY...
SUPERMAN?

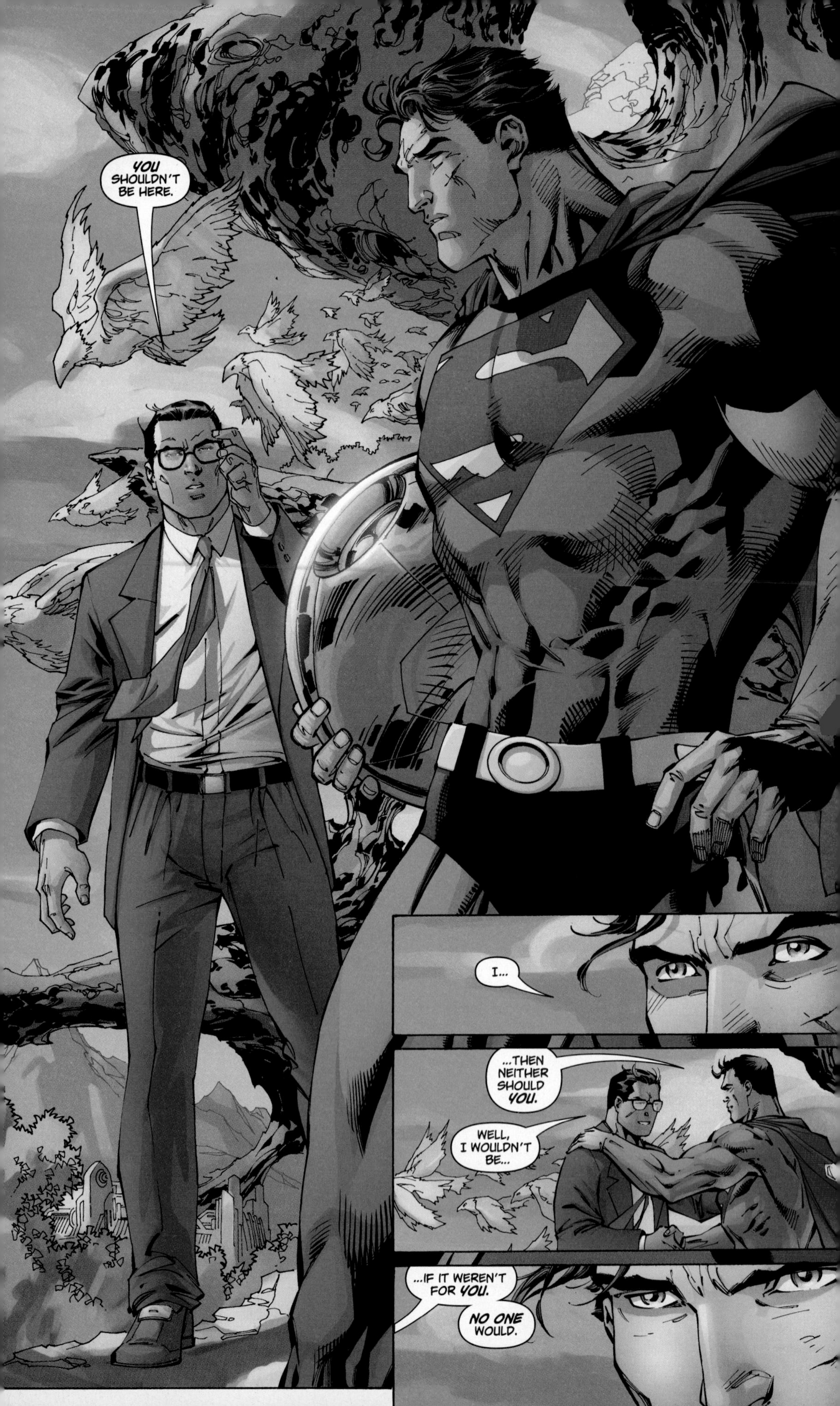

YOU SHOULDN'T BE HERE.
I...
...THEN NEITHER SHOULD YOU.
WELL, I WOULDN'T BE...
...IF IT WEREN'T FOR YOU.
NO ONE WOULD.

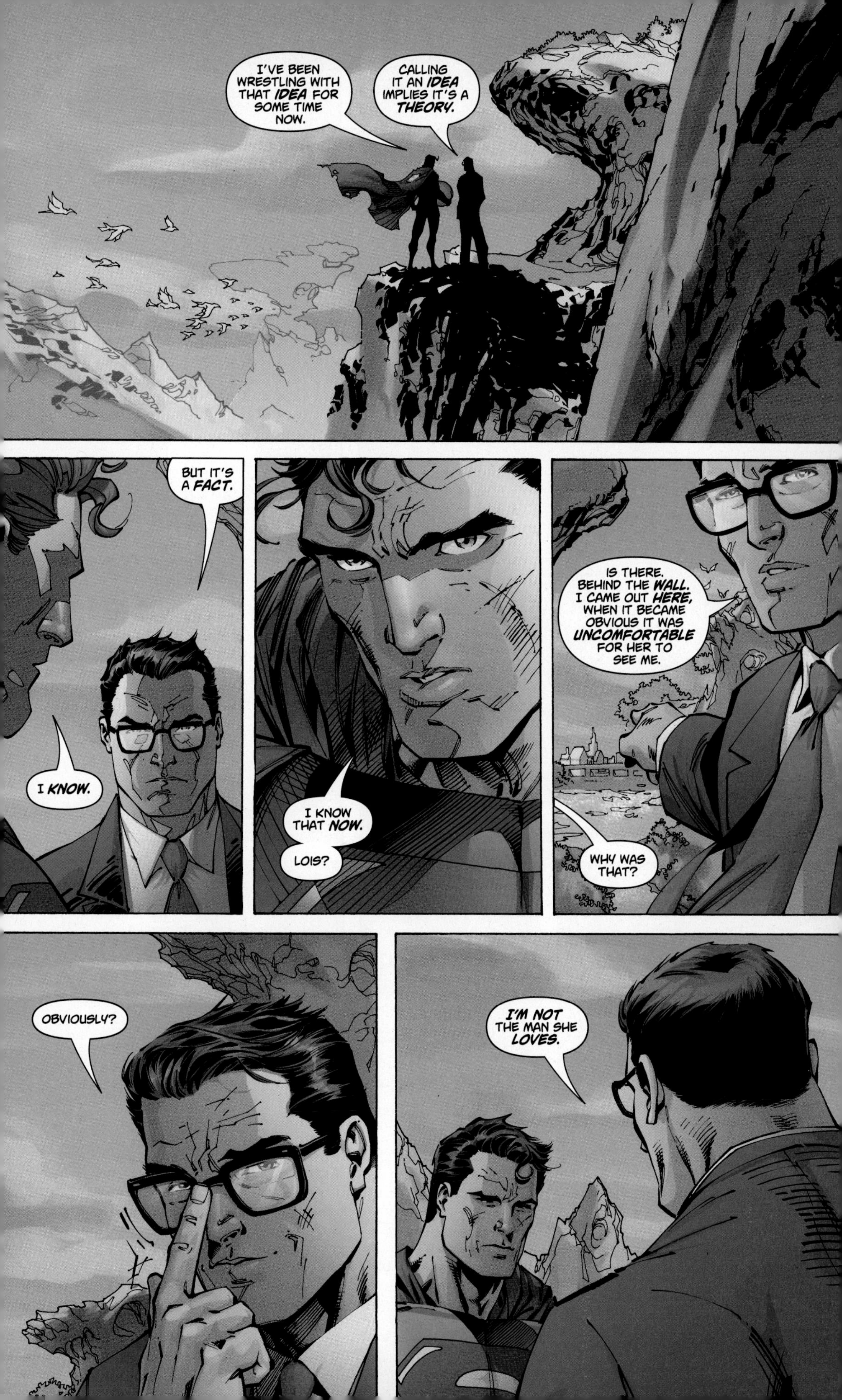
I'VE BEEN WRESTLING WITH THAT IDEA FOR SOME TIME NOW.
CALLING IT AN IDEA IMPLIES IT'S A THEORY.
BUT IT'S A FACT.
I KNOW.
I KNOW THAT NOW.
LOIS?
IS THERE. BEHIND THE WALL. I CAME OUT HERE, WHEN IT BECAME OBVIOUS IT WAS UNCOMFORTABLE FOR HER TO SEE ME.
WHY WAS THAT?
OBVIOUSLY?
I'M NOT THE MAN SHE LOVES.

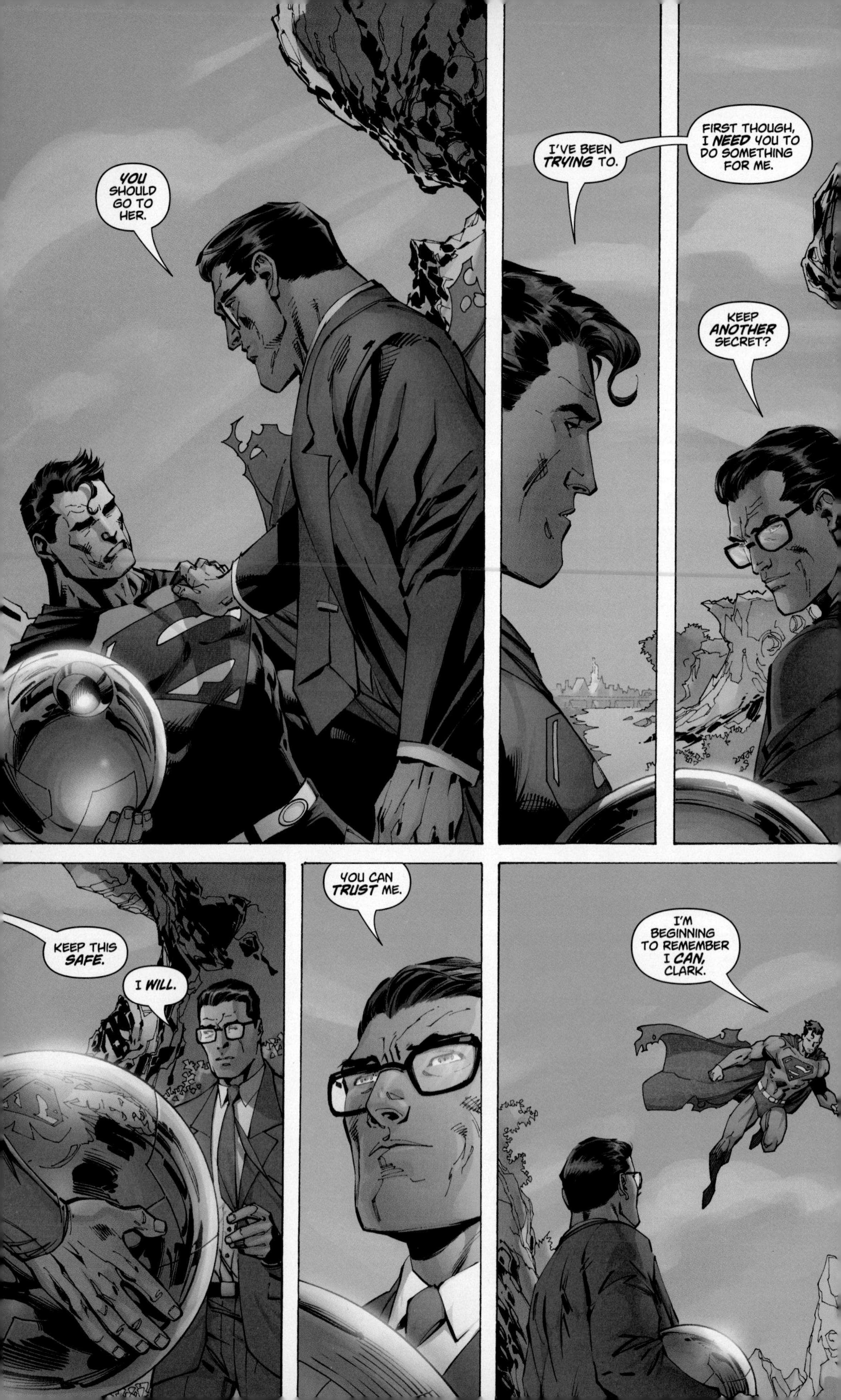

YOU SHOULD GO TO HER.
I'VE BEEN TRYING TO.
FIRST THOUGH, I NEED YOU TO DO SOMETHING FOR ME.
KEEP ANOTHER SECRET?
KEEP THIS SAFE.
I WILL.
YOU CAN TRUST ME.
I'M BEGINNING TO REMEMBER I CAN, CLARK.

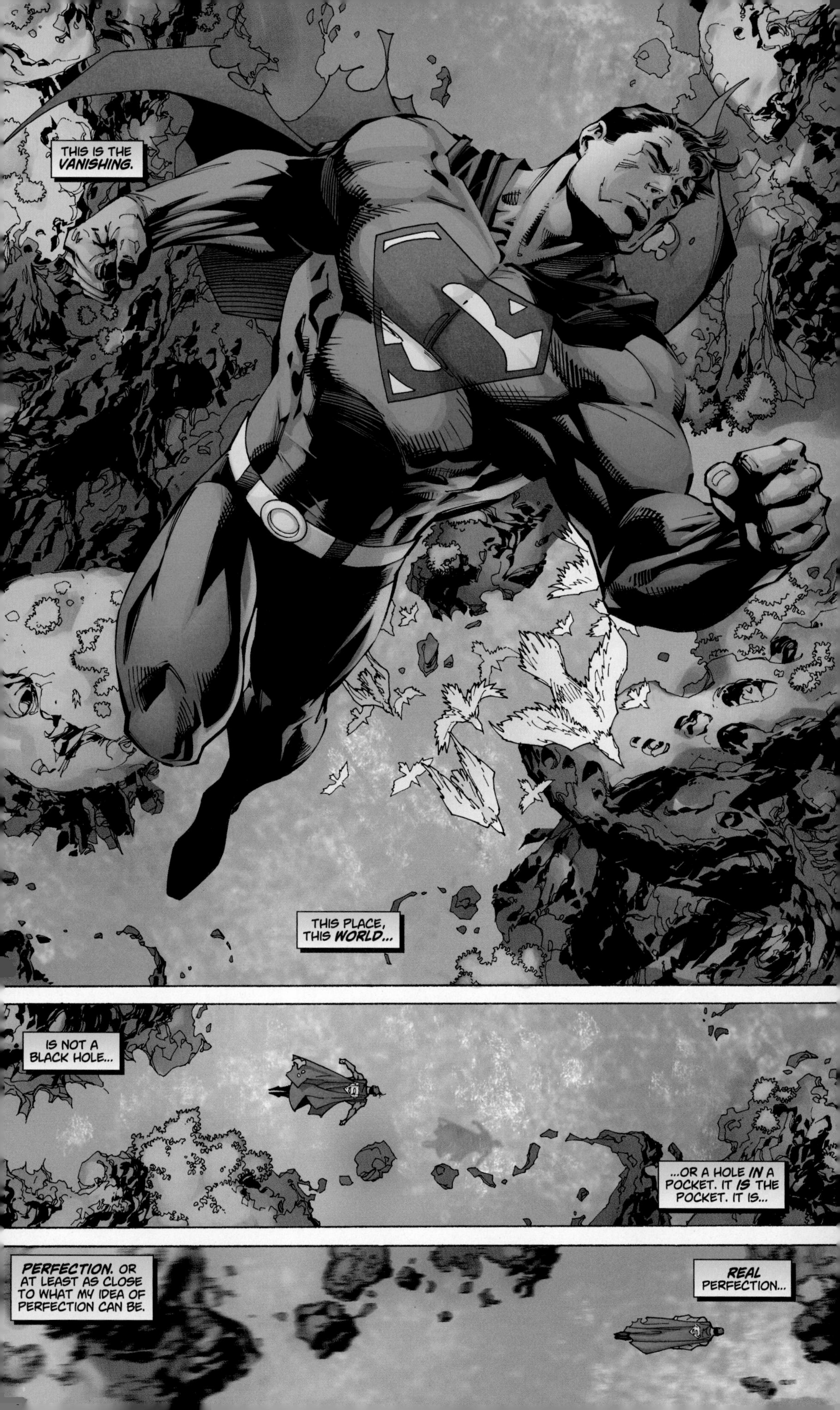
THIS IS THE *VANISHING.*
THIS PLACE, THIS *WORLD...*
IS NOT A BLACK HOLE...
...OR A HOLE *IN* A POCKET. IT *IS* THE POCKET. IT IS...
PERFECTION. OR AT LEAST AS CLOSE TO WHAT MY IDEA OF PERFECTION CAN BE.
REAL PERFECTION...

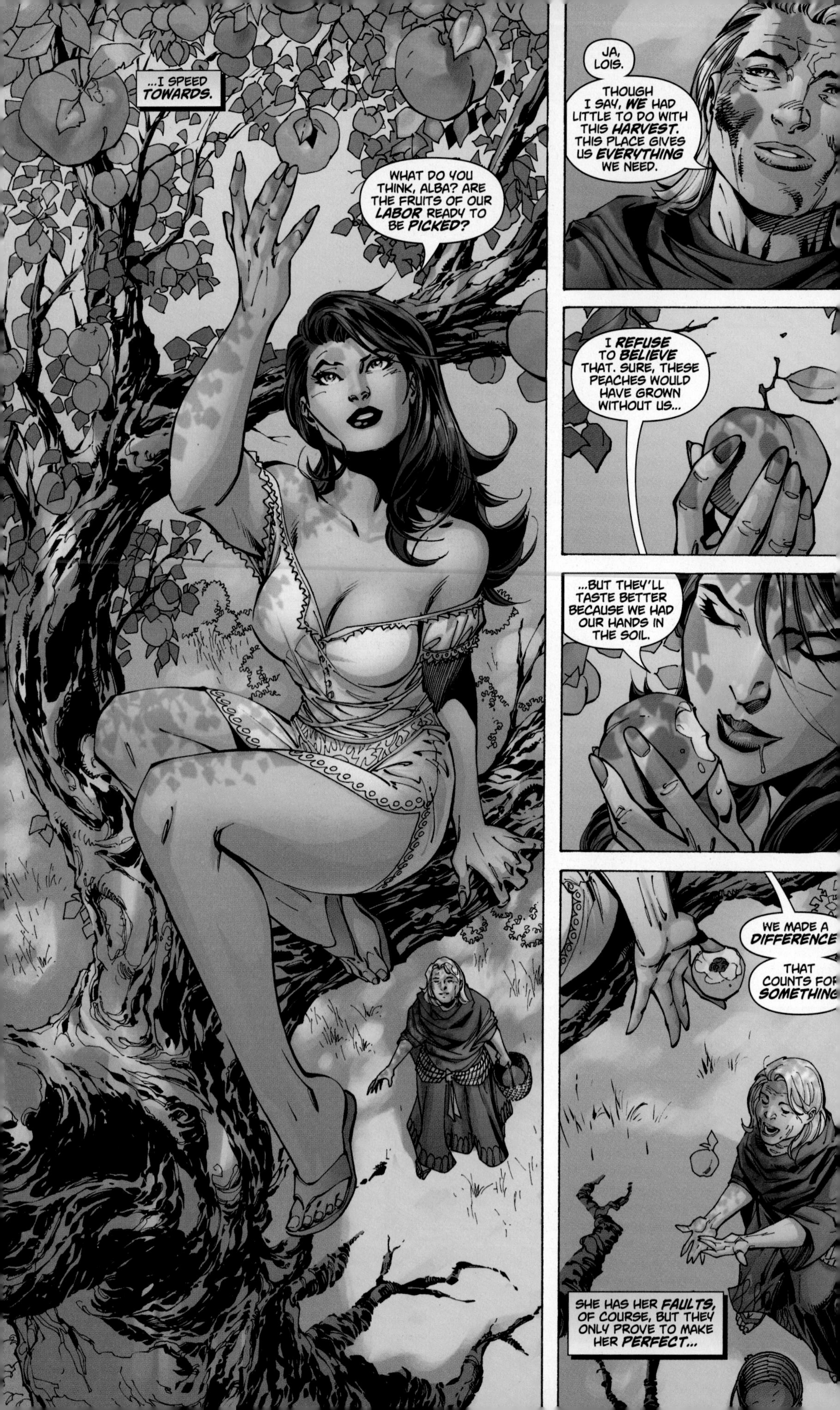

...I SPEED TOWARDS.
WHAT DO YOU THINK, ALBA? ARE THE FRUITS OF OUR LABOR READY TO BE PICKED?
JA, LOIS.
THOUGH I SAY, WE HAD LITTLE TO DO WITH THIS HARVEST. THIS PLACE GIVES US EVERYTHING WE NEED.
I REFUSE TO BELIEVE THAT. SURE, THESE PEACHES WOULD HAVE GROWN WITHOUT US...
...BUT THEY'LL TASTE BETTER BECAUSE WE HAD OUR HANDS IN THE SOIL.
WE MADE A DIFFERENCE
THAT COUNTS FOR SOMETHING
SHE HAS HER FAULTS, OF COURSE, BUT THEY ONLY PROVE TO MAKE HER PERFECT...

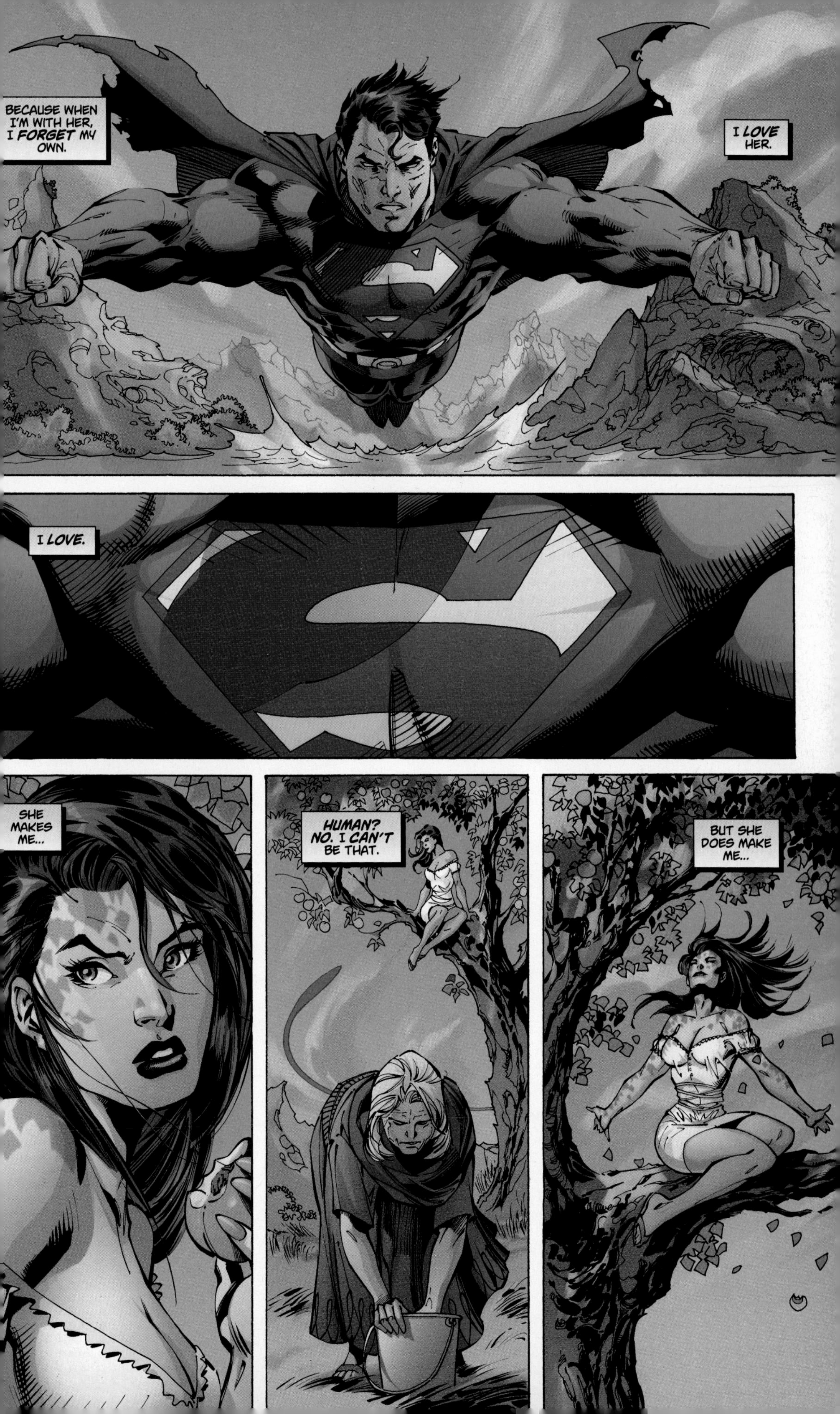
BECAUSE WHEN I'M WITH HER, I *FORGET* MY OWN.
I *LOVE* HER.
I *LOVE.*
SHE MAKES ME...
HUMAN? NO. I *CAN'T* BE THAT.
BUT SHE DOES MAKE ME...

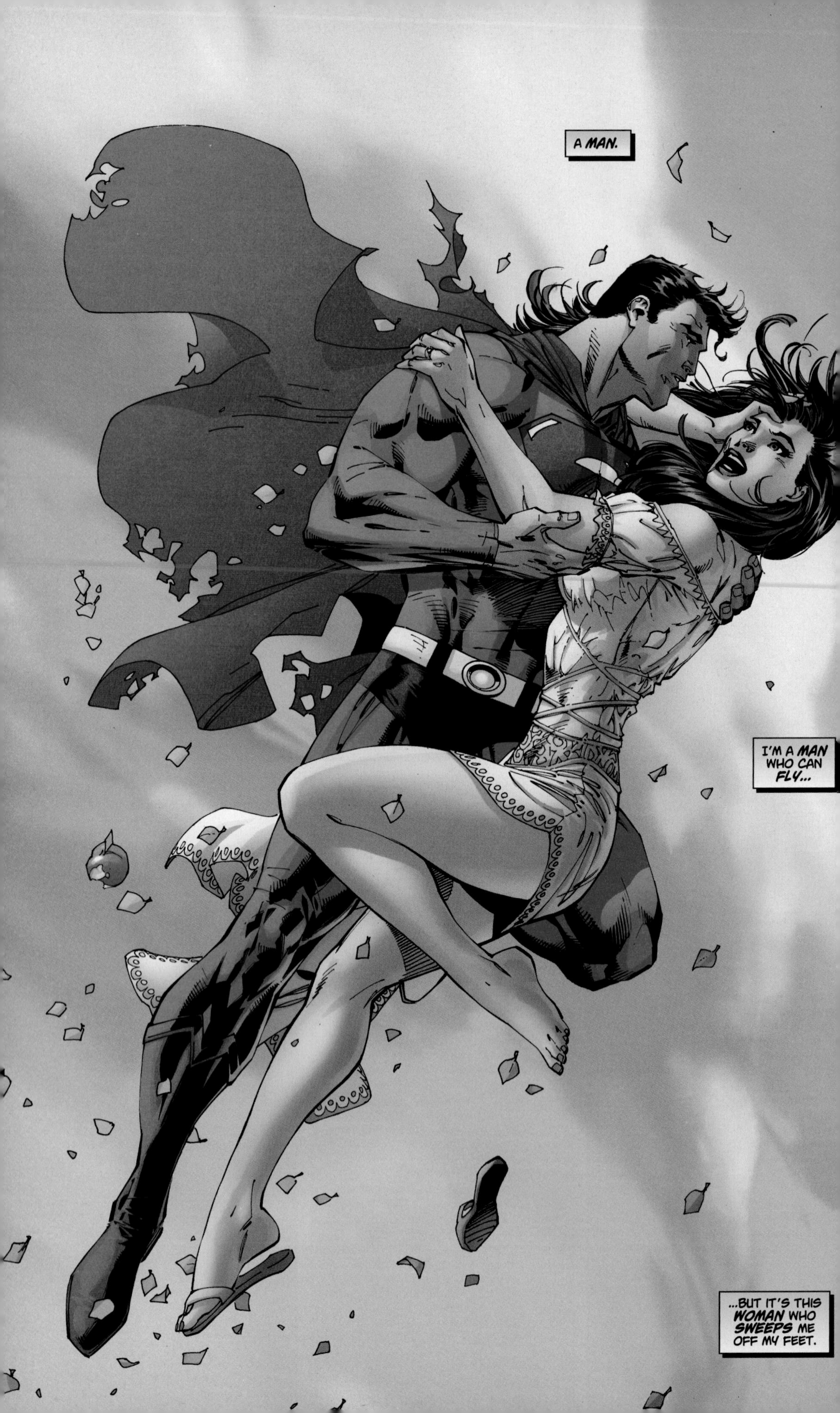
A MAN.
I'M A MAN WHO CAN FLY...
...BUT IT'S THIS WOMAN WHO SWEEPS ME OFF MY FEET.

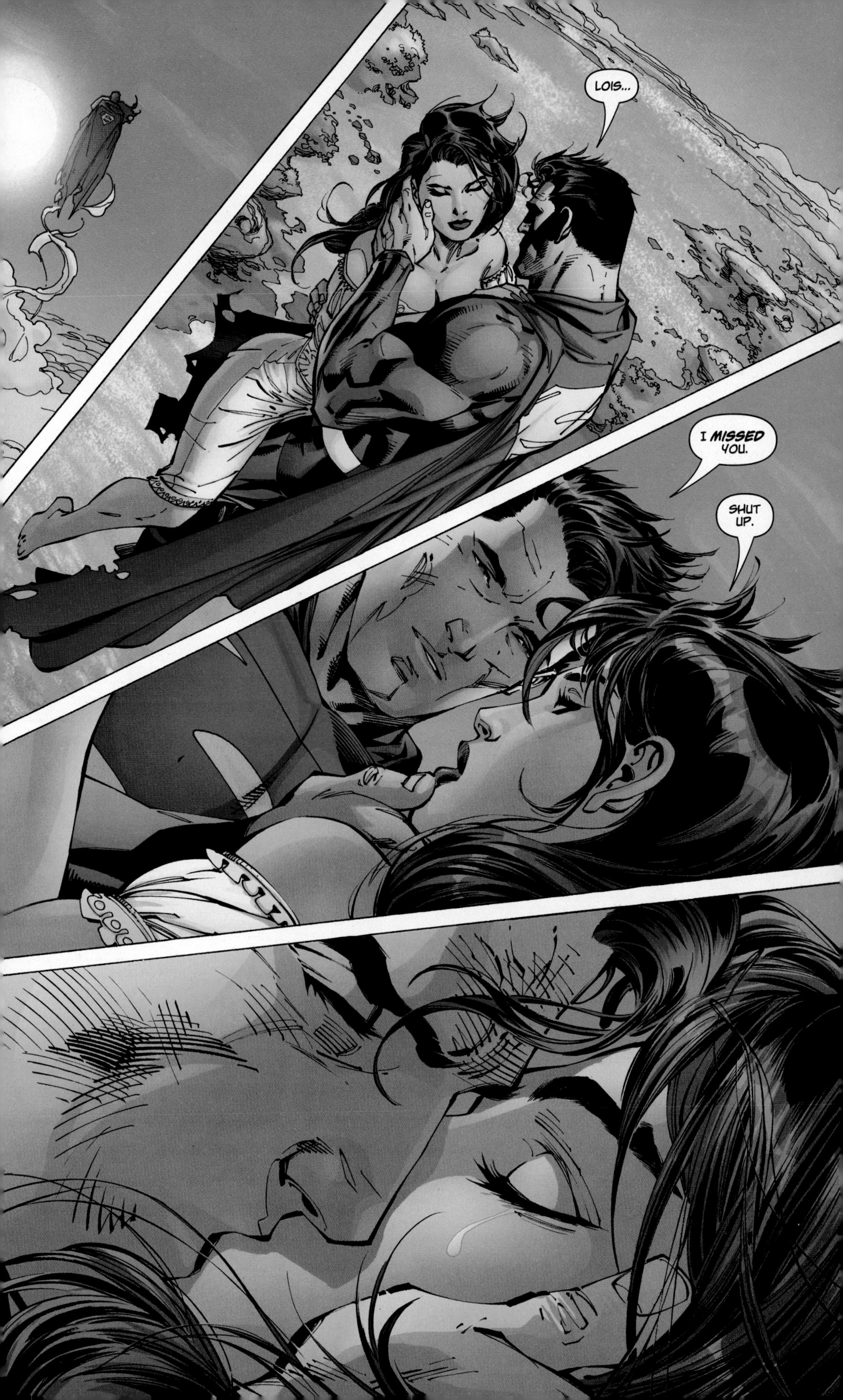
LOIS...
I MISSED YOU.
SHUT UP.

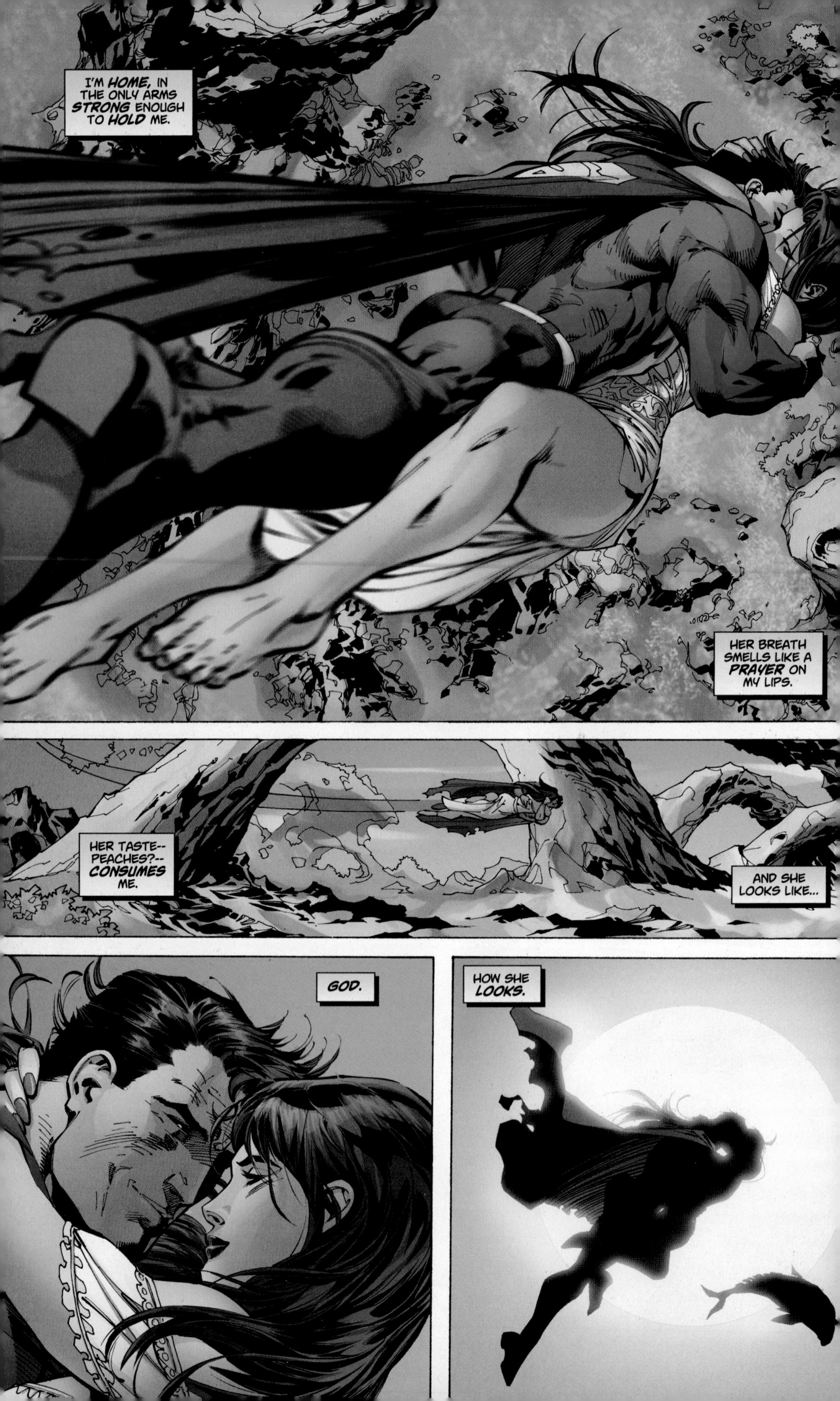
I'M HOME, IN THE ONLY ARMS STRONG ENOUGH TO HOLD ME.
HER BREATH SMELLS LIKE A PRAYER ON MY LIPS.
HER TASTE-- PEACHES?-- CONSUMES ME.
AND SHE LOOKS LIKE...
GOD.
HOW SHE LOOKS.

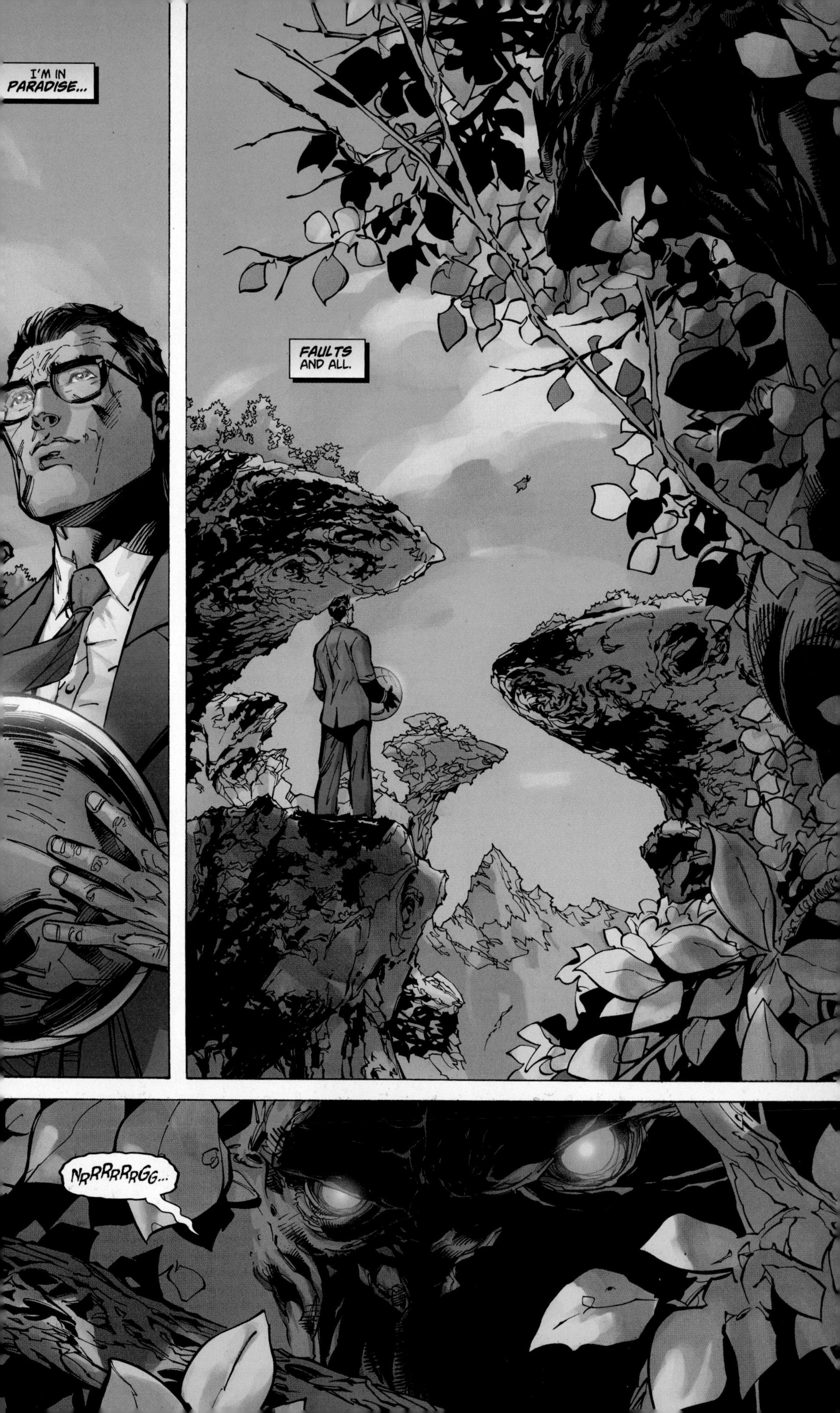
I'M IN PARADISE...
FAULTS AND ALL.
NRRRRRRGG...

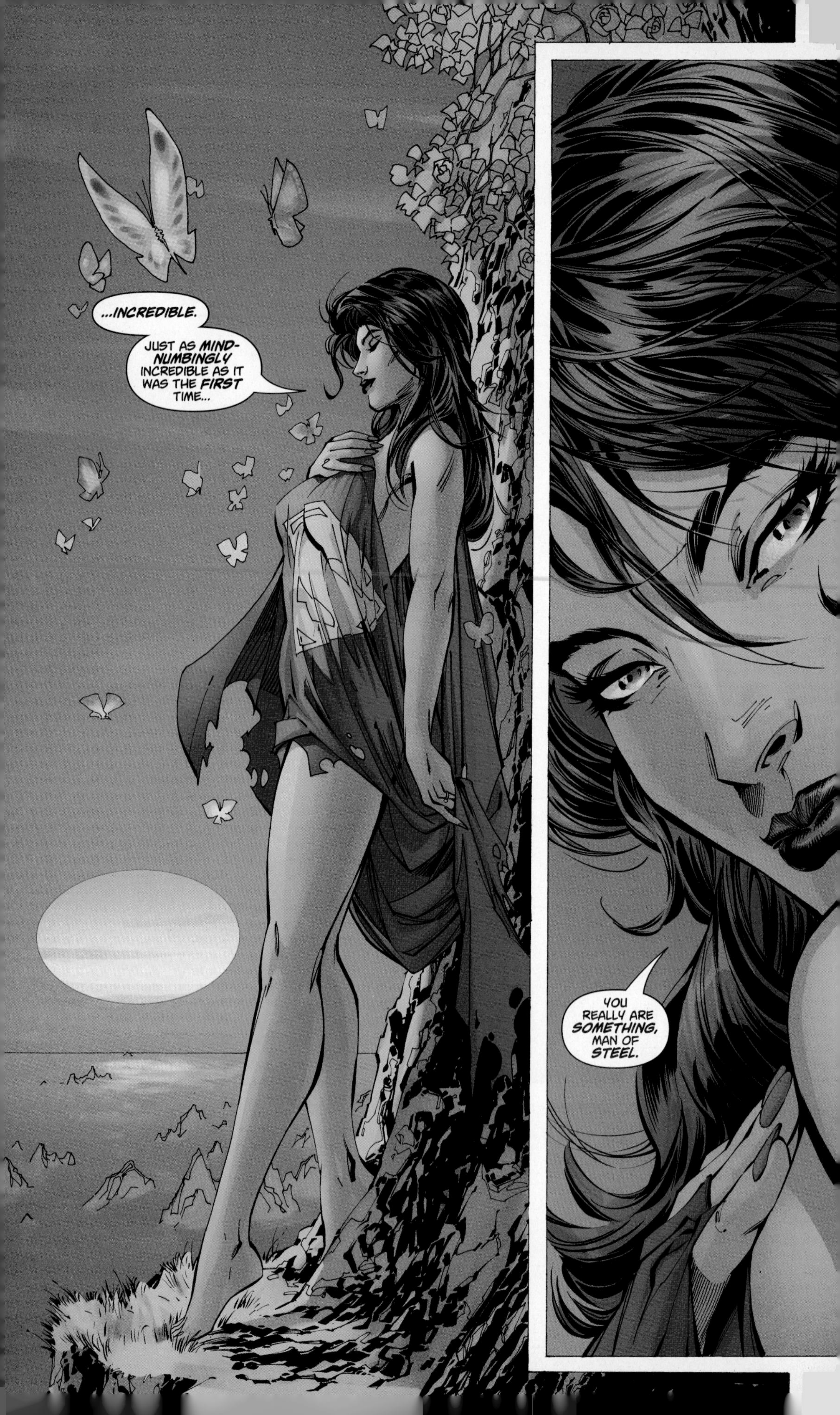
...INCREDIBLE.
JUST AS MIND-NUMBINGLY INCREDIBLE AS IT WAS THE FIRST TIME...
YOU REALLY ARE SOMETHING, MAN OF STEEL.

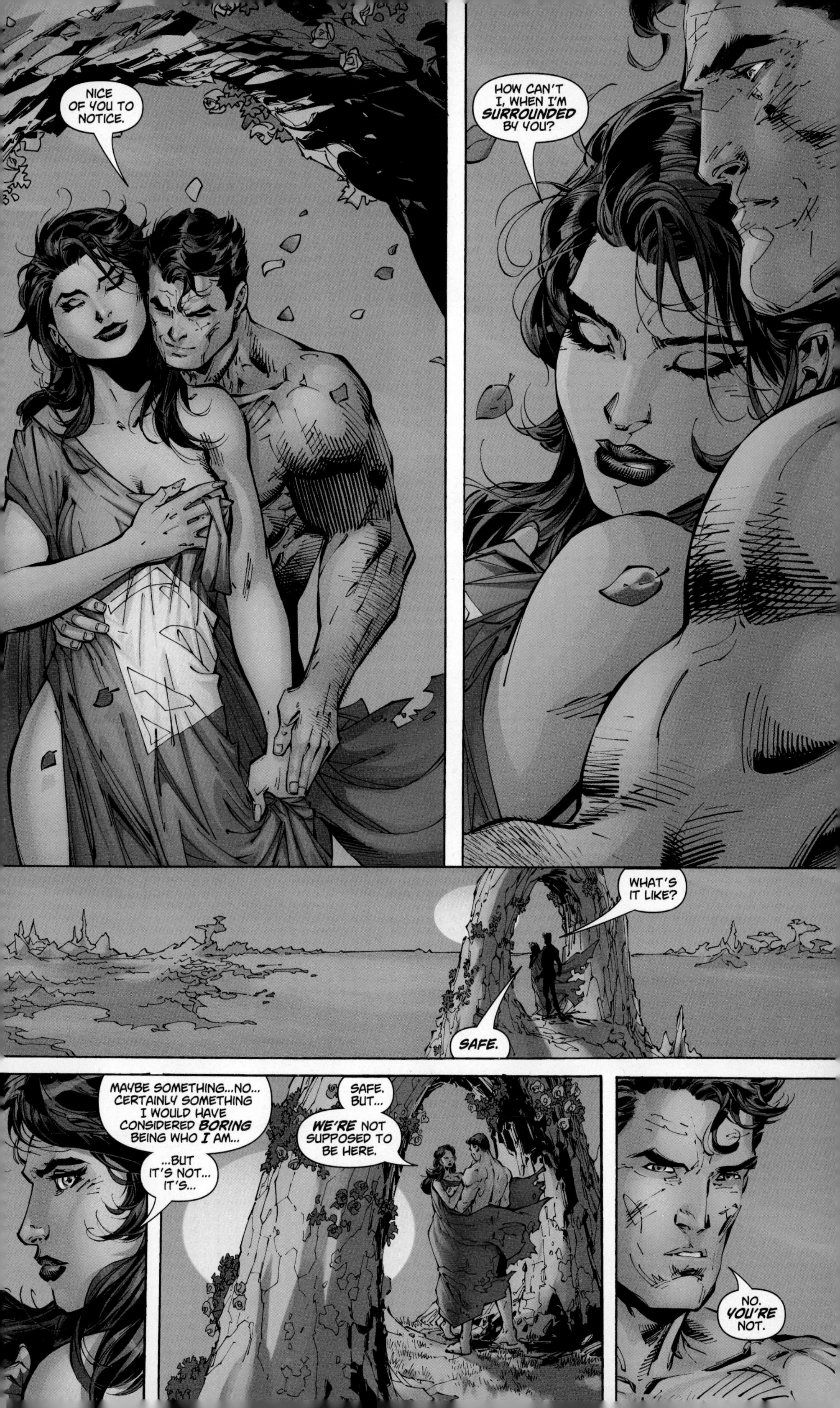
NICE OF YOU TO NOTICE.
HOW CAN'T I, WHEN I'M SURROUNDED BY YOU?
WHAT'S IT LIKE?
SAFE.
MAYBE SOMETHING...NO... CERTAINLY SOMETHING I WOULD HAVE CONSIDERED BORING BEING WHO I AM...
...BUT IT'S NOT... IT'S...
SAFE. BUT...
WE'RE NOT SUPPOSED TO BE HERE.
NO. YOU'RE NOT.

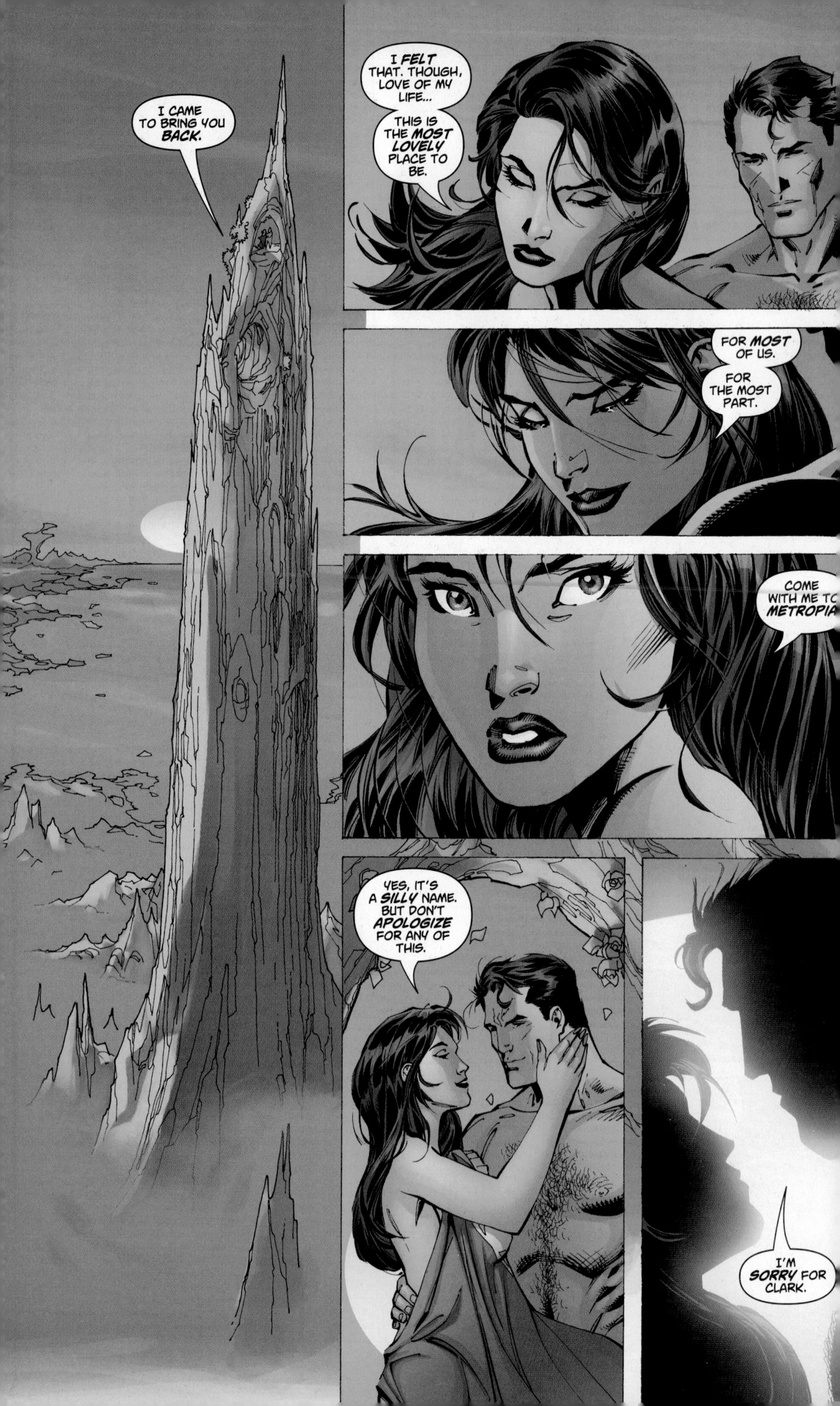

I CAME TO BRING YOU BACK.
I FELT THAT. THOUGH, LOVE OF MY LIFE...
THIS IS THE MOST LOVELY PLACE TO BE.
FOR MOST OF US.
FOR THE MOST PART.
COME WITH ME TO METROPIA
YES, IT'S A SILLY NAME. BUT DON'T APOLOGIZE FOR ANY OF THIS.
I'M SORRY FOR CLARK.

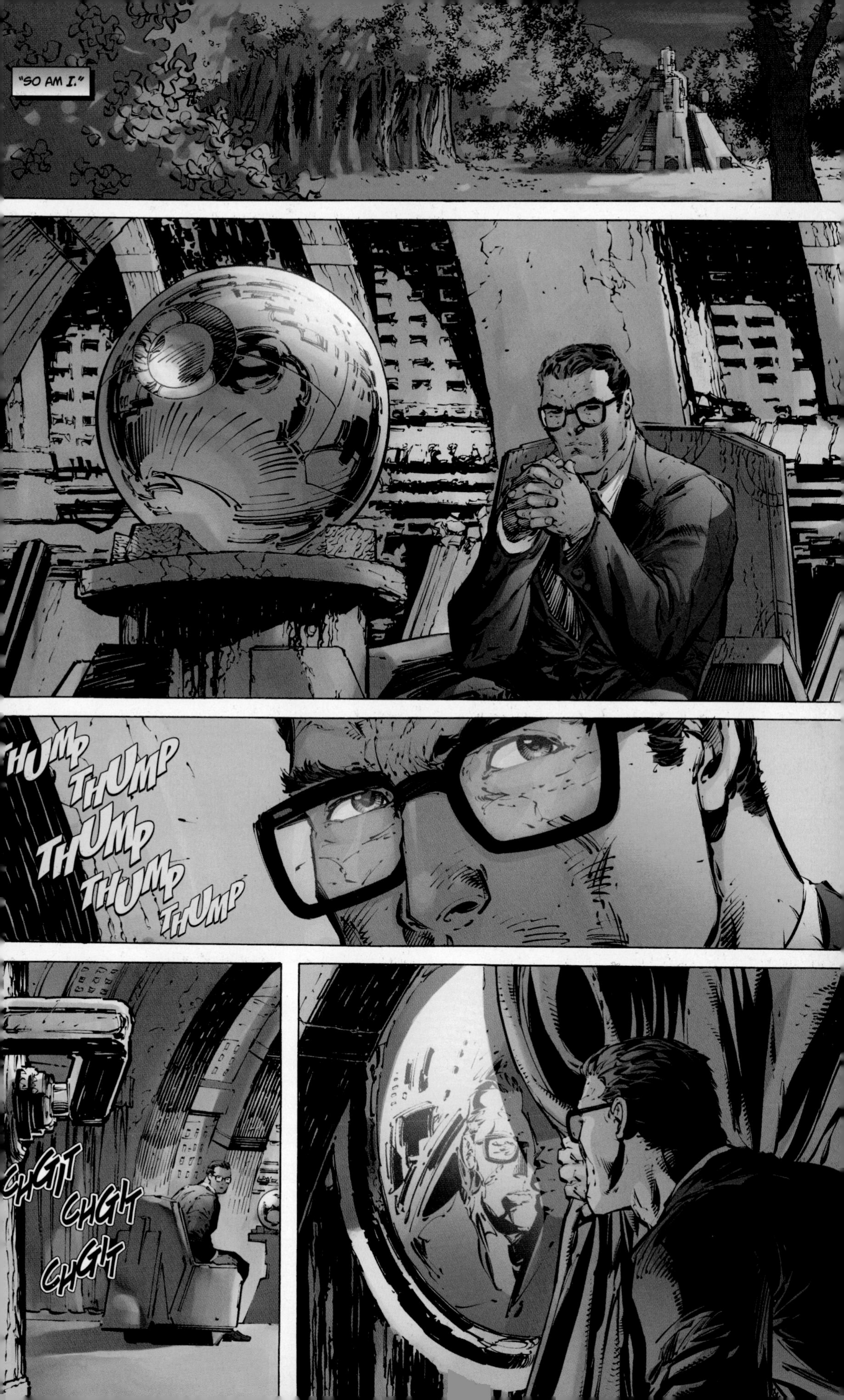
"SO AM I."
THUMP THUMP
THUMP
THUMP
THUMP
CHGIT
CHGIT
CHGIT

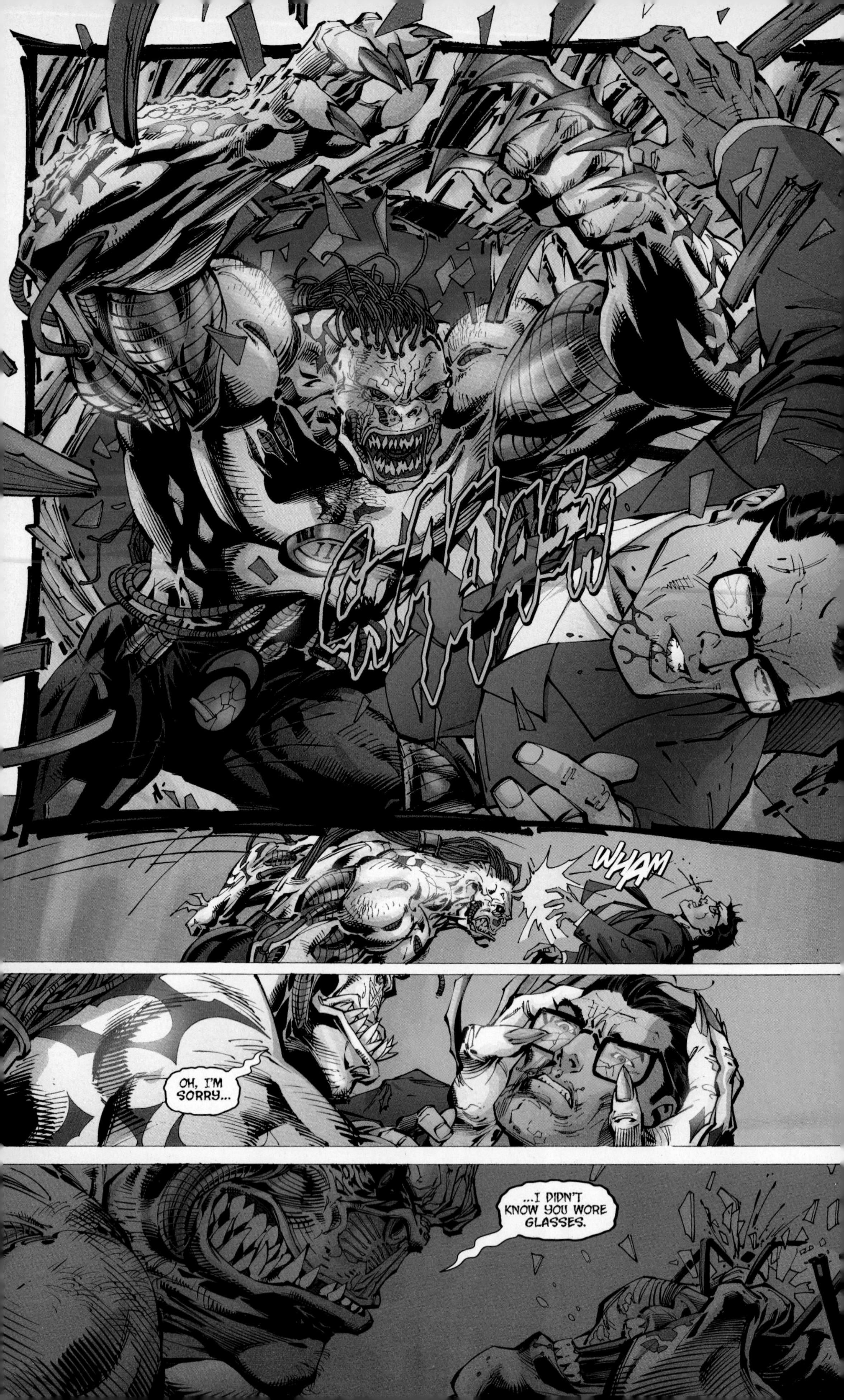
WHAM
OH, I'M SORRY...
...I DIDN'T KNOW YOU WORE GLASSES.

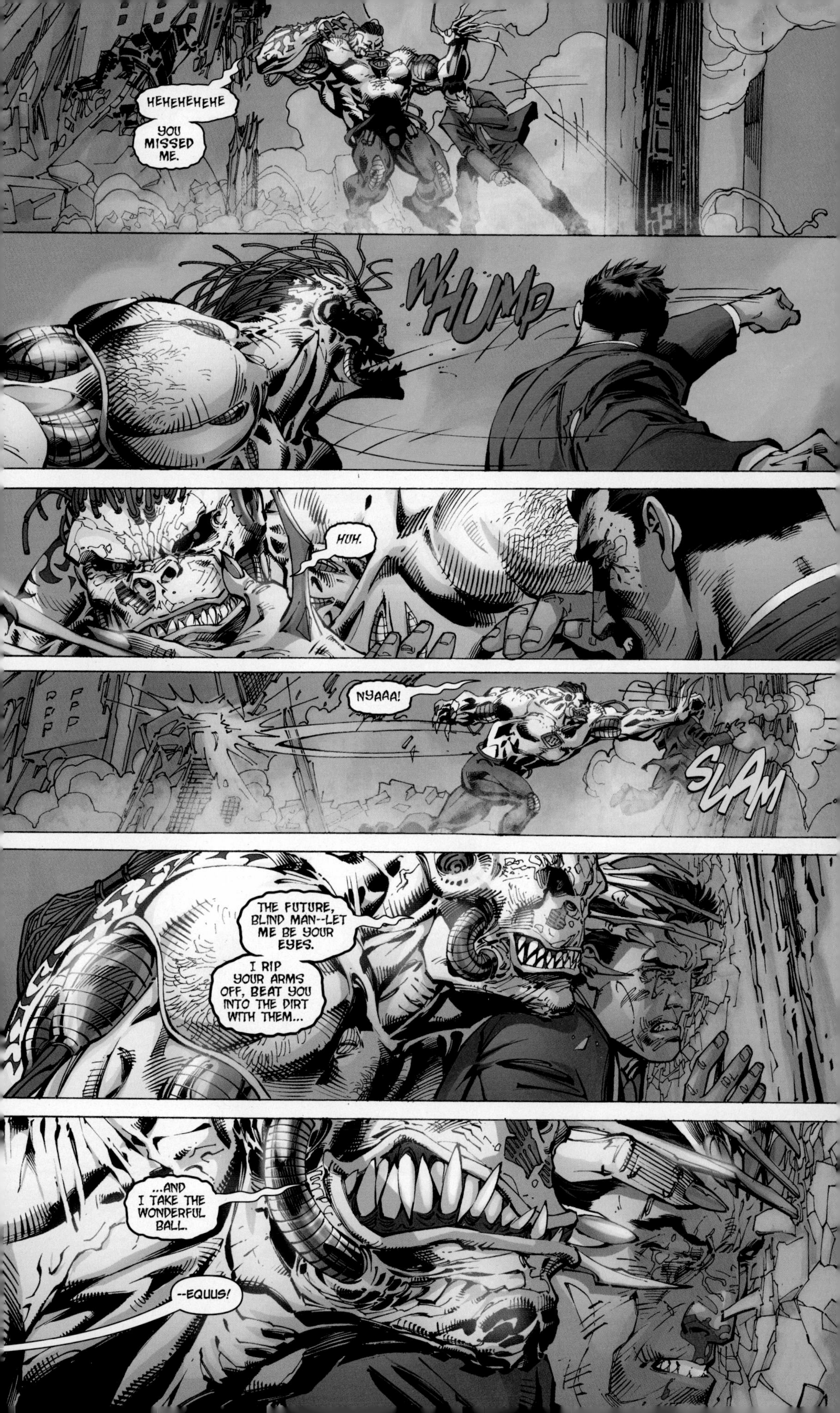
HEHEHEHEHE
YOU MISSED ME.
WHUMP
HUH.
NYAAA!
SLAM
THE FUTURE, BLIND MAN--LET ME BE YOUR EYES.
I RIP YOUR ARMS OFF, BEAT YOU INTO THE DIRT WITH THEM...
...AND I TAKE THE WONDERFUL BALL.
--EQUUS!

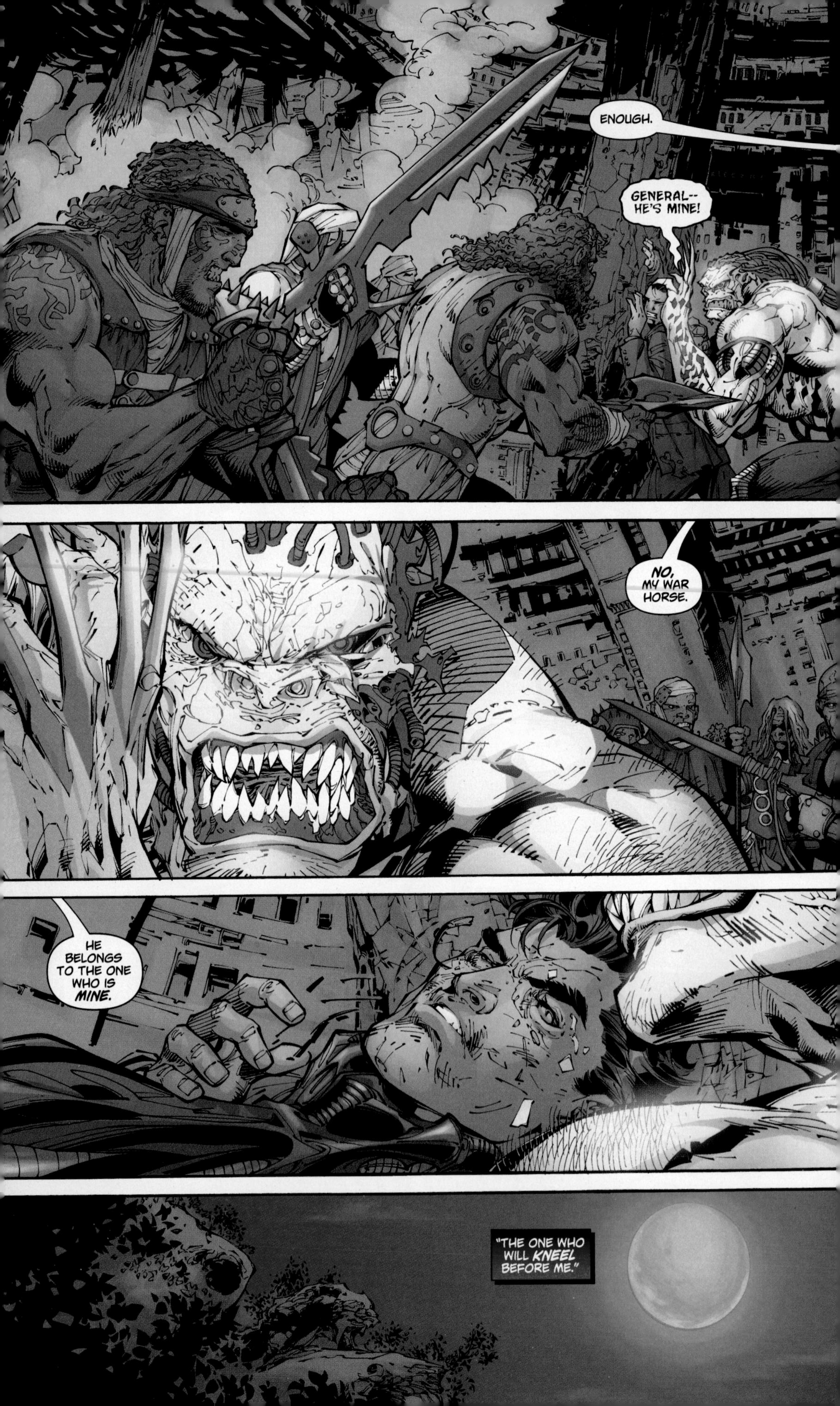
ENOUGH.
GENERAL-- HE'S MINE!
NO, MY WAR HORSE.
HE BELONGS TO THE ONE WHO IS MINE.
"THE ONE WHO WILL KNEEL BEFORE ME."

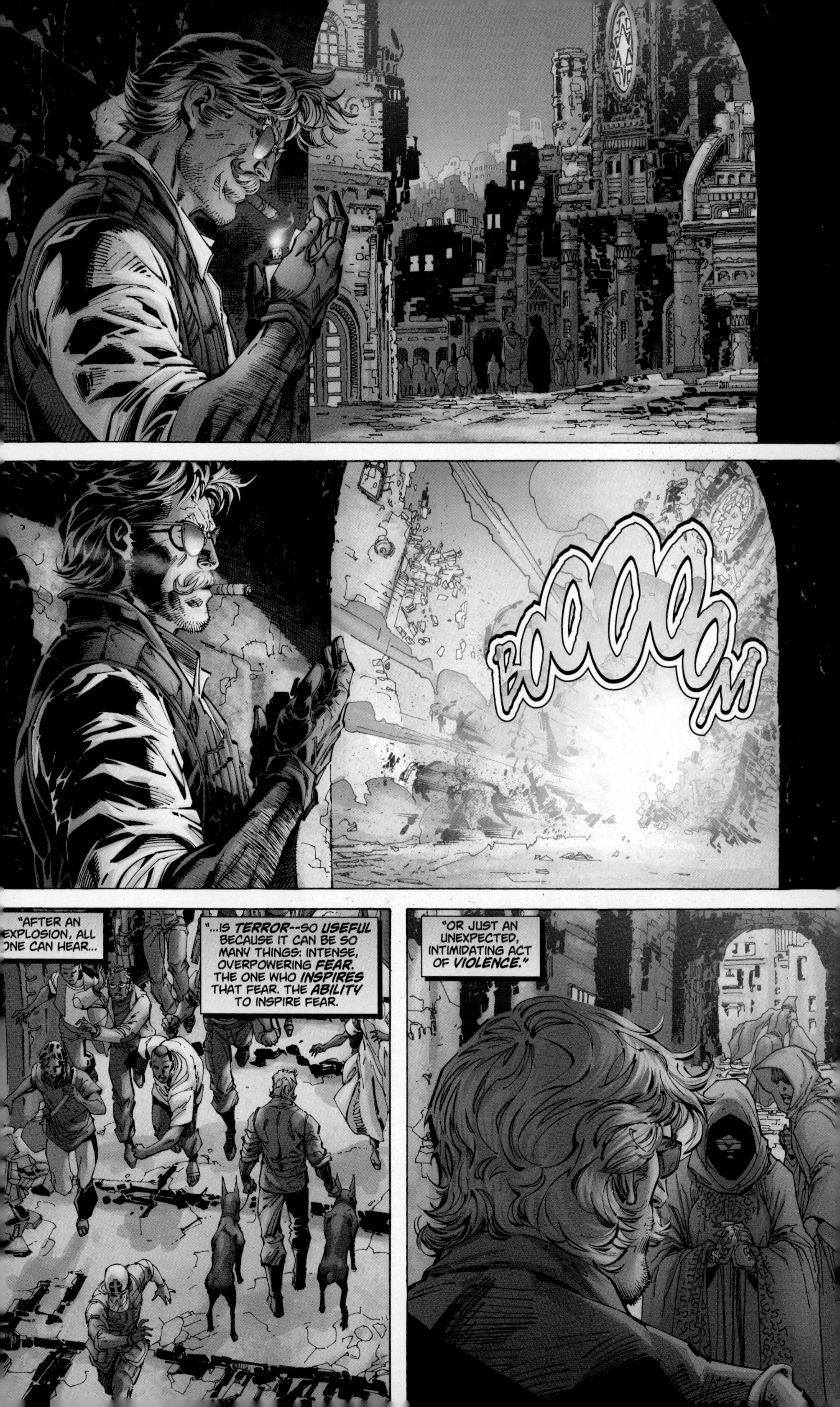
BOOOOOM
"AFTER AN EXPLOSION, ALL ONE CAN HEAR...
"...IS TERROR--SO USEFUL BECAUSE IT CAN BE SO MANY THINGS: INTENSE, OVERPOWERING FEAR. THE ONE WHO INSPIRES THAT FEAR. THE ABILITY TO INSPIRE FEAR.
"OR JUST AN UNEXPECTED, INTIMIDATING ACT OF VIOLENCE."

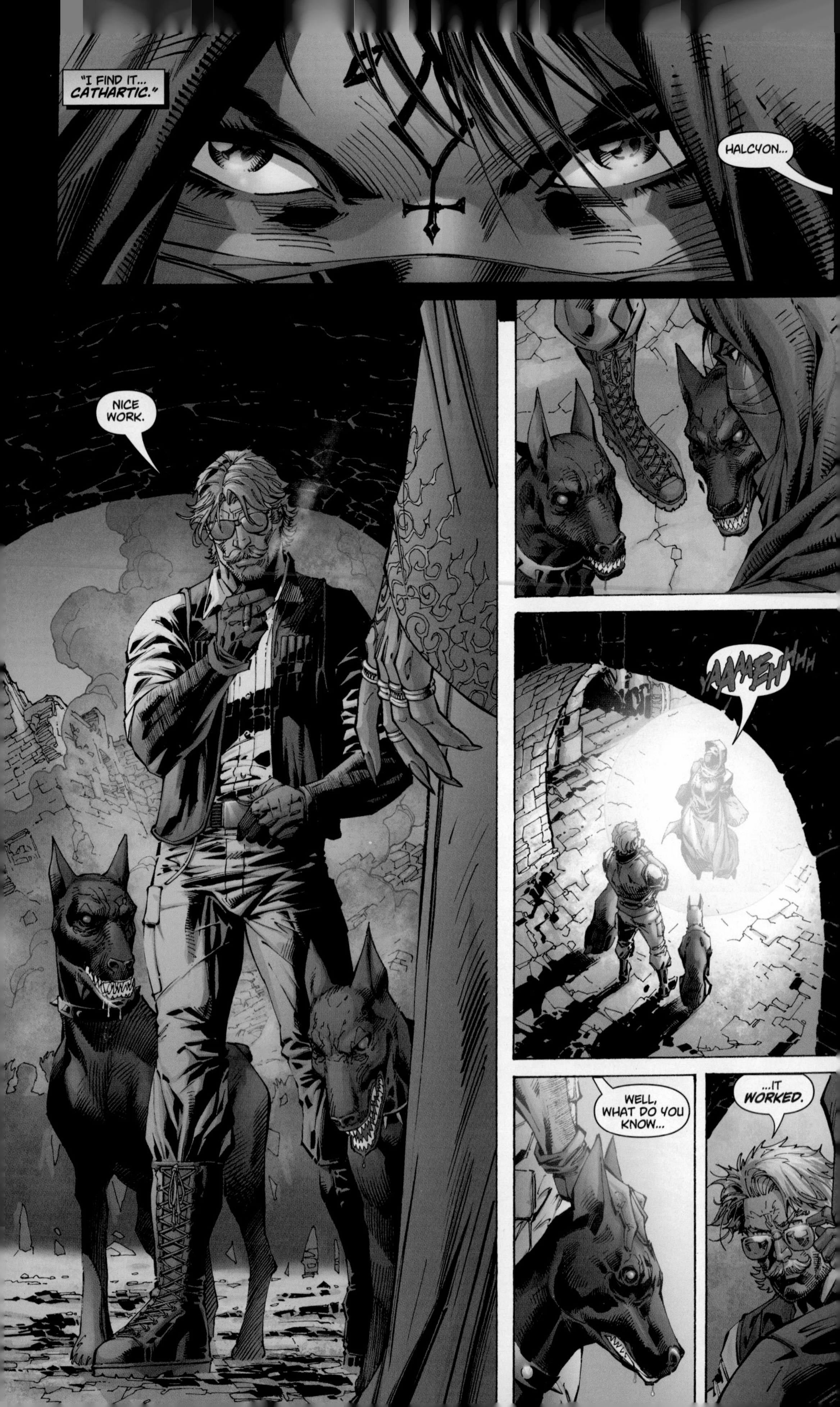
"I FIND IT... CATHARTIC."
HALCYON...
NICE WORK.
YAAAAEHHHH
WELL, WHAT DO YOU KNOW...
...IT WORKED.

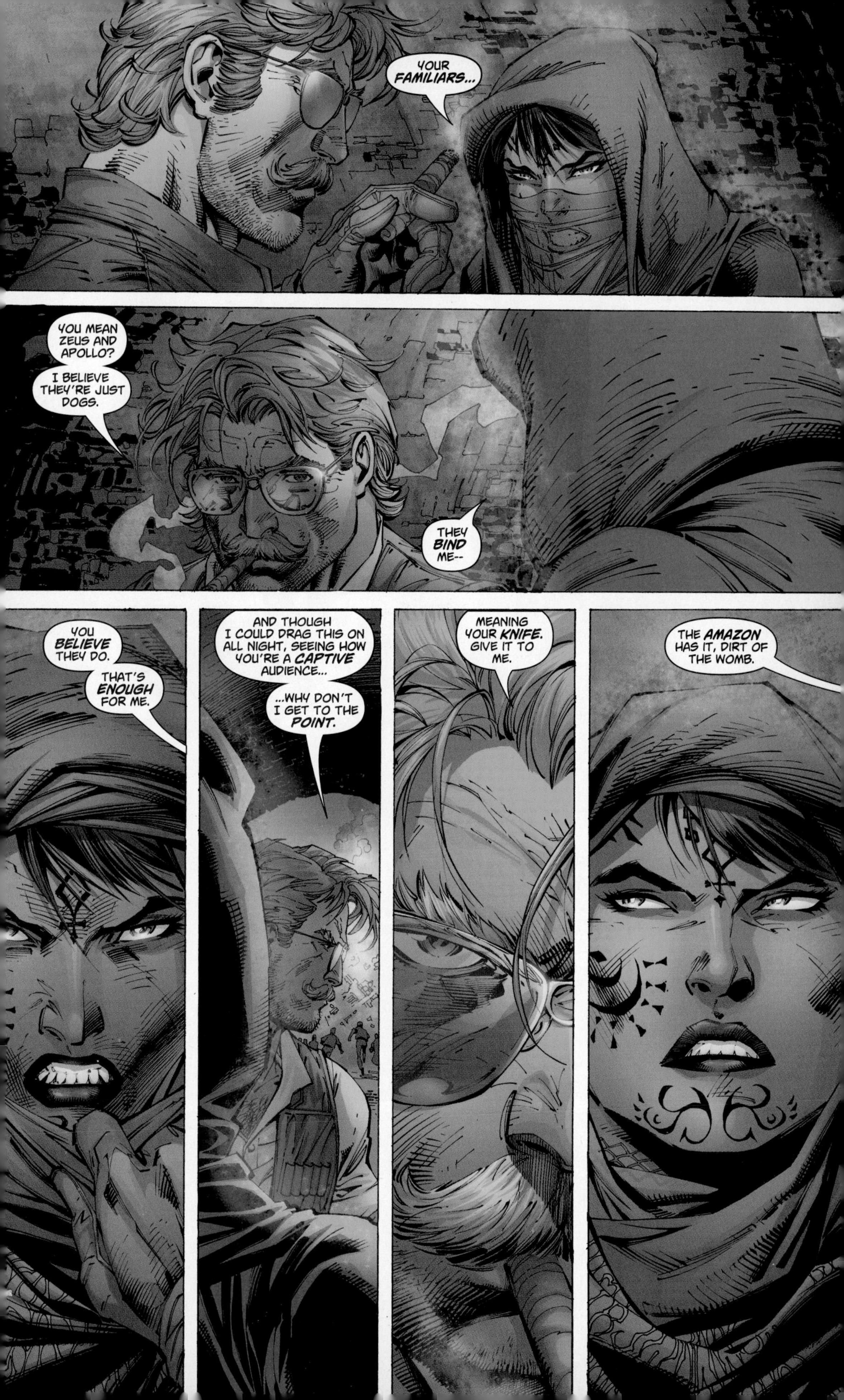
YOUR FAMILIARS...
YOU MEAN ZEUS AND APOLLO?
I BELIEVE THEY'RE JUST DOGS.
THEY BIND ME--
YOU BELIEVE THEY DO.
THAT'S ENOUGH FOR ME.
AND THOUGH I COULD DRAG THIS ON ALL NIGHT, SEEING HOW YOU'RE A CAPTIVE AUDIENCE...
...WHY DON'T I GET TO THE POINT.
MEANING YOUR KNIFE. GIVE IT TO ME.
THE AMAZON HAS IT, DIRT OF THE WOMB.

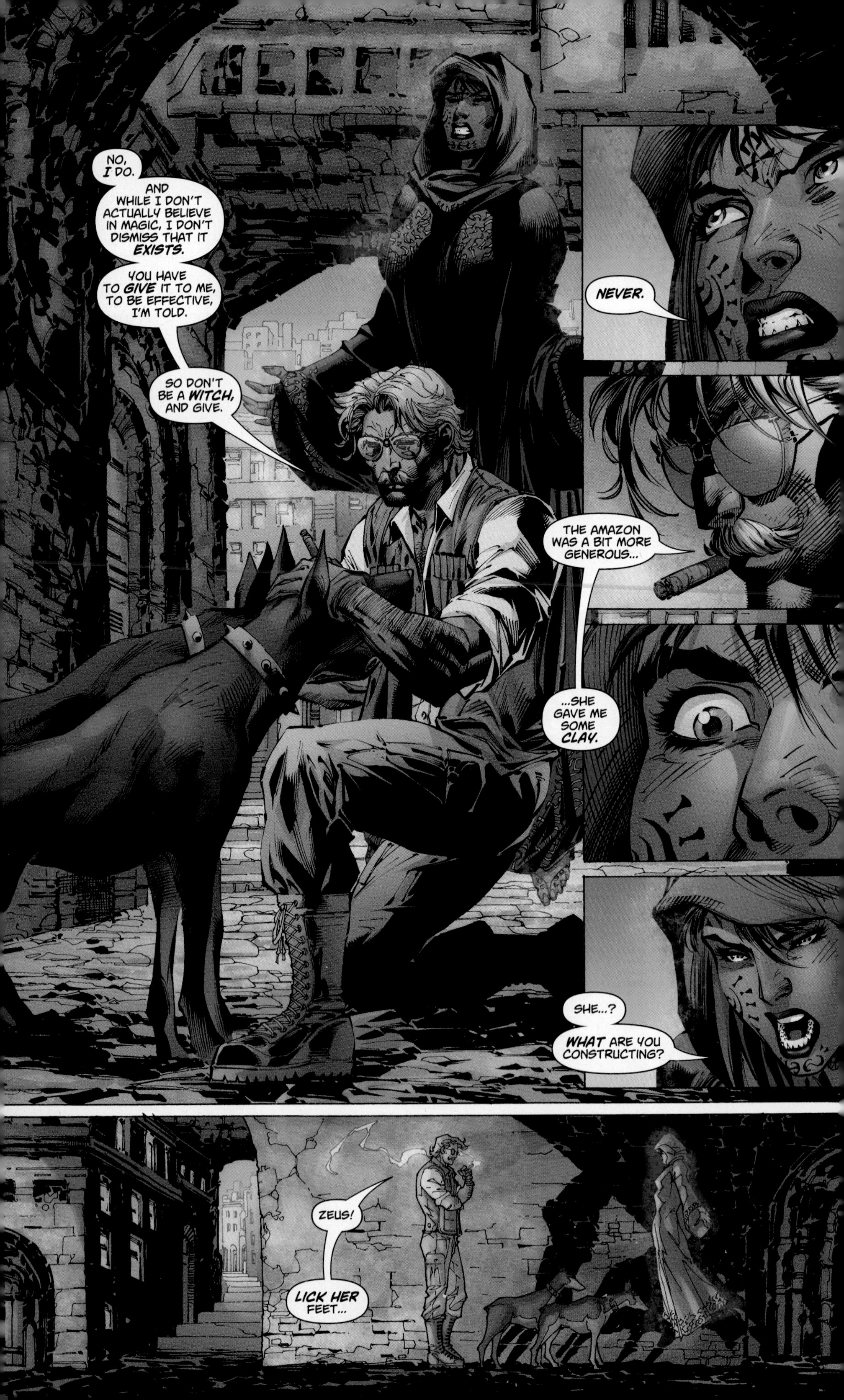
NO, I DO.
AND WHILE I DON'T ACTUALLY BELIEVE IN MAGIC, I DON'T DISMISS THAT IT EXISTS.
YOU HAVE TO GIVE IT TO ME, TO BE EFFECTIVE, I'M TOLD.
SO DON'T BE A WITCH, AND GIVE.
NEVER.
THE AMAZON WAS A BIT MORE GENEROUS...
...SHE GAVE ME SOME CLAY.
SHE...?
WHAT ARE YOU CONSTRUCTING?
ZEUS!
LICK HER FEET...

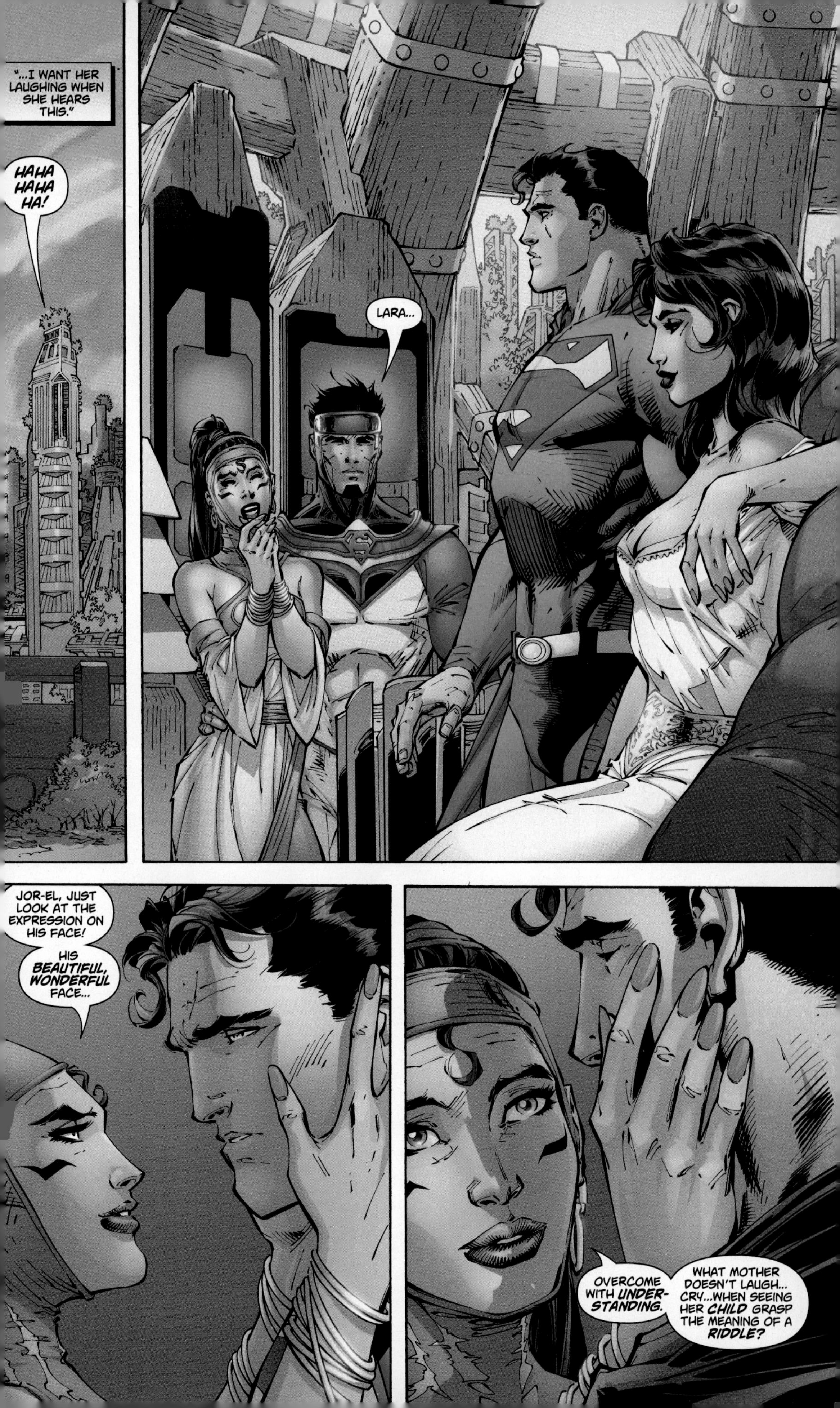
"...I WANT HER LAUGHING WHEN SHE HEARS THIS."
HAHA HAHA HA!
LARA...
JOR-EL, JUST LOOK AT THE EXPRESSION ON HIS FACE!
HIS BEAUTIFUL, WONDERFUL FACE...
OVERCOME WITH UNDER-STANDING.
WHAT MOTHER DOESN'T LAUGH... CRY...WHEN SEEING HER CHILD GRASP THE MEANING OF A RIDDLE?

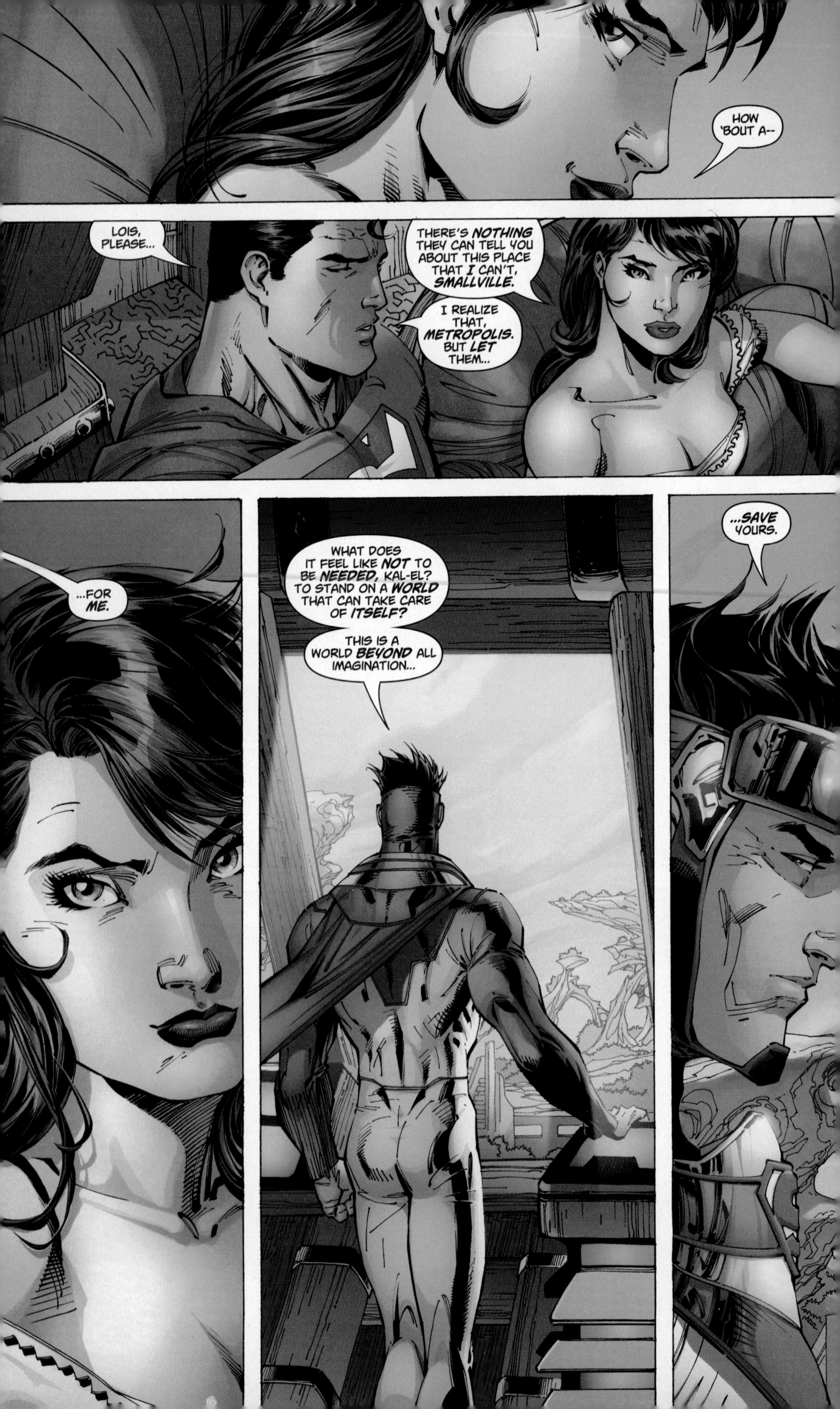
HOW 'BOUT A--
LOIS, PLEASE...
THERE'S NOTHING THEY CAN TELL YOU ABOUT THIS PLACE THAT I CAN'T, SMALLVILLE.
I REALIZE THAT, METROPOLIS. BUT LET THEM...
...FOR ME.
WHAT DOES IT FEEL LIKE NOT TO BE NEEDED, KAL-EL? TO STAND ON A WORLD THAT CAN TAKE CARE OF ITSELF?
THIS IS A WORLD BEYOND ALL IMAGINATION...
...SAVE YOURS.

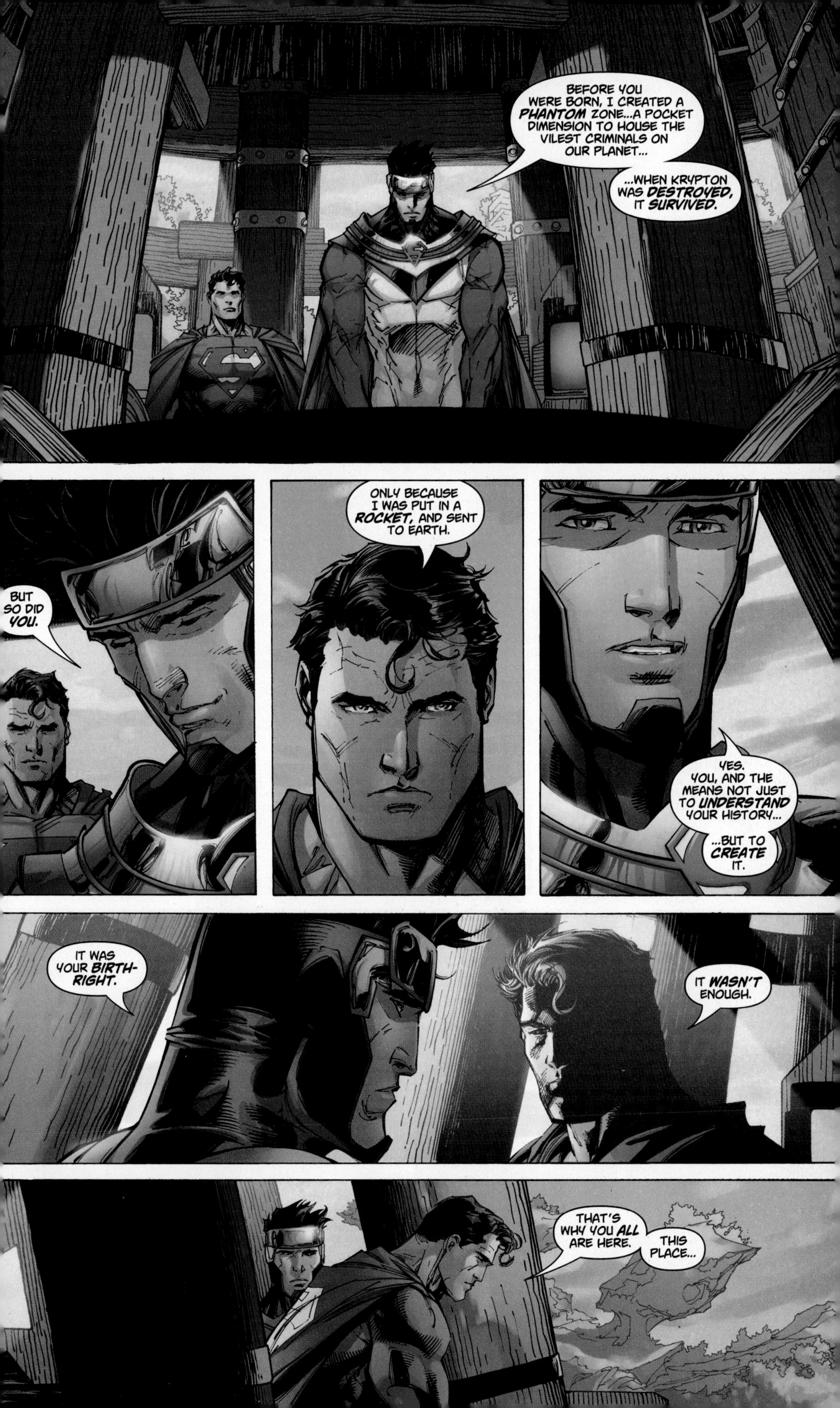

BEFORE YOU WERE BORN, I CREATED A PHANTOM ZONE...A POCKET DIMENSION TO HOUSE THE VILEST CRIMINALS ON OUR PLANET...
...WHEN KRYPTON WAS DESTROYED, IT SURVIVED.
BUT SO DID YOU.
ONLY BECAUSE I WAS PUT IN A ROCKET, AND SENT TO EARTH.
YES. YOU, AND THE MEANS NOT JUST TO UNDERSTAND YOUR HISTORY...
...BUT TO CREATE IT.
IT WAS YOUR BIRTHRIGHT.
IT WASN'T ENOUGH.
THAT'S WHY YOU ALL ARE HERE.
THIS PLACE...

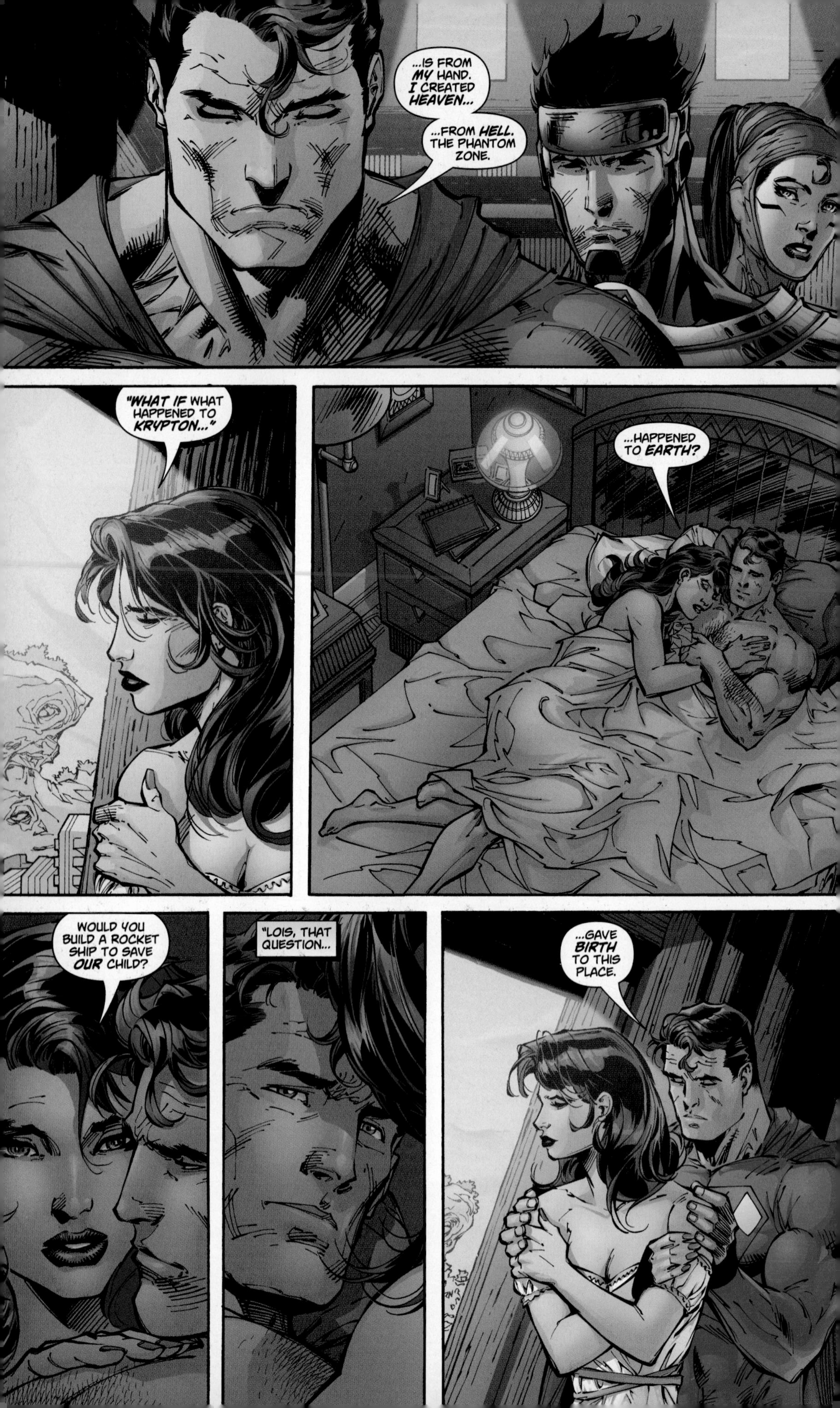
...IS FROM MY HAND. I CREATED HEAVEN...
...FROM HELL. THE PHANTOM ZONE.
"WHAT IF WHAT HAPPENED TO KRYPTON..."
...HAPPENED TO EARTH?
WOULD YOU BUILD A ROCKET SHIP TO SAVE OUR CHILD?
"LOIS, THAT QUESTION...
...GAVE BIRTH TO THIS PLACE.

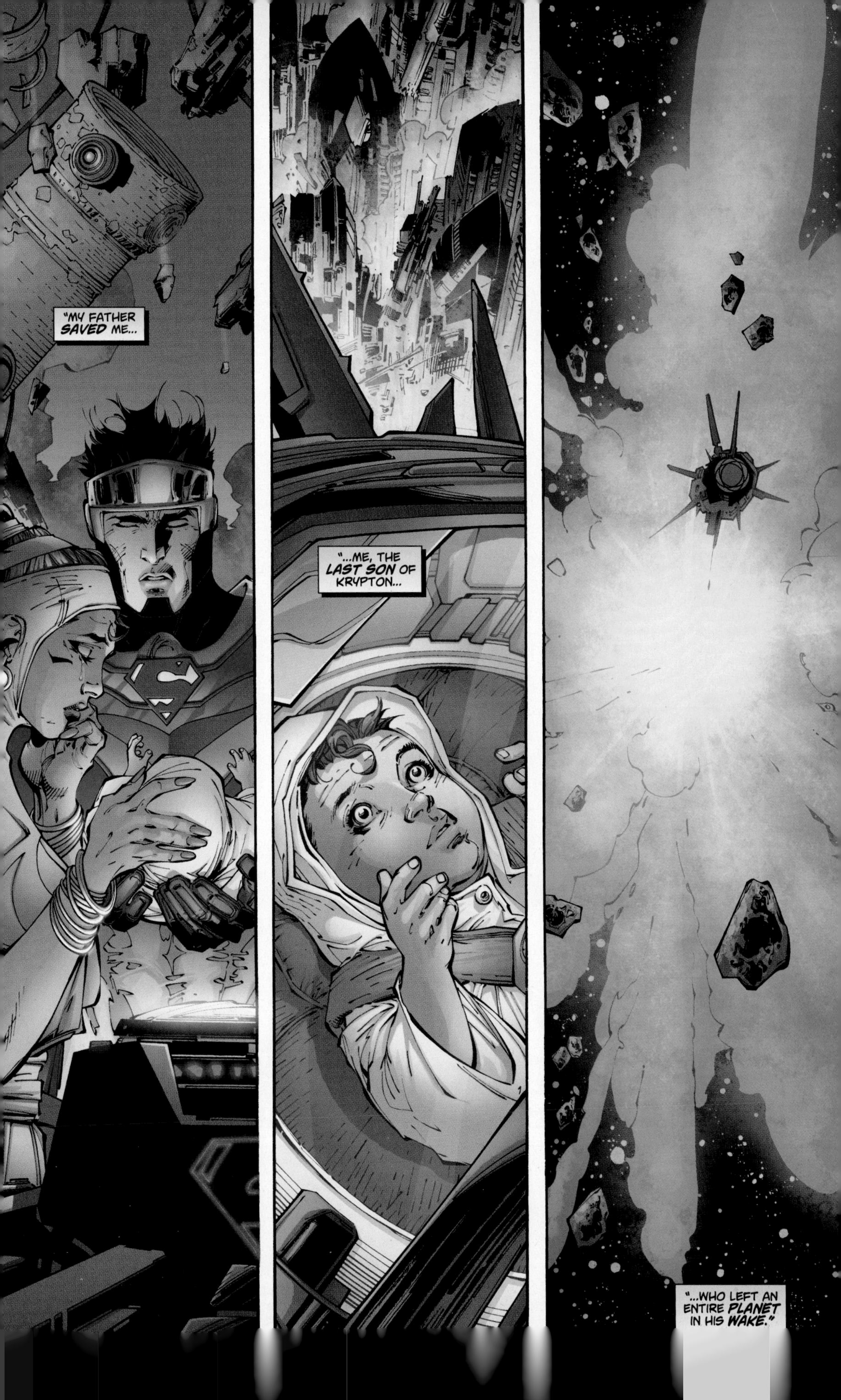
"MY FATHER SAVED ME...
"...ME, THE LAST SON OF KRYPTON...
"...WHO LEFT AN ENTIRE PLANET IN HIS WAKE."

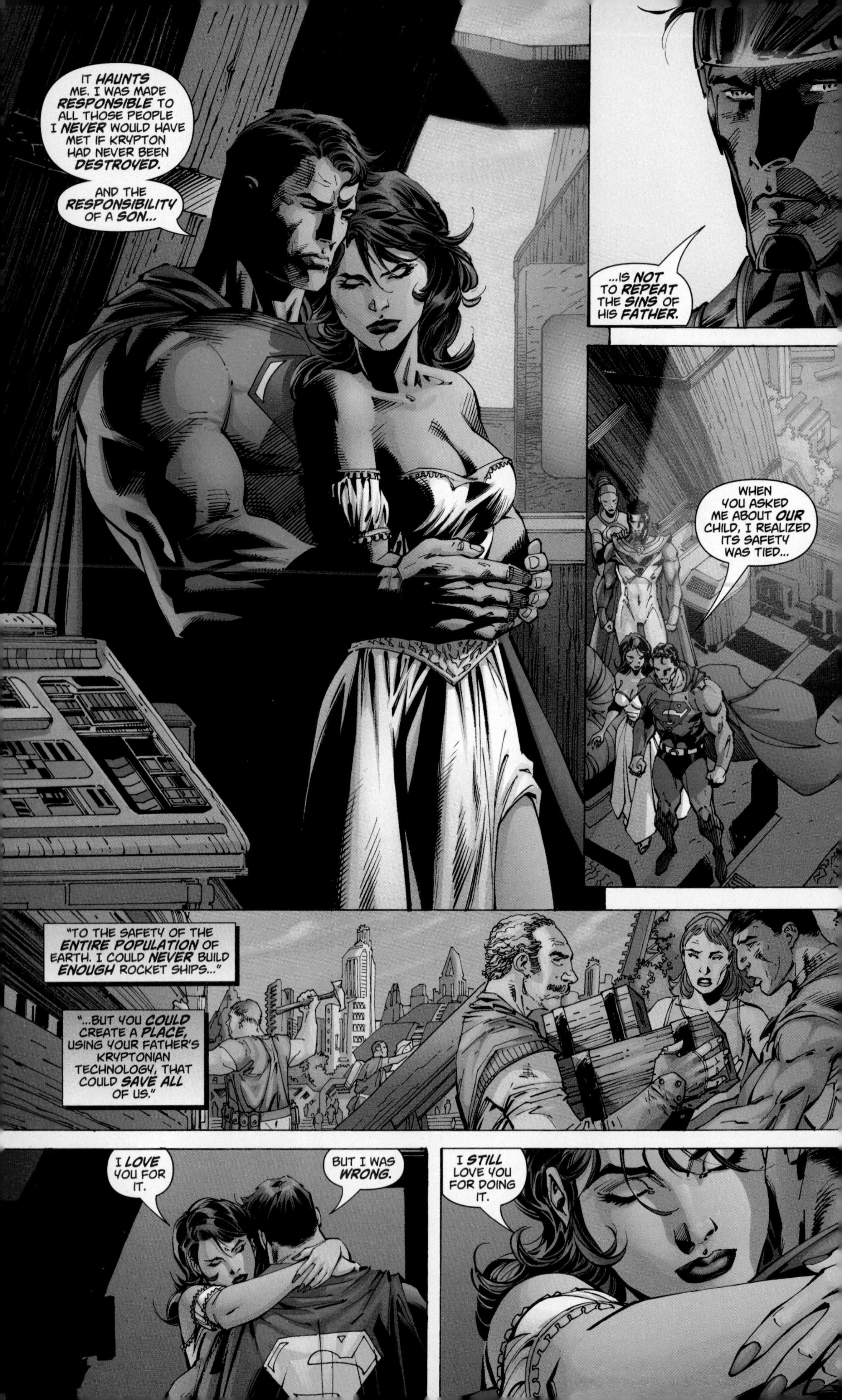

IT HAUNTS ME. I WAS MADE RESPONSIBLE TO ALL THOSE PEOPLE I NEVER WOULD HAVE MET IF KRYPTON HAD NEVER BEEN DESTROYED.
AND THE RESPONSIBILITY OF A SON...
...IS NOT TO REPEAT THE SINS OF HIS FATHER.
WHEN YOU ASKED ME ABOUT OUR CHILD, I REALIZED ITS SAFETY WAS TIED...
"TO THE SAFETY OF THE ENTIRE POPULATION OF EARTH. I COULD NEVER BUILD ENOUGH ROCKET SHIPS..."
"...BUT YOU COULD CREATE A PLACE, USING YOUR FATHER'S KRYPTONIAN TECHNOLOGY, THAT COULD SAVE ALL OF US."
I LOVE YOU FOR IT.
BUT I WAS WRONG.
I STILL LOVE YOU FOR DOING IT.

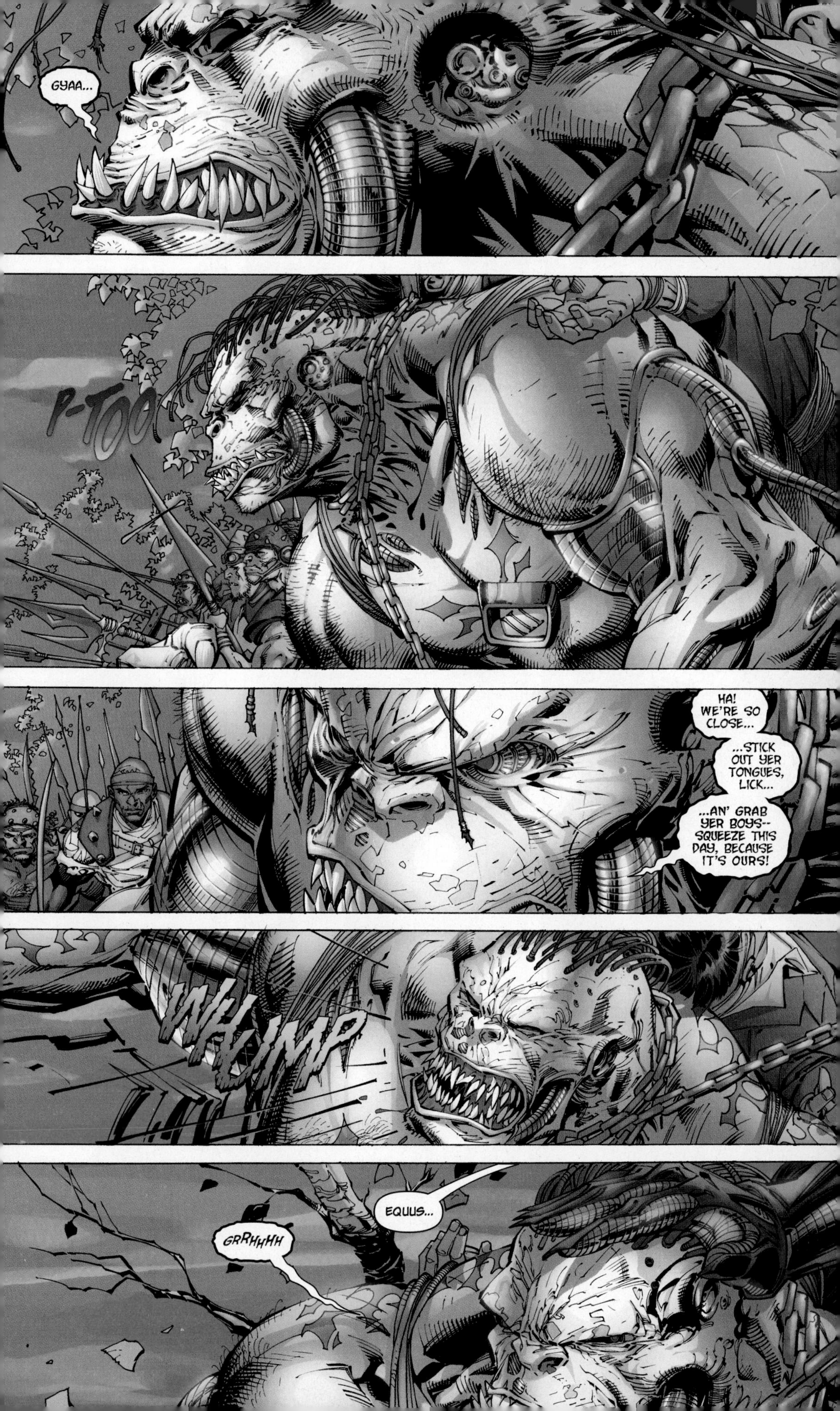

GYAA...
P-TOO
HA! WE'RE SO CLOSE...
...STICK OUT YER TONGUES, LICK...
...AN' GRAB YER BOYS-- SQUEEZE THIS DAY, BECAUSE IT'S OURS!
WHUMP
EQUUS...
GRRHHHH

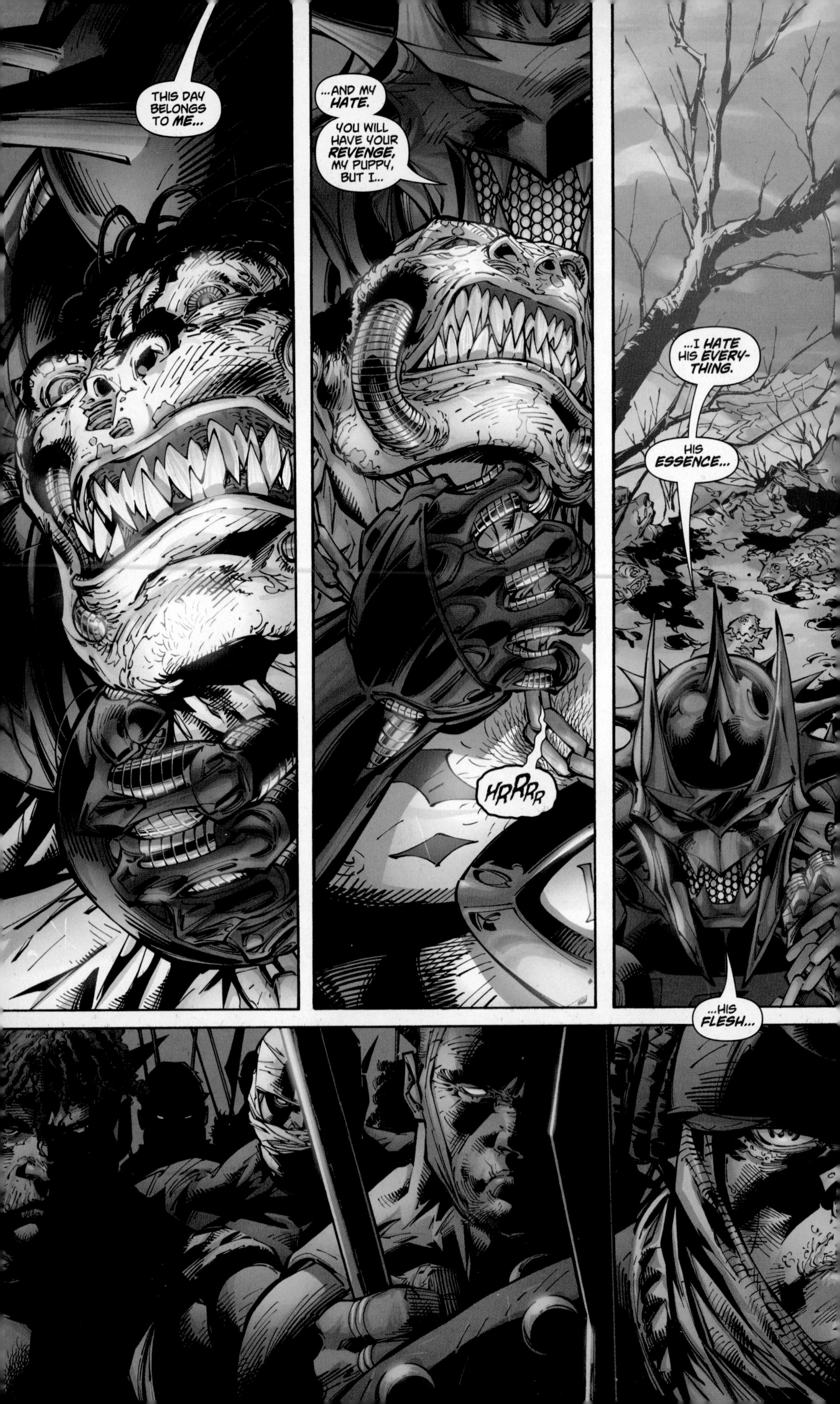

THIS DAY BELONGS TO ME...
...AND MY HATE.
YOU WILL HAVE YOUR REVENGE, MY PUPPY, BUT I...
HRRRR
...I HATE HIS EVERY-THING.
HIS ESSENCE...
...HIS FLESH...

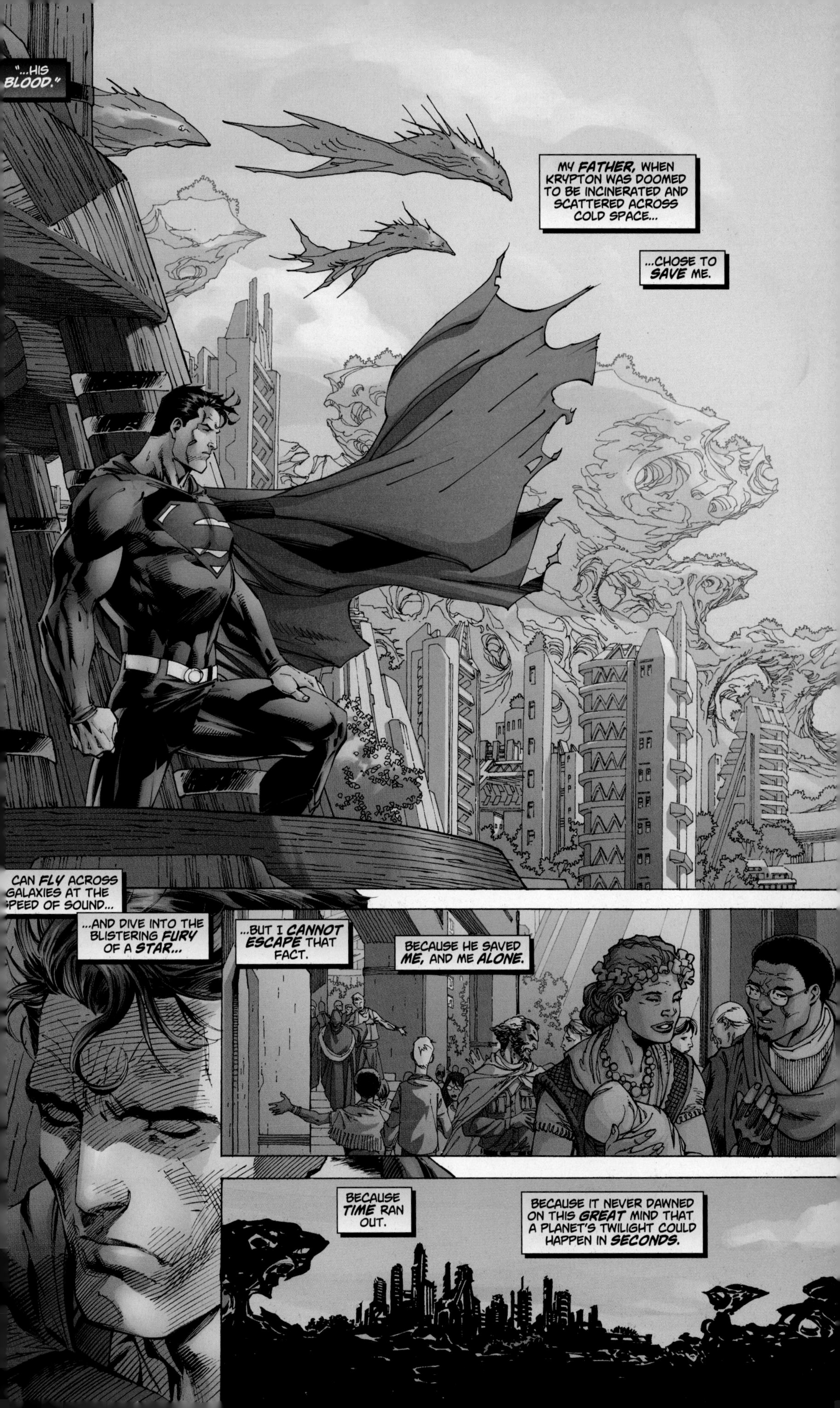
"...HIS BLOOD."
MY FATHER, WHEN KRYPTON WAS DOOMED TO BE INCINERATED AND SCATTERED ACROSS COLD SPACE...
...CHOSE TO SAVE ME.
CAN FLY ACROSS GALAXIES AT THE SPEED OF SOUND...
...AND DIVE INTO THE BLISTERING FURY OF A STAR...
...BUT I CANNOT ESCAPE THAT FACT.
BECAUSE HE SAVED ME, AND ME ALONE.
BECAUSE TIME RAN OUT.
BECAUSE IT NEVER DAWNED ON THIS GREAT MIND THAT A PLANET'S TWILIGHT COULD HAPPEN IN SECONDS.

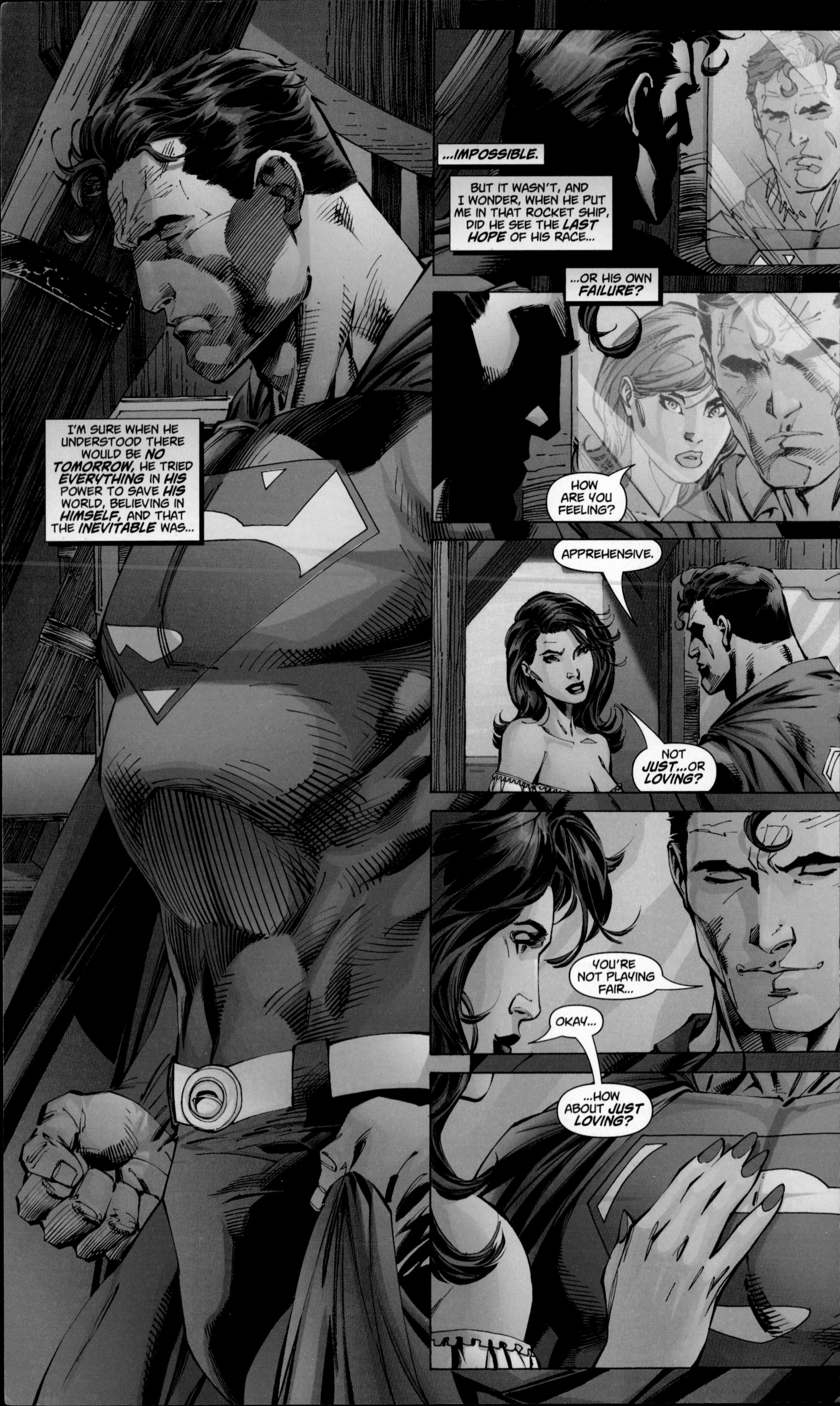
I'M SURE WHEN HE UNDERSTOOD THERE WOULD BE NO TOMORROW, HE TRIED EVERYTHING IN HIS POWER TO SAVE HIS WORLD, BELIEVING IN HIMSELF, AND THAT THE INEVITABLE WAS...
...IMPOSSIBLE.
BUT IT WASN'T, AND I WONDER, WHEN HE PUT ME IN THAT ROCKET SHIP, DID HE SEE THE LAST HOPE OF HIS RACE...
...OR HIS OWN FAILURE?
HOW ARE YOU FEELING?
APPREHENSIVE.
NOT JUST...OR LOVING?
YOU'RE NOT PLAYING FAIR...
OKAY...
...HOW ABOUT JUST LOVING?

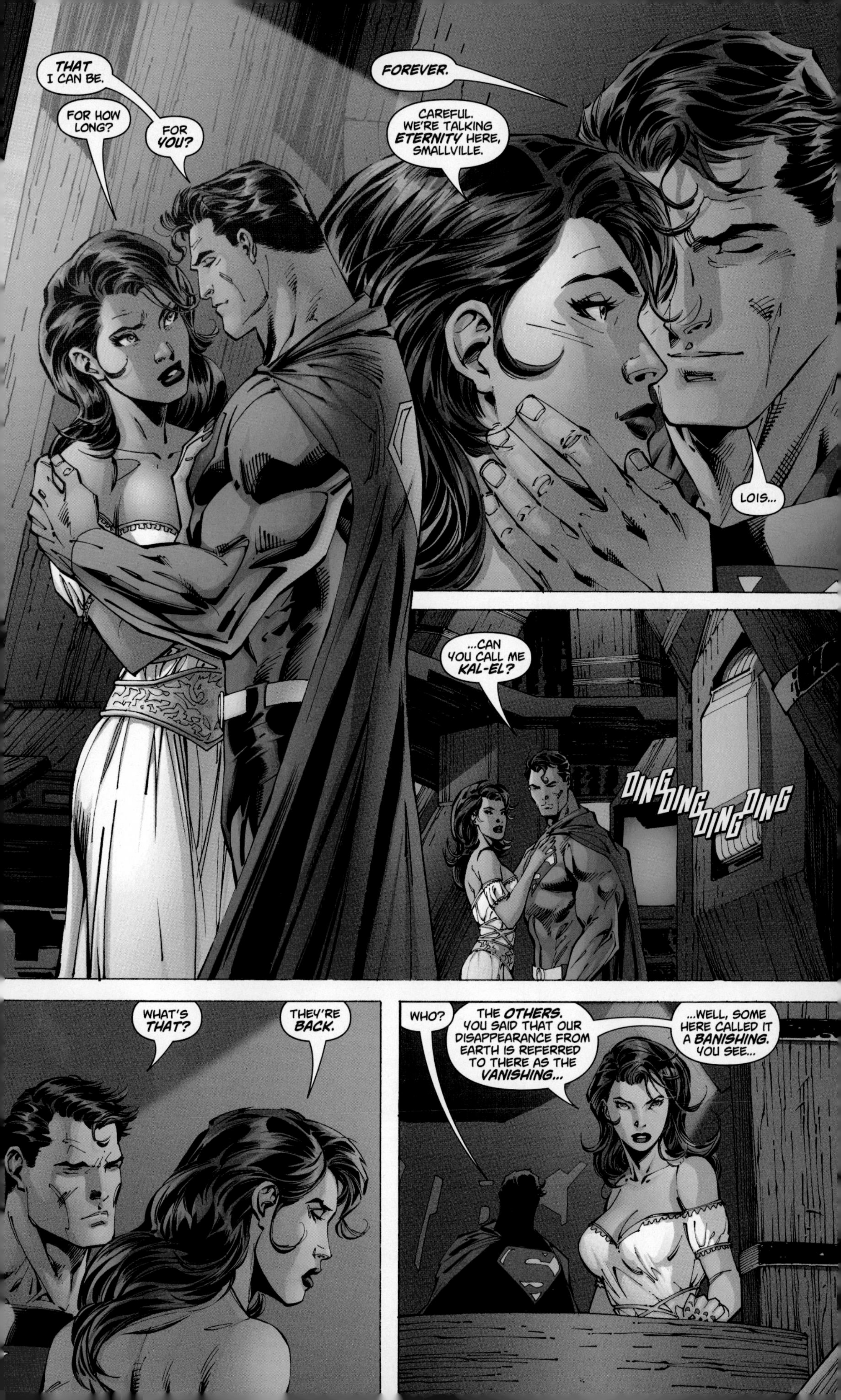

THAT I CAN BE.
FOR HOW LONG?
FOR YOU?
FOREVER.
CAREFUL. WE'RE TALKING ETERNITY HERE, SMALLVILLE.
LOIS...
...CAN YOU CALL ME KAL-EL?
DING DING DING DING
WHAT'S THAT?
THEY'RE BACK.
WHO?
THE OTHERS. YOU SAID THAT OUR DISAPPEARANCE FROM EARTH IS REFERRED TO THERE AS THE VANISHING...
...WELL, SOME HERE CALLED IT A BANISHING. YOU SEE...

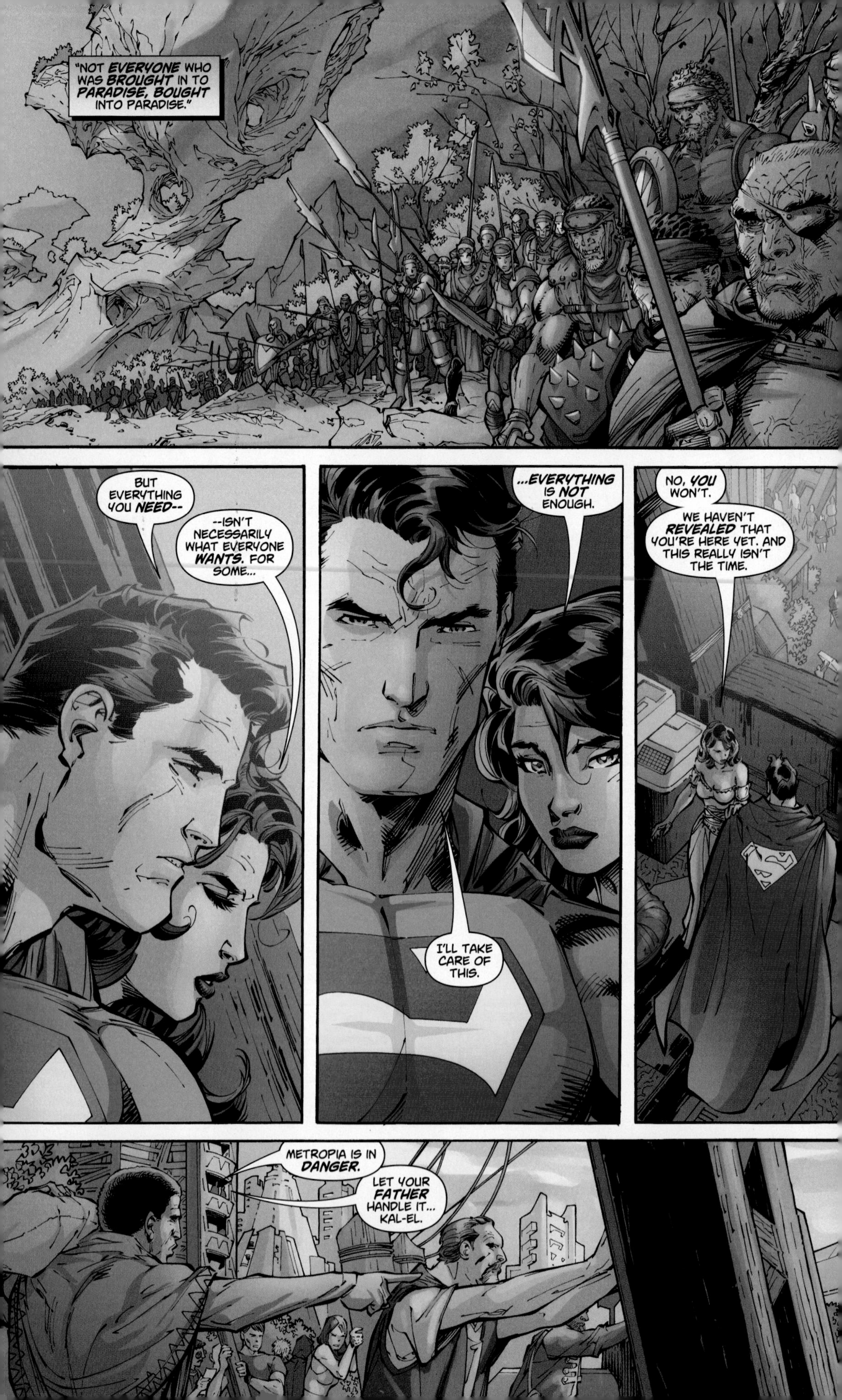
"NOT EVERYONE WHO WAS BROUGHT IN TO PARADISE, BOUGHT INTO PARADISE."
BUT EVERYTHING YOU NEED--
--ISN'T NECESSARILY WHAT EVERYONE WANTS. FOR SOME...
...EVERYTHING IS NOT ENOUGH.
I'LL TAKE CARE OF THIS.
NO, YOU WON'T.
WE HAVEN'T REVEALED THAT YOU'RE HERE YET. AND THIS REALLY ISN'T THE TIME.
METROPIA IS IN DANGER.
LET YOUR FATHER HANDLE IT... KAL-EL.

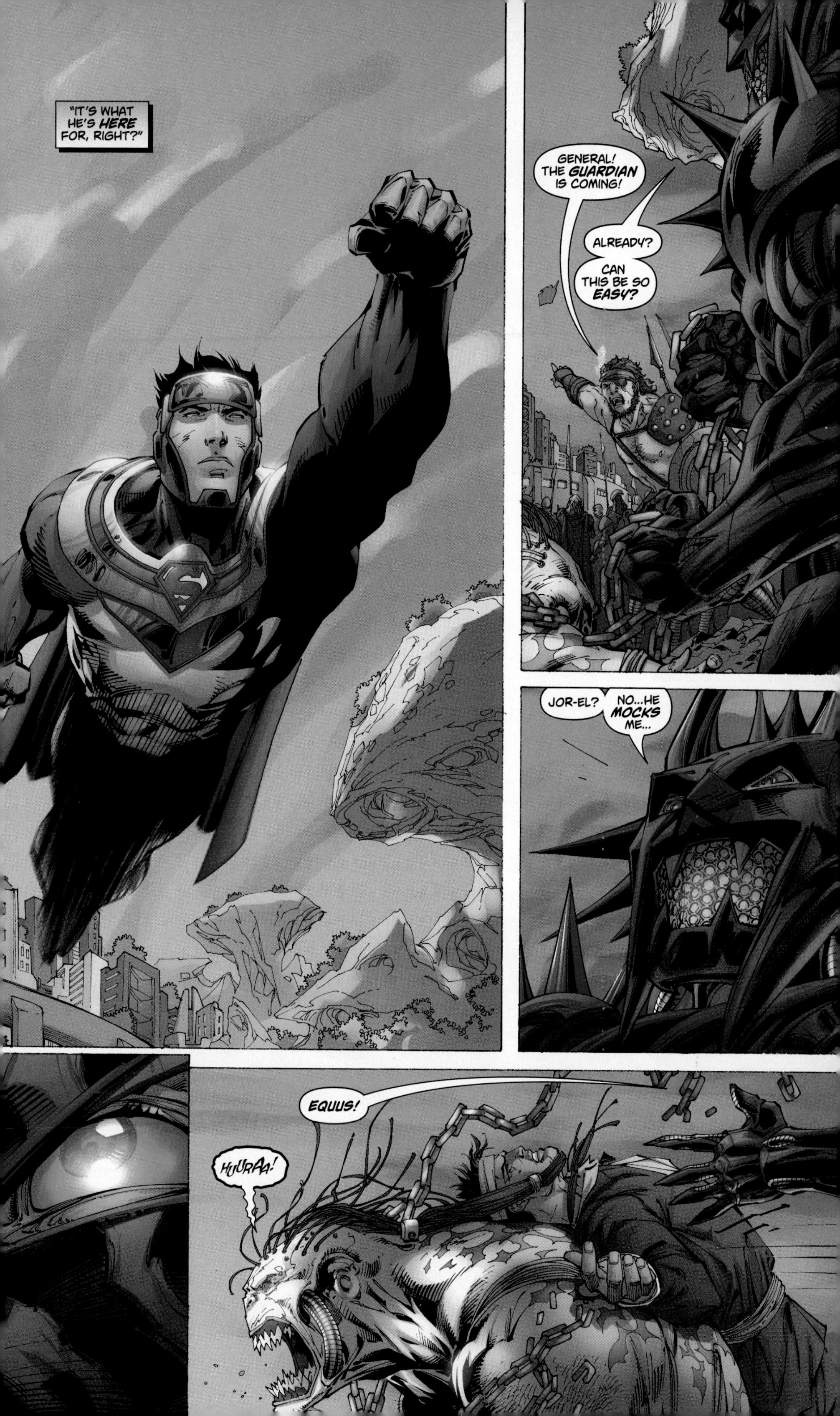
"IT'S WHAT HE'S *HERE* FOR, RIGHT?"
GENERAL! THE *GUARDIAN* IS COMING!
ALREADY?
CAN THIS BE SO *EASY?*
JOR-EL?
NO...HE *MOCKS* ME...
EQUUS!
HUURAA!

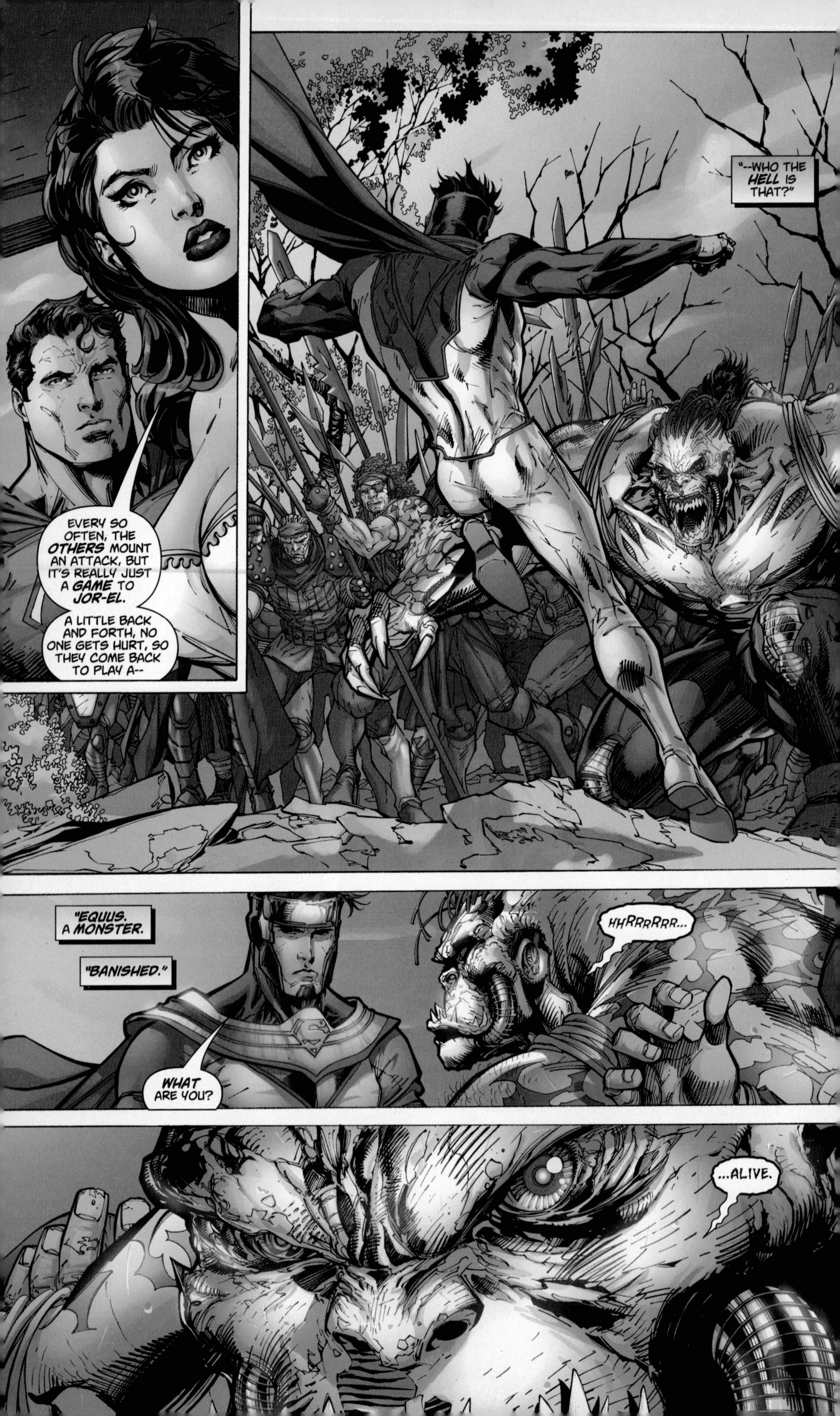
EVERY SO OFTEN, THE OTHERS MOUNT AN ATTACK, BUT IT'S REALLY JUST A GAME TO JOR-EL.
A LITTLE BACK AND FORTH, NO ONE GETS HURT, SO THEY COME BACK TO PLAY A--
"--WHO THE HELL IS THAT?"
"EQUUS. A MONSTER.
"BANISHED."
HHRRRRRR...
WHAT ARE YOU?
...ALIVE.

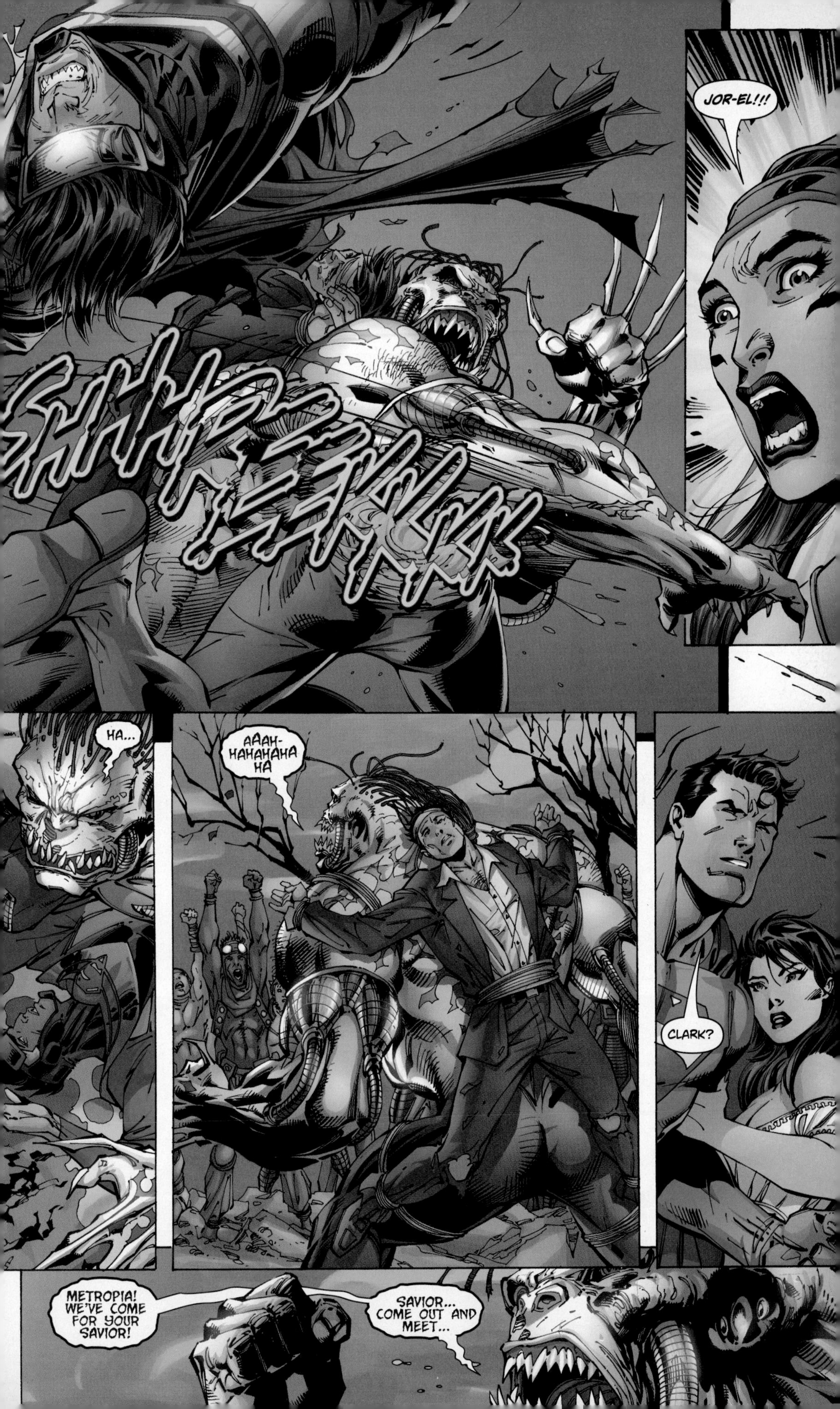
JOR-EL!!!
SHHRRAKKK
HA...
AAAH-HAHAHAHA HA
CLARK?
METROPIA! WE'VE COME FOR YOUR SAVIOR!
SAVIOR... COME OUT AND MEET...

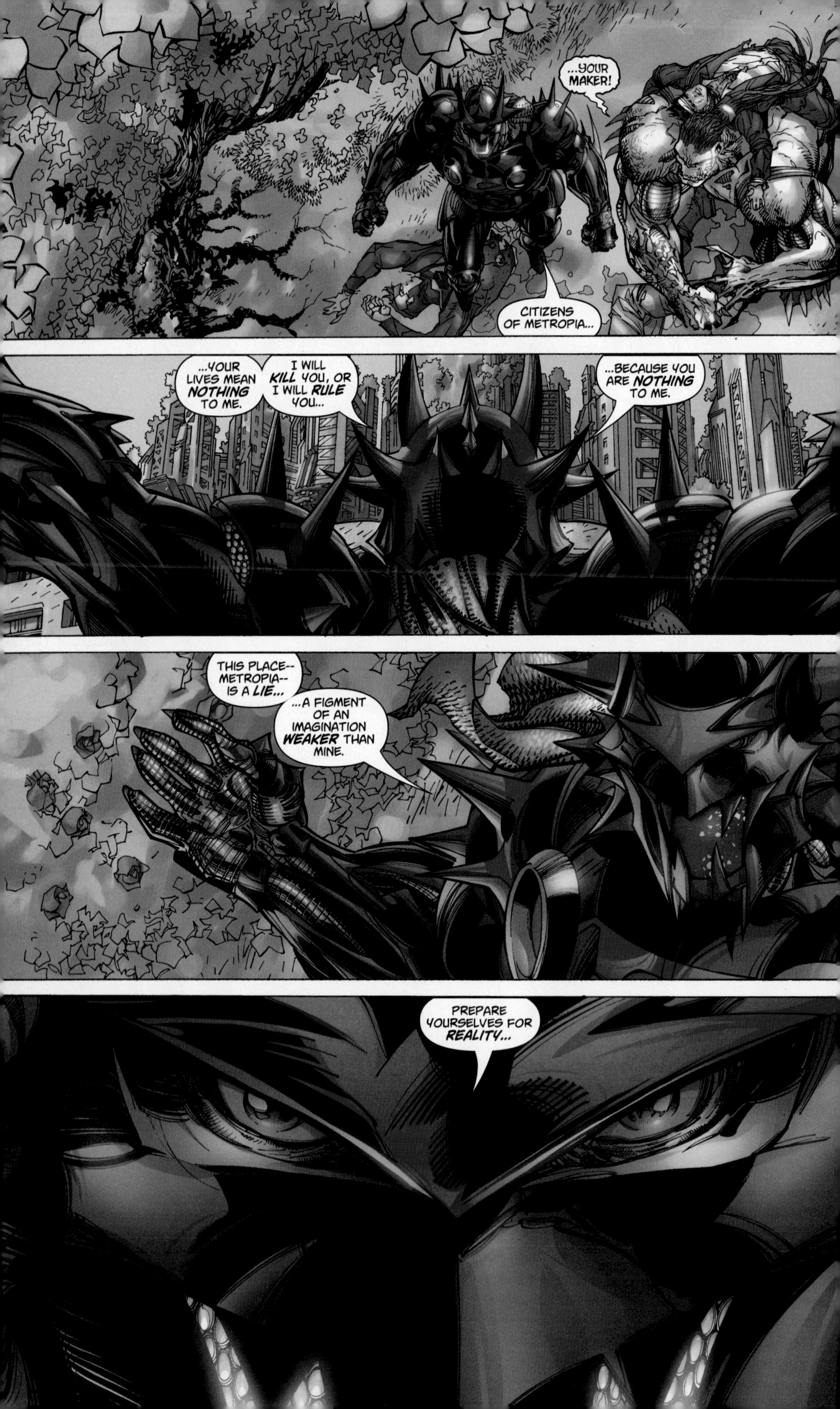

...YOUR MAKER!
CITIZENS OF METROPIA...
...YOUR LIVES MEAN NOTHING TO ME.
I WILL KILL YOU, OR I WILL RULE YOU...
...BECAUSE YOU ARE NOTHING TO ME.
THIS PLACE-- METROPIA-- IS A LIE...
...A FIGMENT OF AN IMAGINATION WEAKER THAN MINE.
PREPARE YOURSELVES FOR REALITY...

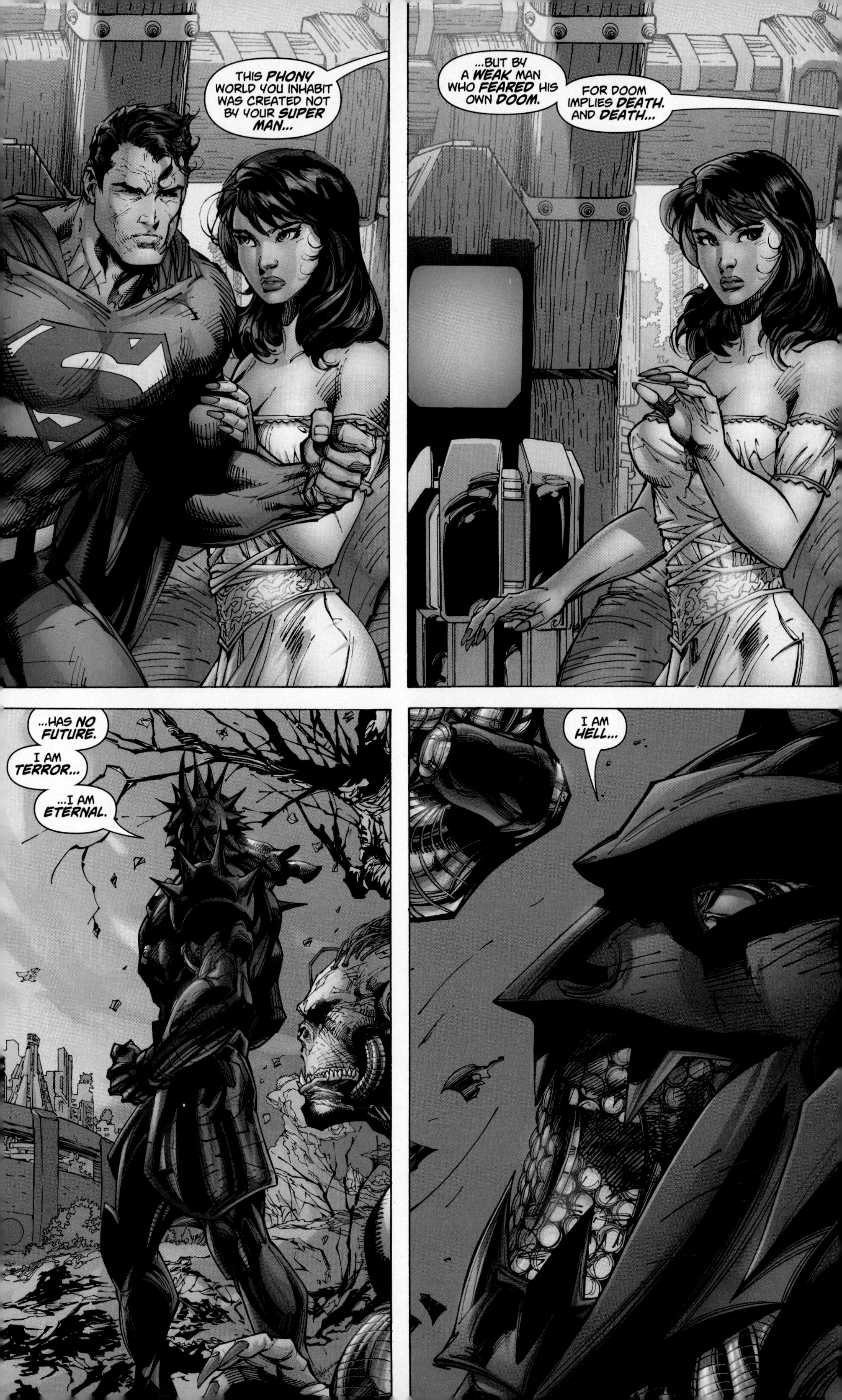
THIS PHONY WORLD YOU INHABIT WAS CREATED NOT BY YOUR SUPER MAN...
...BUT BY A WEAK MAN WHO FEARED HIS OWN DOOM.
FOR DOOM IMPLIES DEATH. AND DEATH...
...HAS NO FUTURE.
I AM TERROR...
...I AM ETERNAL.
I AM HELL...

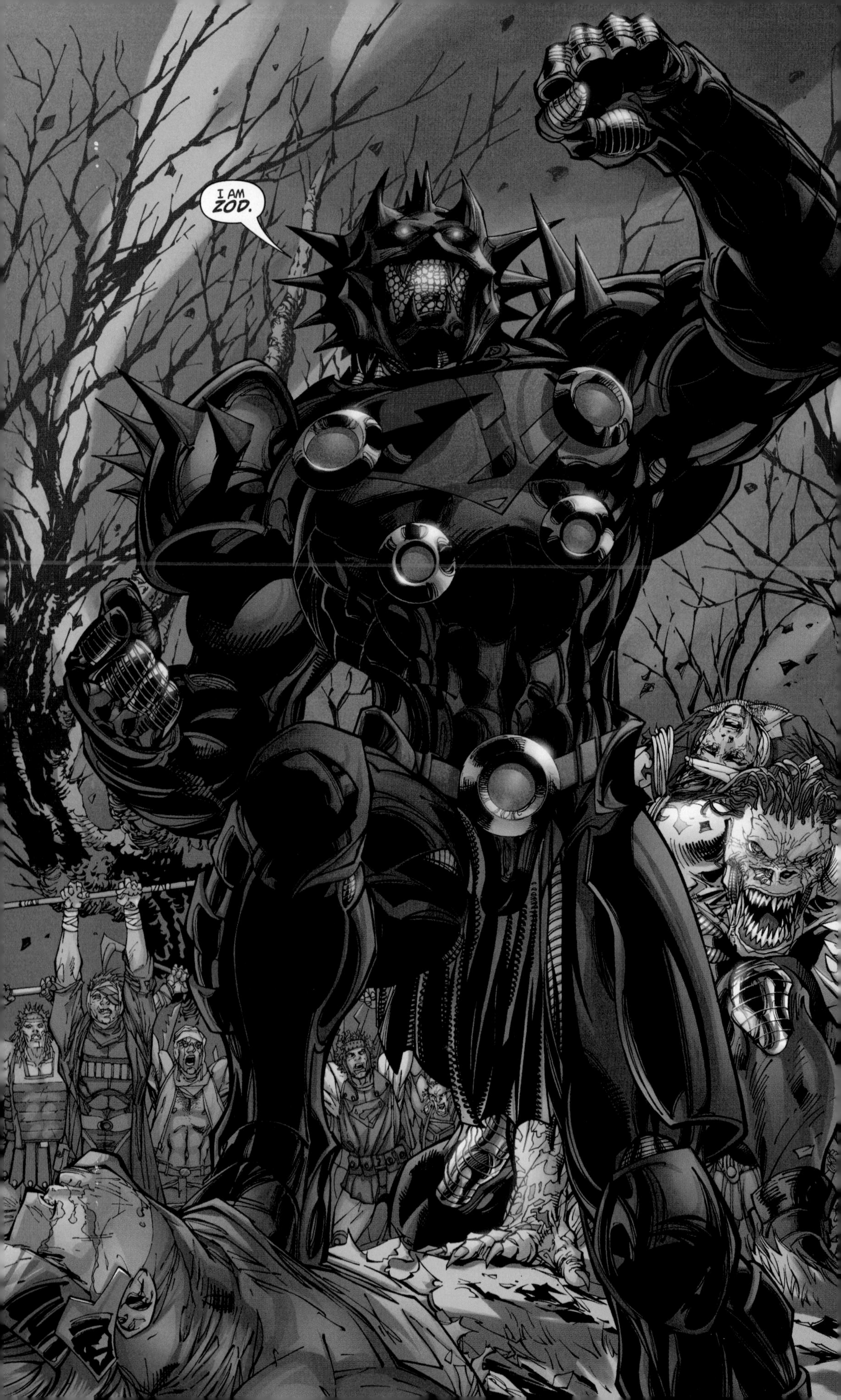

I AM ZOD.

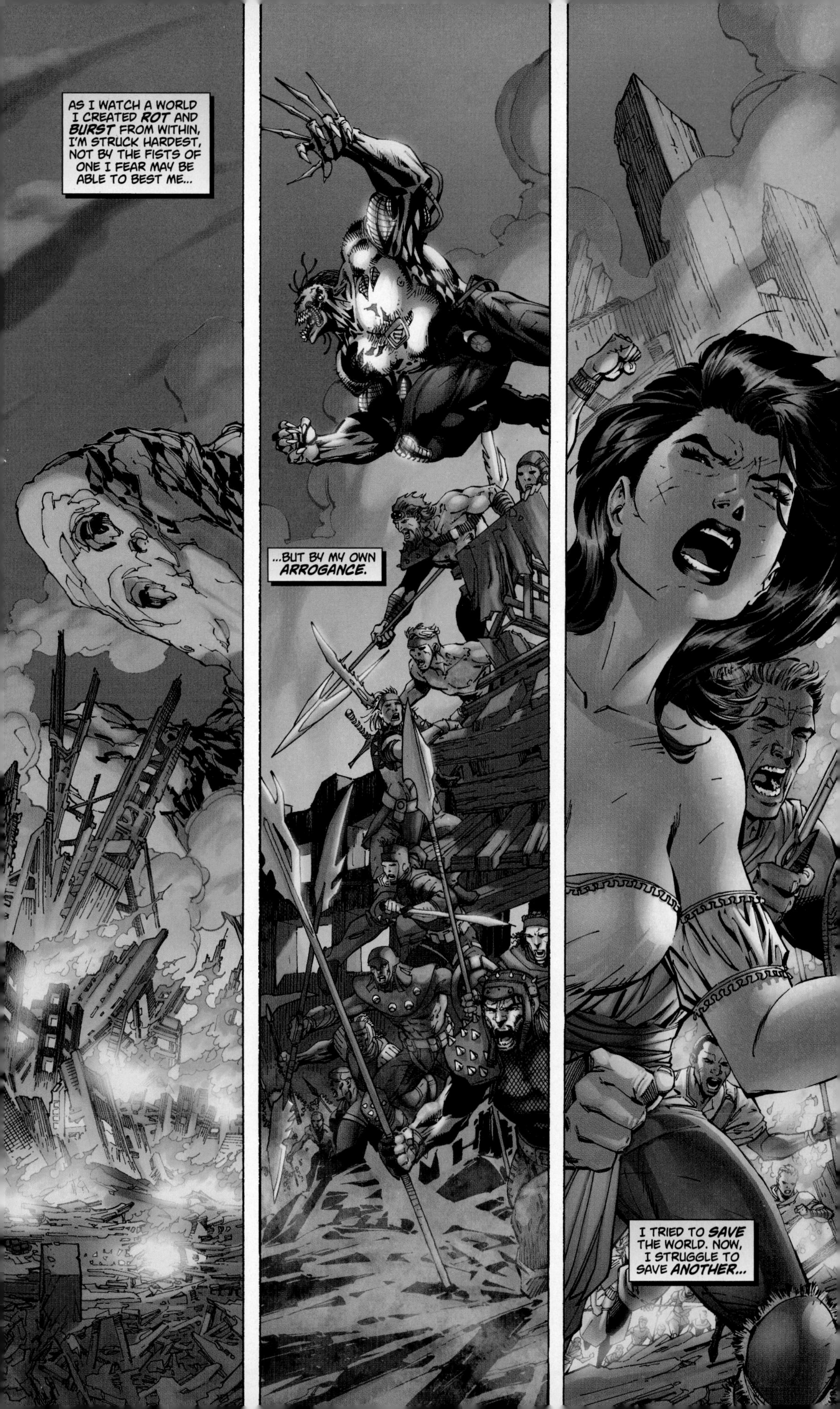
AS I WATCH A WORLD I CREATED ROT AND BURST FROM WITHIN, I'M STRUCK HARDEST, NOT BY THE FISTS OF ONE I FEAR MAY BE ABLE TO BEST ME...
...BUT BY MY OWN ARROGANCE.
I TRIED TO SAVE THE WORLD. NOW, I STRUGGLE TO SAVE ANOTHER...

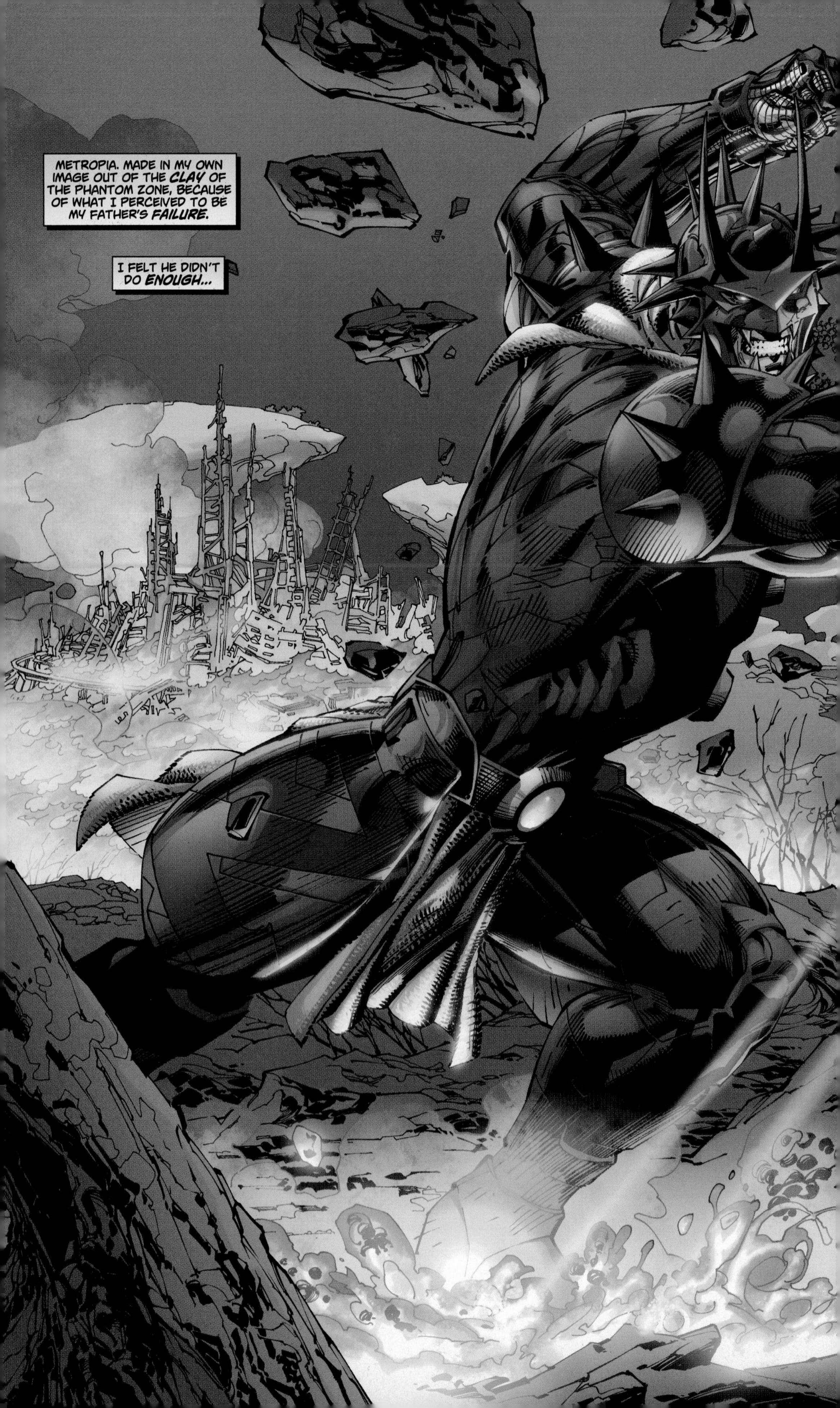
METROPIA. MADE IN MY OWN IMAGE OUT OF THE CLAY OF THE PHANTOM ZONE, BECAUSE OF WHAT I PERCEIVED TO BE MY FATHER'S FAILURE.
I FELT HE DIDN'T DO ENOUGH...

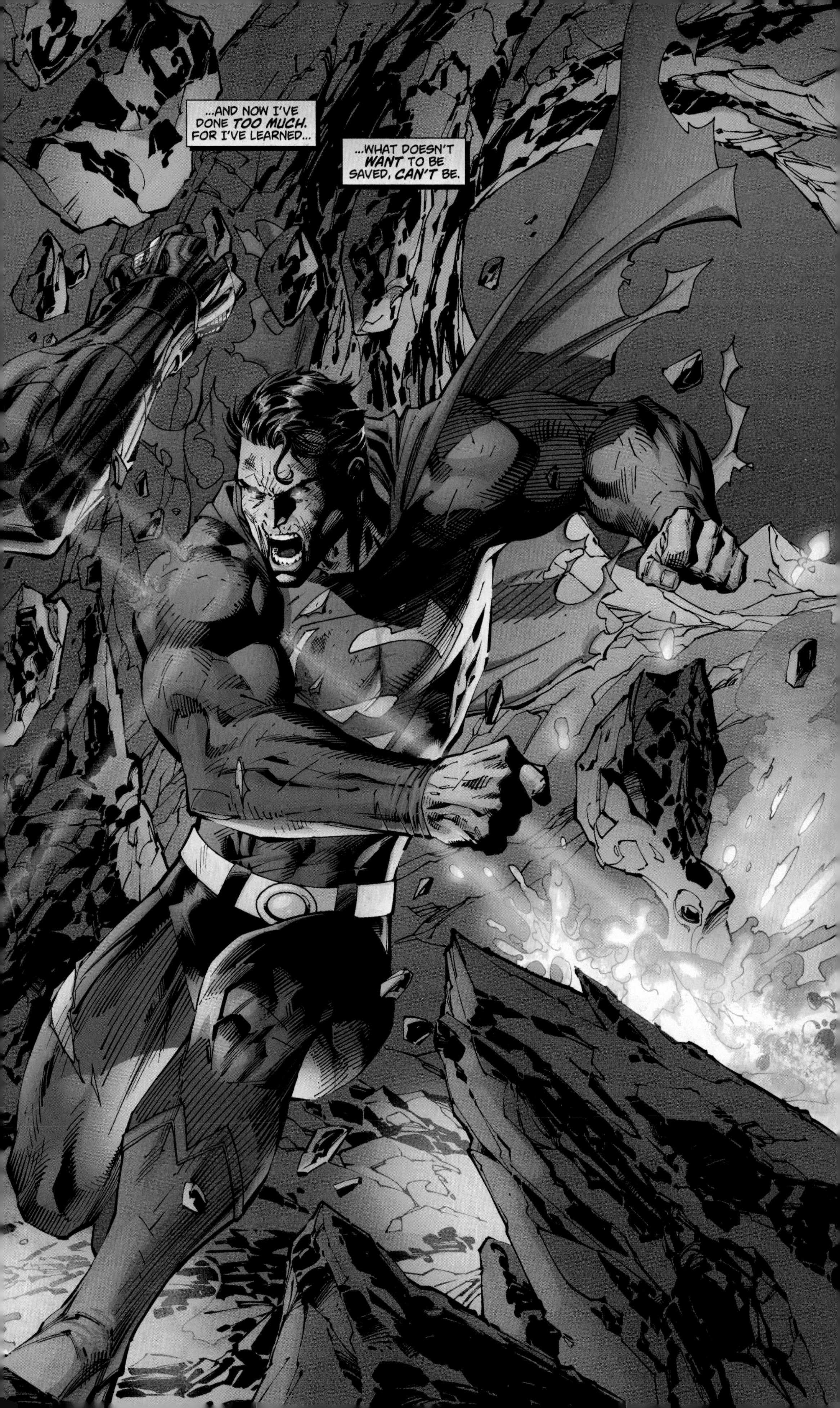
...AND NOW I'VE DONE *TOO MUCH*. FOR I'VE LEARNED...
...WHAT DOESN'T *WANT* TO BE SAVED, *CAN'T* BE.

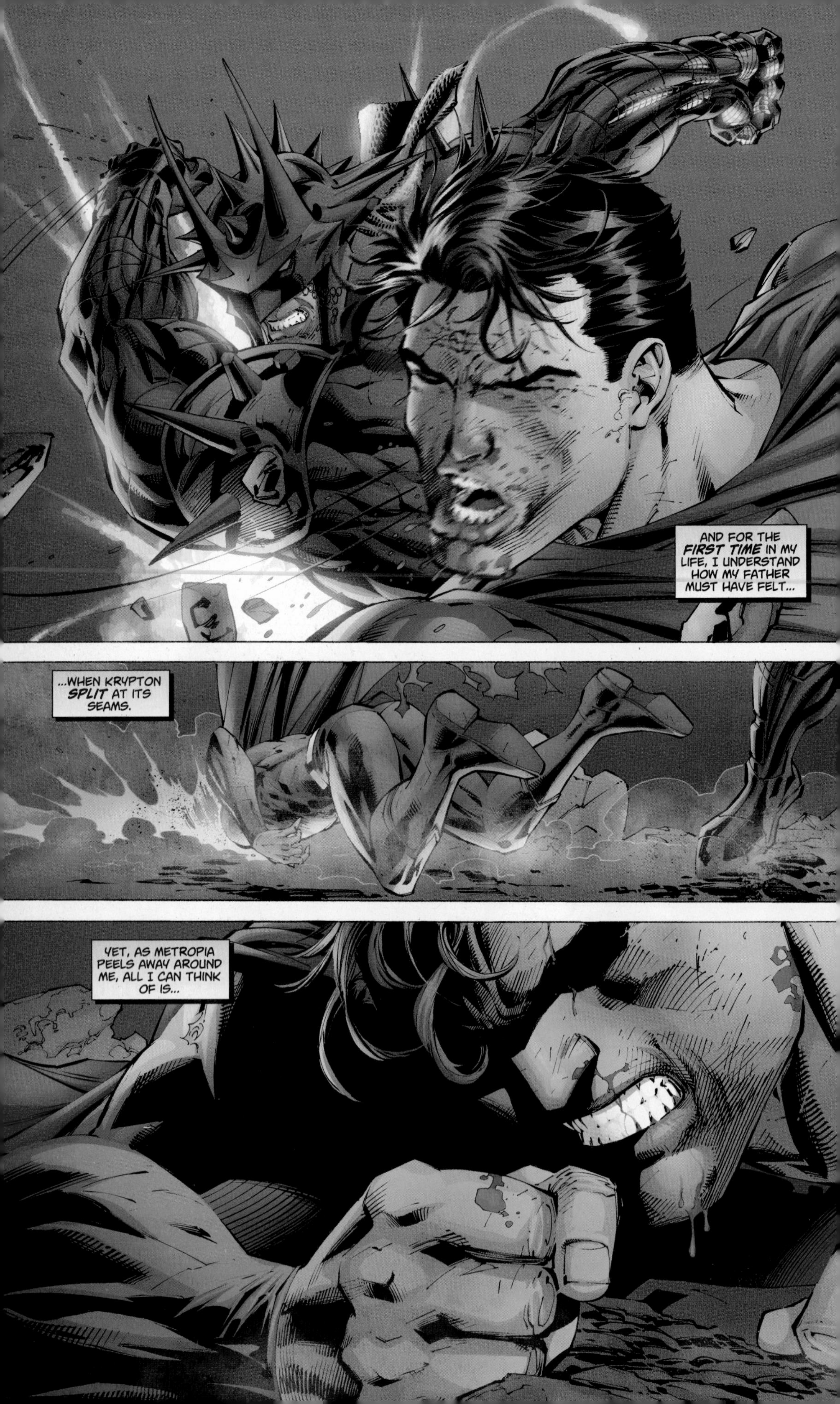
AND FOR THE FIRST TIME IN MY LIFE, I UNDERSTAND HOW MY FATHER MUST HAVE FELT...
...WHEN KRYPTON SPLIT AT ITS SEAMS.
YET, AS METROPIA PEELS AWAY AROUND ME, ALL I CAN THINK OF IS...

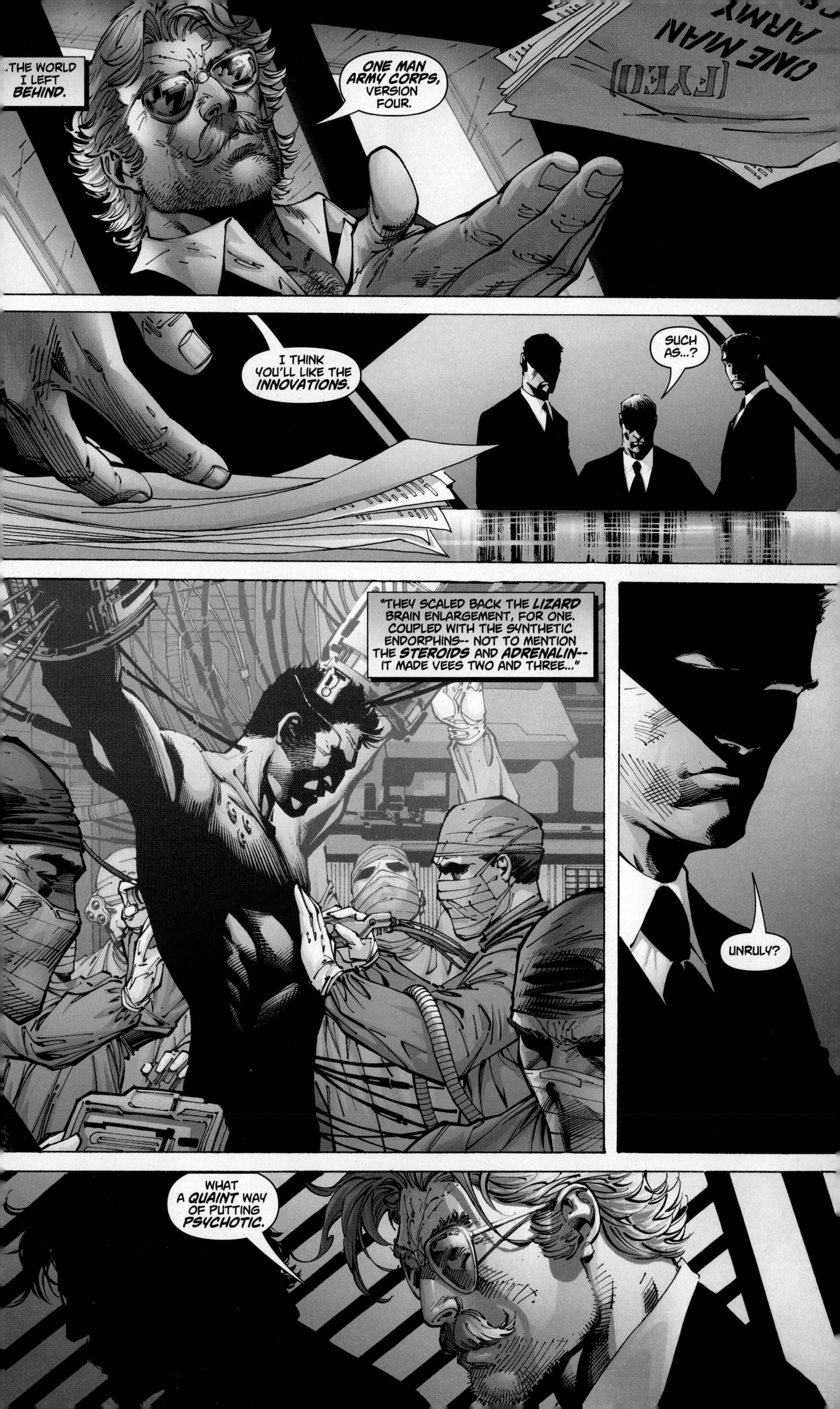

...THE WORLD I LEFT BEHIND.
ONE MAN ARMY CORPS, VERSION FOUR.
ONE MAN ARMY
(FYEO)
I THINK YOU'LL LIKE THE INNOVATIONS.
SUCH AS...?
"THEY SCALED BACK THE LIZARD BRAIN ENLARGEMENT, FOR ONE. COUPLED WITH THE SYNTHETIC ENDORPHINS-- NOT TO MENTION THE STEROIDS AND ADRENALIN-- IT MADE VEES TWO AND THREE..."
UNRULY?
WHAT A QUAINT WAY OF PUTTING PSYCHOTIC.

THE HAPTIC, OLIGOTRONIC, AND HINGE TECH HAVE ALL BEEN RETAINED, BUT--WITH A *BONUS*...

...NANOPARTICLE MAGNETO-RHEOLOGICAL FLUIDS, HOUSED IN A CARBON NANOTUBULAR VASCULATURE SYSTEM. YOU COULD *KILL* HIM...

...AND HE *WOULDN'T DIE.*

AS PER ONE OF YOUR REQUESTS, THE *VOODOO* ENHANCEMENTS HAVE BEEN *INCREASED.*

IT'S NOT *VOODOO*, MR. ORR.

RIGHT.

WHERE VEE-THREE HAD-- THIS IS REALLY HARD FOR ME TO SAY-- THE SKELETAL WINGS OF A *FALLEN ANGEL* EMBEDDED IN ITS FOREARMS...

WHERE'D YOU GET *THAT*, ANYWAY?

PLEASE CONTINUE, MR. ORR.

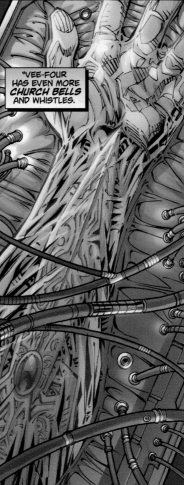

"VEE-FOUR HAS EVEN MORE *CHURCH BELLS* AND WHISTLES.

"AND A *CRICKET.*"

"EXCUSE ME?"

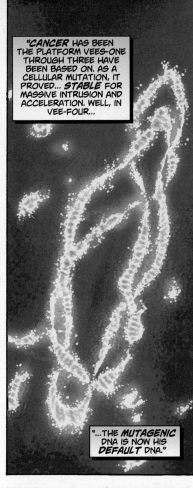

"CANCER HAS BEEN THE PLATFORM VEES-ONE THROUGH THREE HAVE BEEN BASED ON. AS A CELLULAR MUTATION, IT PROVED... *STABLE* FOR MASSIVE INTRUSION AND ACCELERATION. WELL, IN VEE-FOUR...

"...THE *MUTAGENIC* DNA IS NOW HIS *DEFAULT* DNA."

"WE'VE *CURED* CANCER?"

"THAT'S *ONE* WAY OF PUTTING IT. ANOTHER IS...

"...YOU'VE *HARNESSED* IT."

WELL, IT ALL LOOKS *PROMISING*, BUT UNFORTUNATELY...

...WE'VE DECIDED TO GO IN *ANOTHER* DIRECTION.

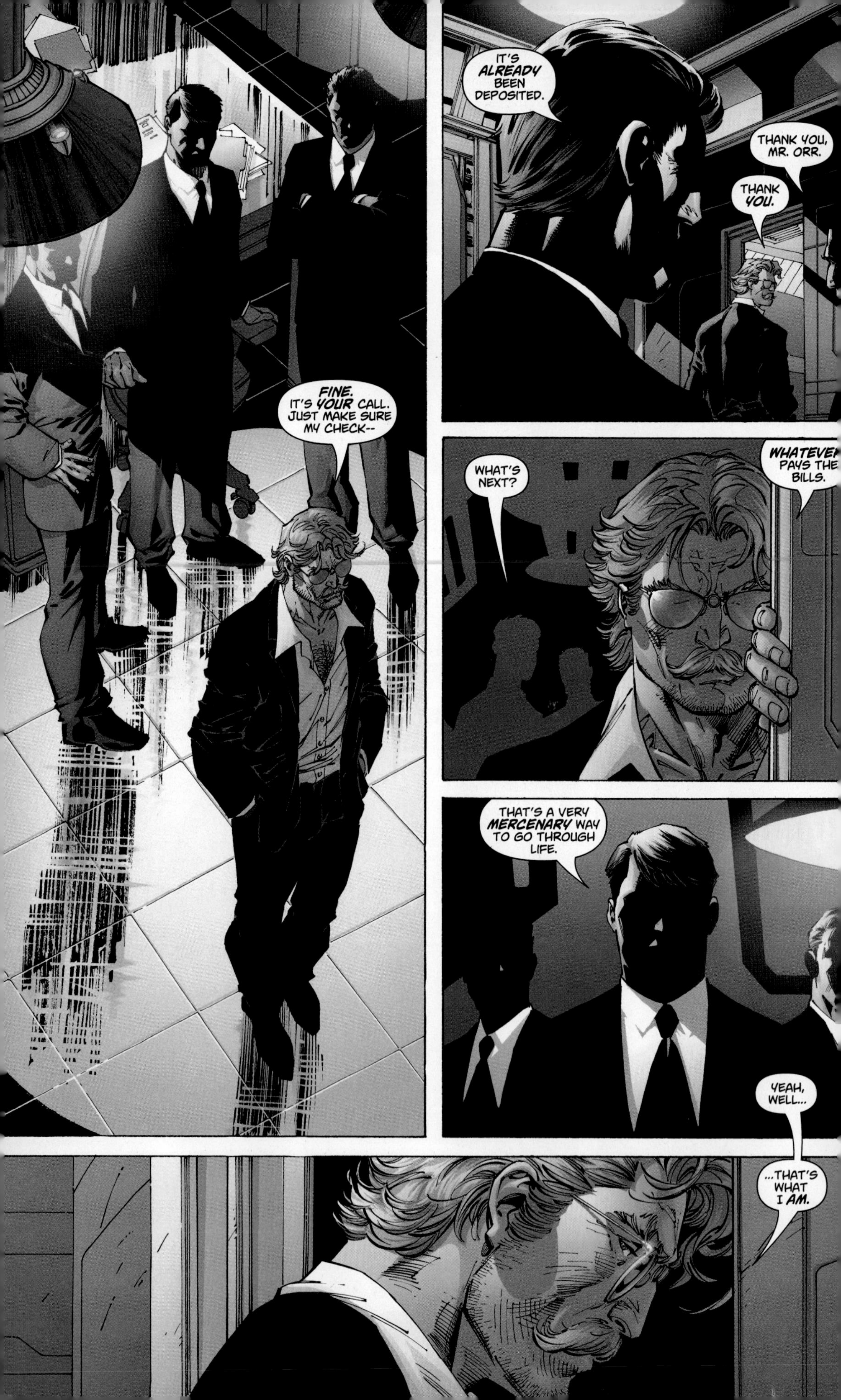

FINE. IT'S YOUR CALL. JUST MAKE SURE MY CHECK--
IT'S ALREADY BEEN DEPOSITED.
THANK YOU, MR. ORR.
THANK YOU.
WHAT'S NEXT?
WHATEVER PAYS THE BILLS.
THAT'S A VERY MERCENARY WAY TO GO THROUGH LIFE.
YEAH, WELL...
...THAT'S WHAT I AM.

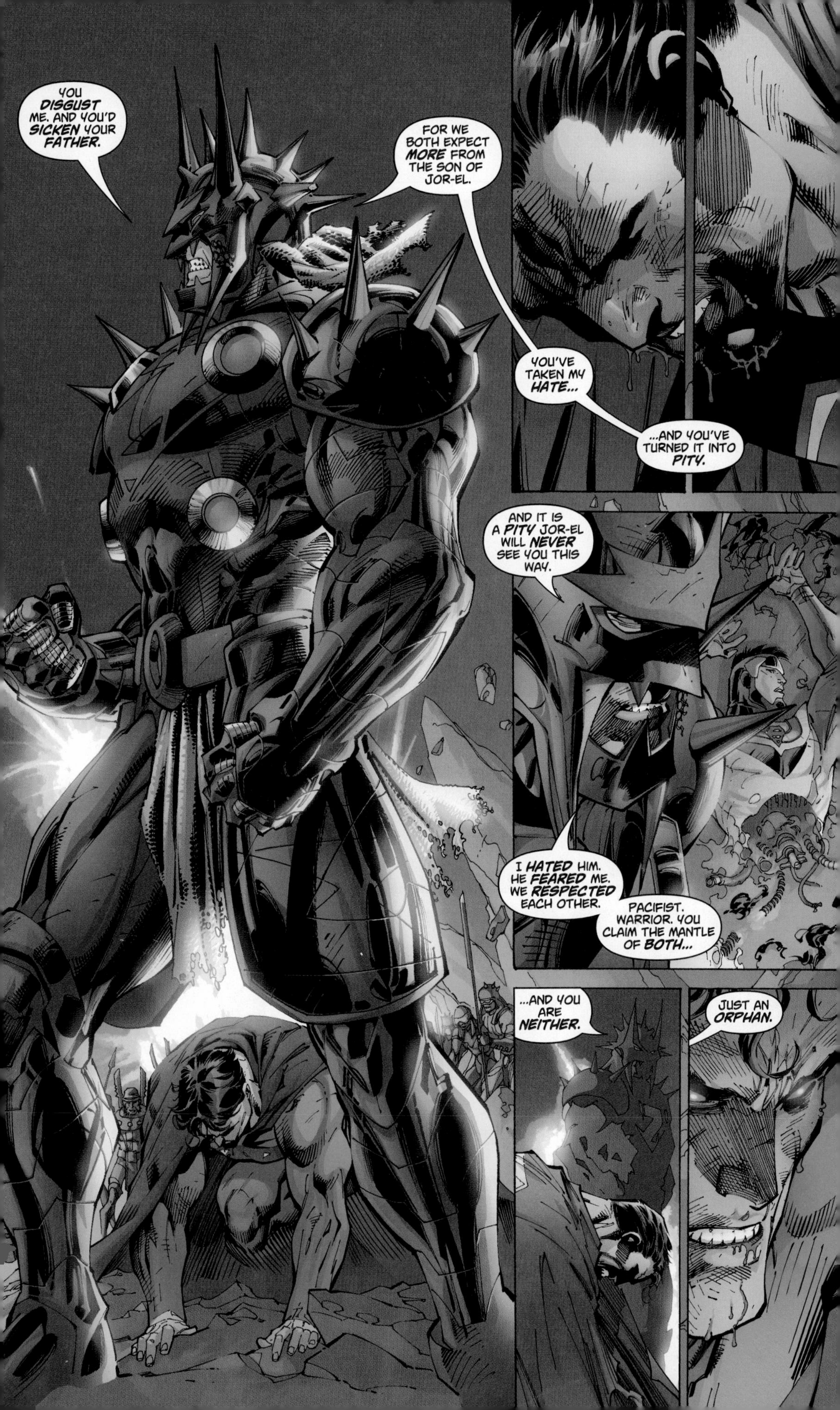
YOU DISGUST ME. AND YOU'D SICKEN YOUR FATHER.
FOR WE BOTH EXPECT MORE FROM THE SON OF JOR-EL.
YOU'VE TAKEN MY HATE...
...AND YOU'VE TURNED IT INTO PITY.
AND IT IS A PITY JOR-EL WILL NEVER SEE YOU THIS WAY.
I HATED HIM. HE FEARED ME. WE RESPECTED EACH OTHER.
PACIFIST. WARRIOR. YOU CLAIM THE MANTLE OF BOTH...
...AND YOU ARE NEITHER.
JUST AN ORPHAN.

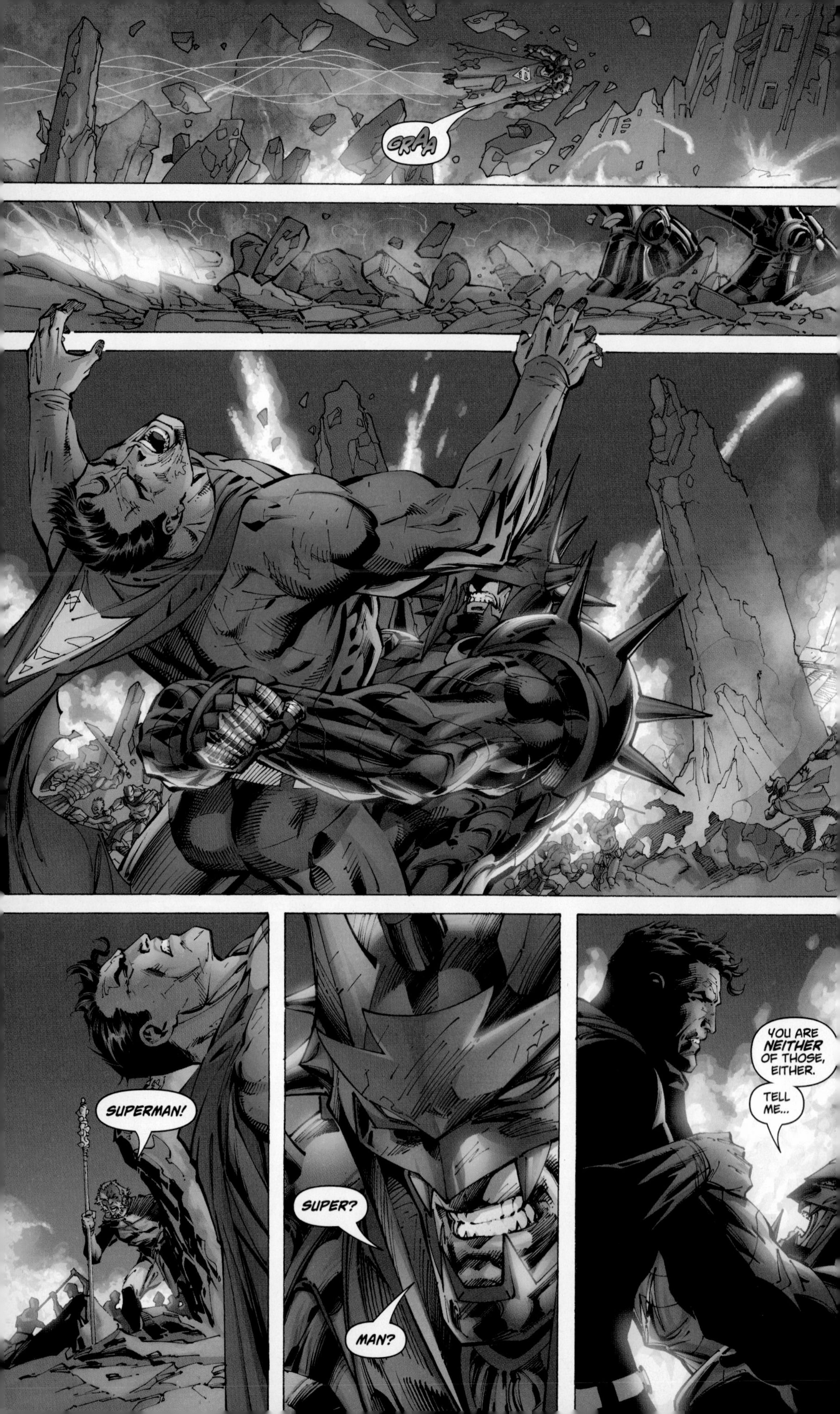
GRAA
SUPERMAN!
SUPER?
MAN?
YOU ARE NEITHER OF THOSE, EITHER.
TELL ME...

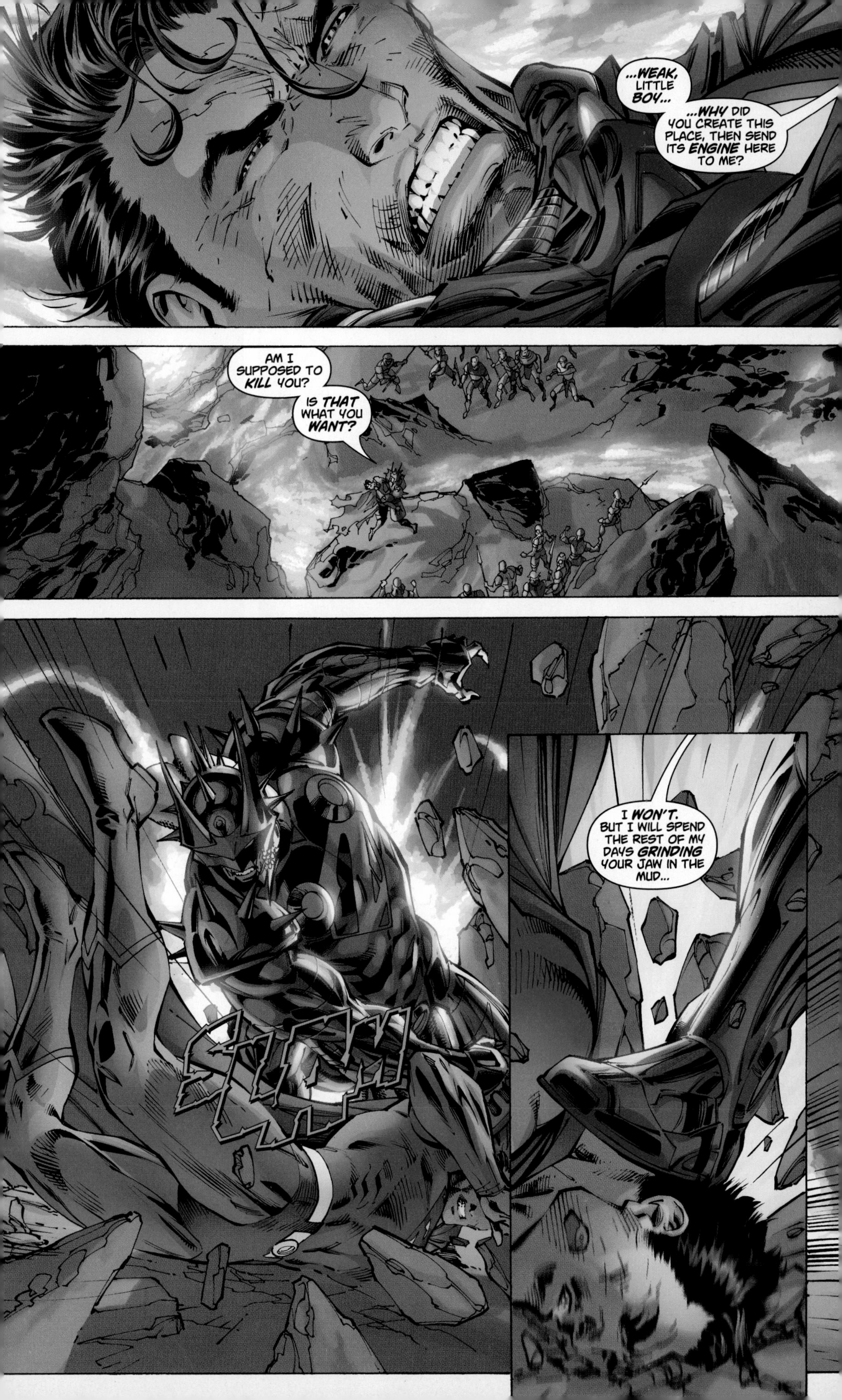

...WEAK, LITTLE BOY...
...WHY DID YOU CREATE THIS PLACE, THEN SEND ITS ENGINE HERE TO ME?
AM I SUPPOSED TO KILL YOU?
IS THAT WHAT YOU WANT?
I WON'T. BUT I WILL SPEND THE REST OF MY DAYS GRINDING YOUR JAW IN THE MUD...

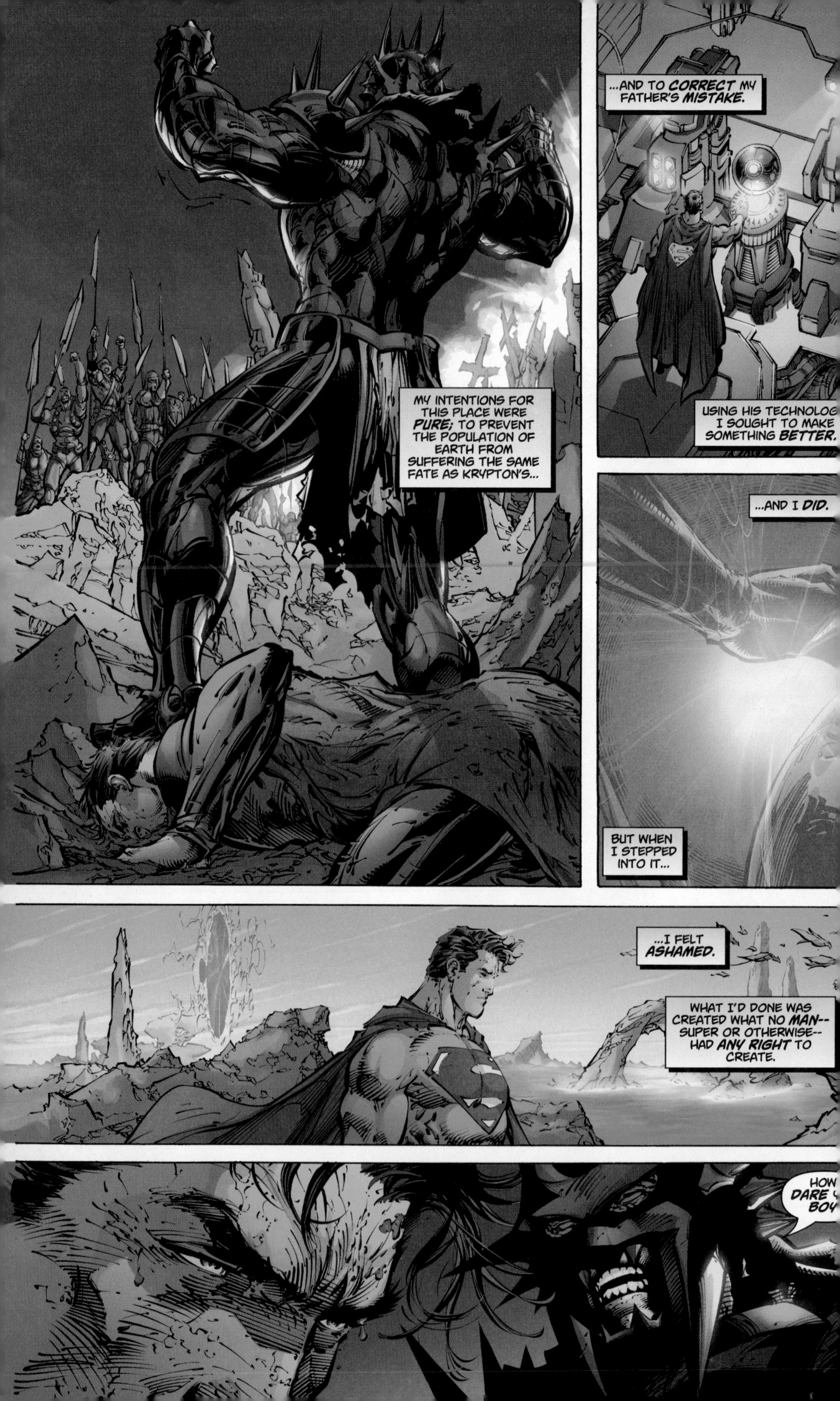
MY INTENTIONS FOR THIS PLACE WERE PURE; TO PREVENT THE POPULATION OF EARTH FROM SUFFERING THE SAME FATE AS KRYPTON'S...
...AND TO CORRECT MY FATHER'S MISTAKE.
USING HIS TECHNOLOG I SOUGHT TO MAKE SOMETHING BETTER.
...AND I DID.
BUT WHEN I STEPPED INTO IT...
...I FELT ASHAMED.
WHAT I'D DONE WAS CREATED WHAT NO MAN-- SUPER OR OTHERWISE-- HAD ANY RIGHT TO CREATE.
HOW DARE BOY

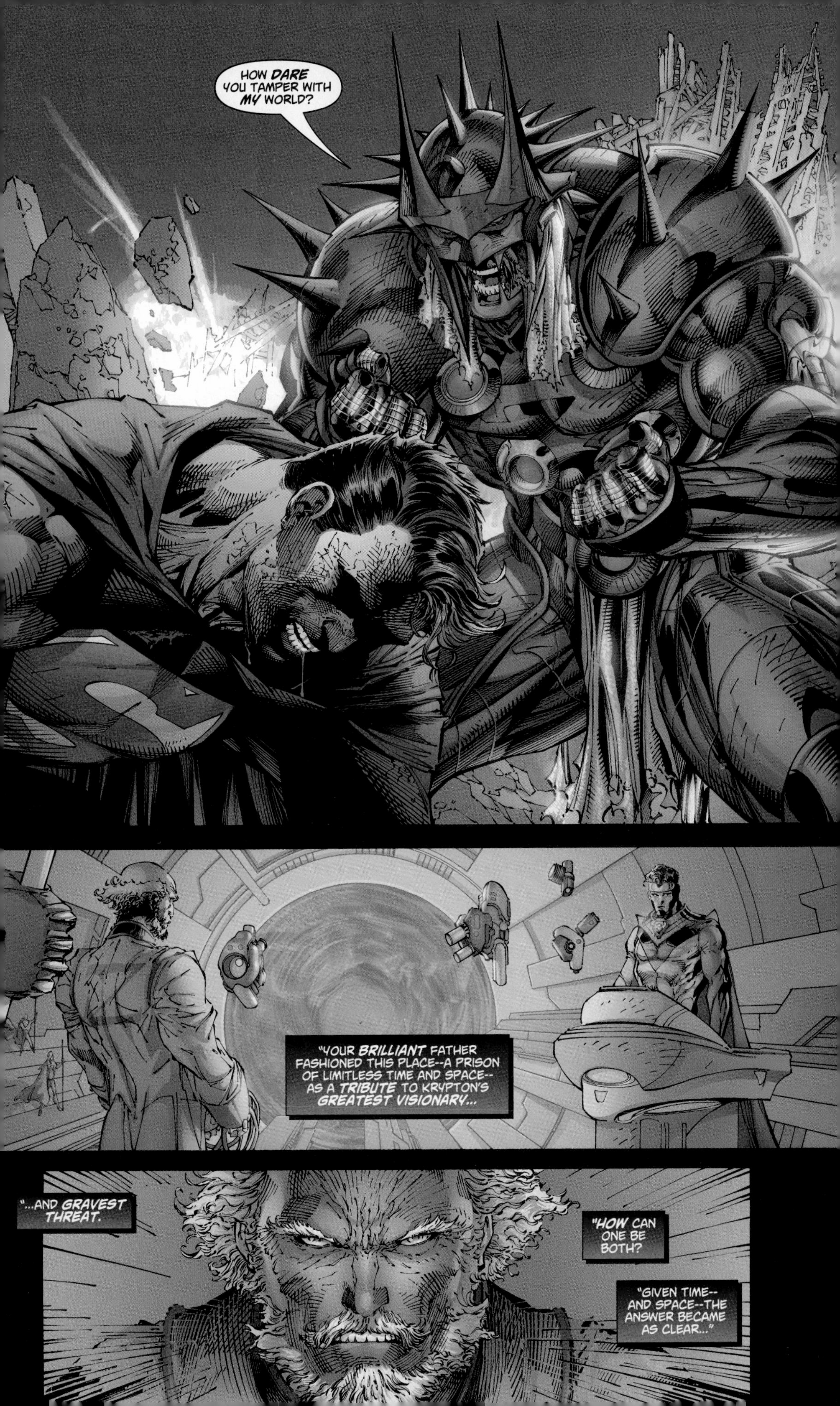
HOW DARE YOU TAMPER WITH MY WORLD?
"YOUR BRILLIANT FATHER FASHIONED THIS PLACE--A PRISON OF LIMITLESS TIME AND SPACE--AS A TRIBUTE TO KRYPTON'S GREATEST VISIONARY...
"...AND GRAVEST THREAT.
"HOW CAN ONE BE BOTH?
"GIVEN TIME--AND SPACE--THE ANSWER BECAME AS CLEAR..."

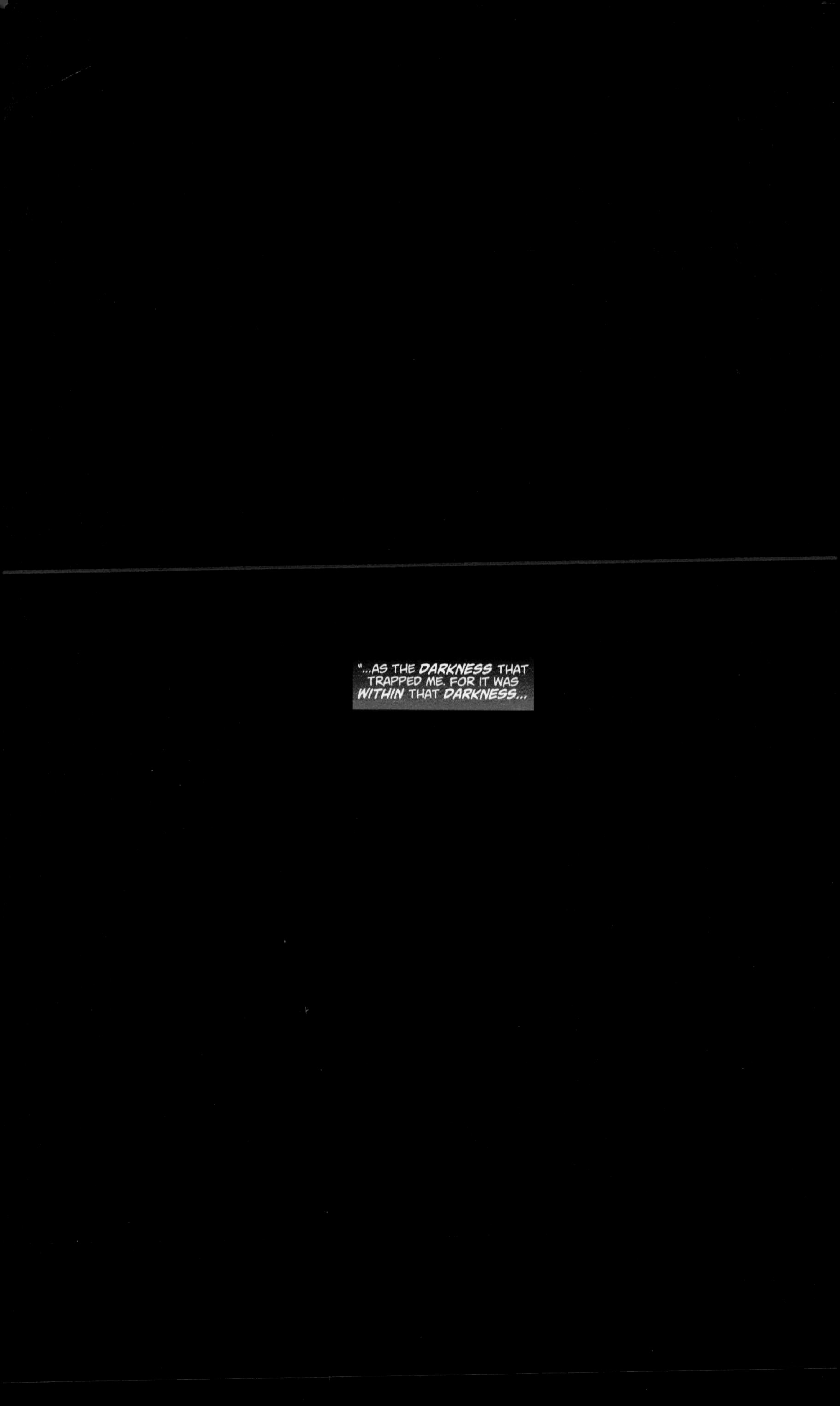
"...AS THE DARKNESS THAT TRAPPED ME. FOR IT WAS WITHIN THAT DARKNESS...

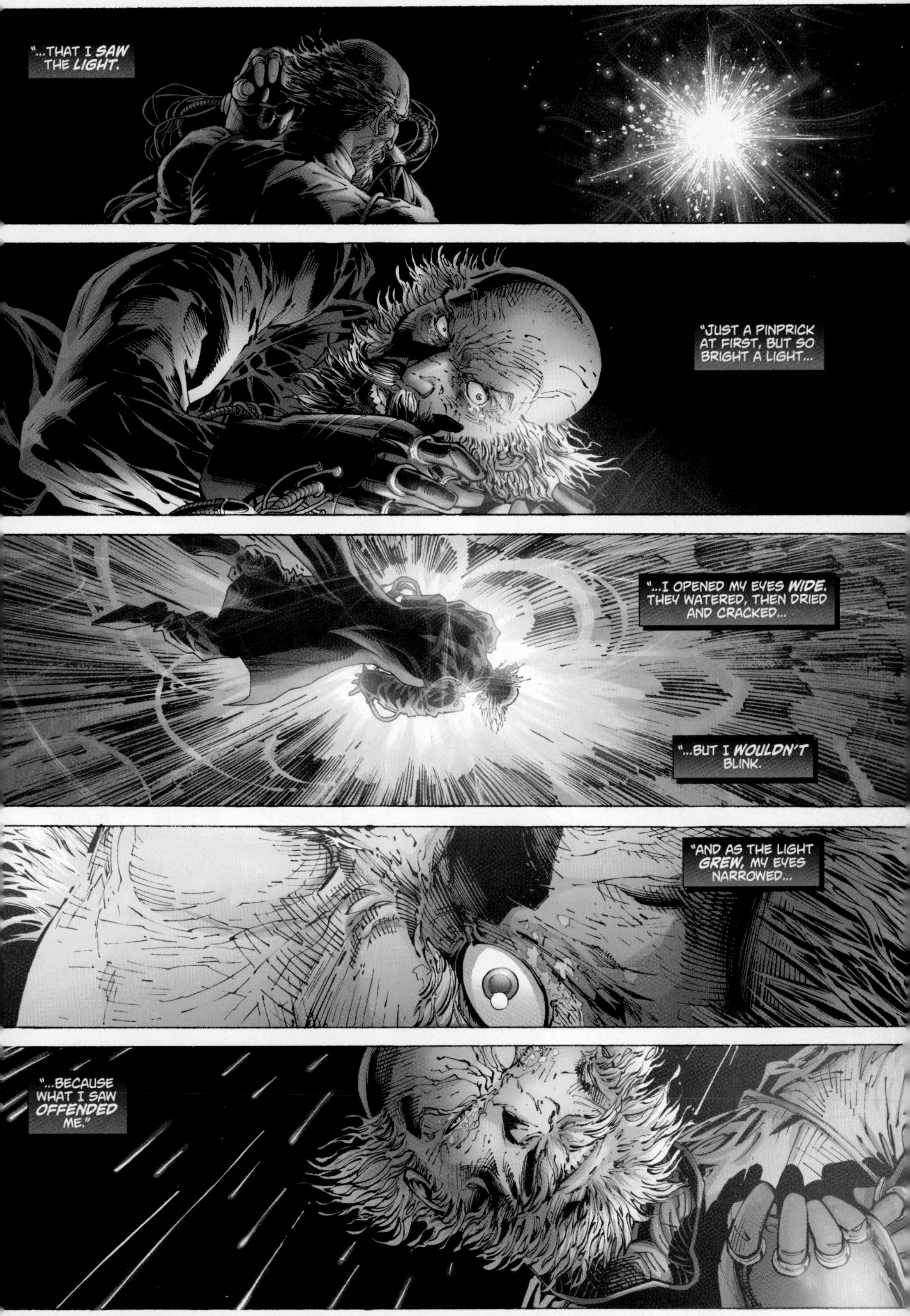
"...THAT I SAW THE LIGHT.
"JUST A PINPRICK AT FIRST, BUT SO BRIGHT A LIGHT...
"...I OPENED MY EYES WIDE. THEY WATERED, THEN DRIED AND CRACKED...
"...BUT I WOULDN'T BLINK.
"AND AS THE LIGHT GREW, MY EYES NARROWED...
"...BECAUSE WHAT I SAW OFFENDED ME."

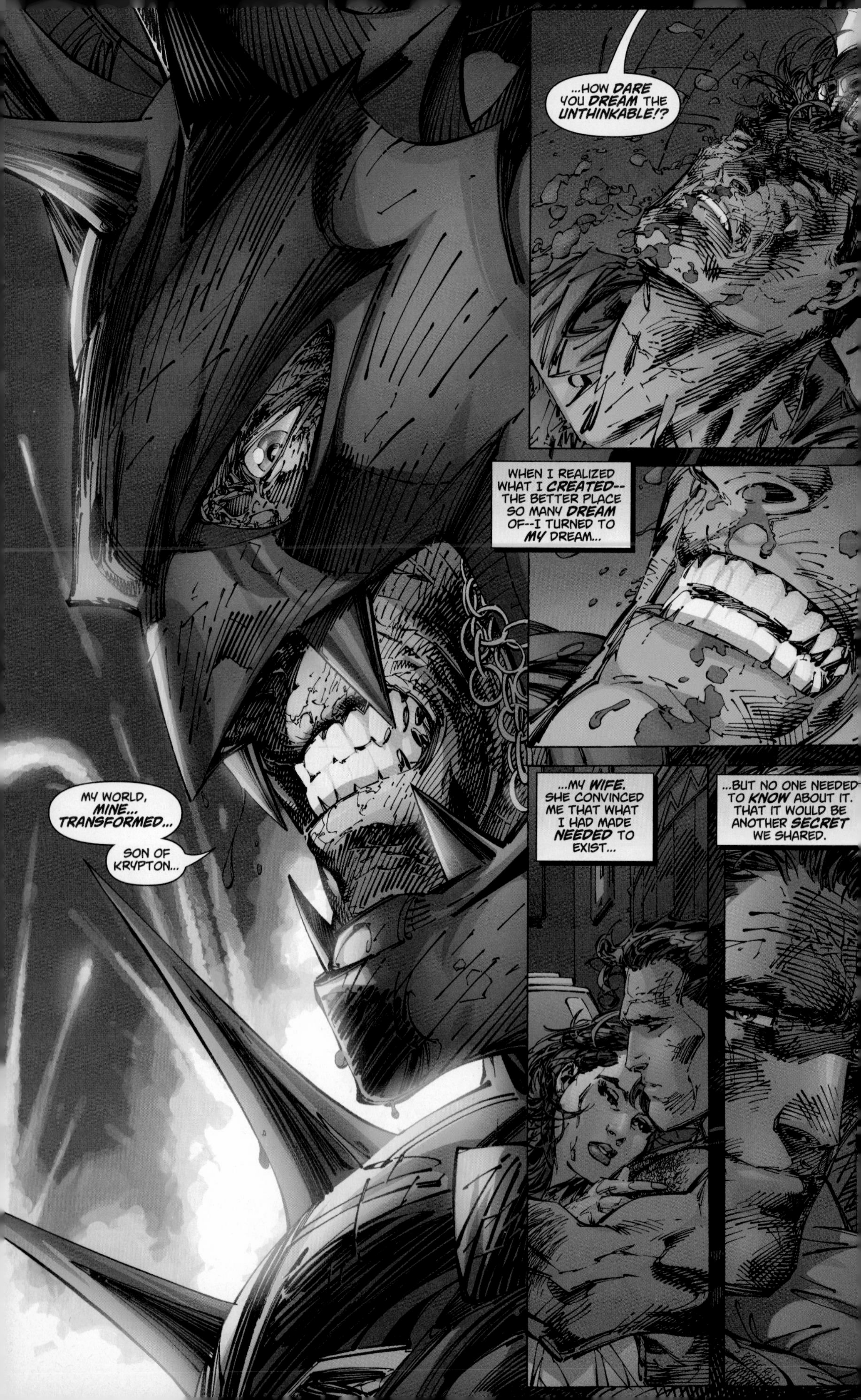

...HOW DARE YOU DREAM THE UNTHINKABLE!?
MY WORLD, MINE... TRANSFORMED...
SON OF KRYPTON...
WHEN I REALIZED WHAT I CREATED-- THE BETTER PLACE SO MANY DREAM OF--I TURNED TO MY DREAM...
...MY WIFE. SHE CONVINCED ME THAT WHAT I HAD MADE NEEDED TO EXIST...
...BUT NO ONE NEEDED TO KNOW ABOUT IT. THAT IT WOULD BE ANOTHER SECRET WE SHARED.

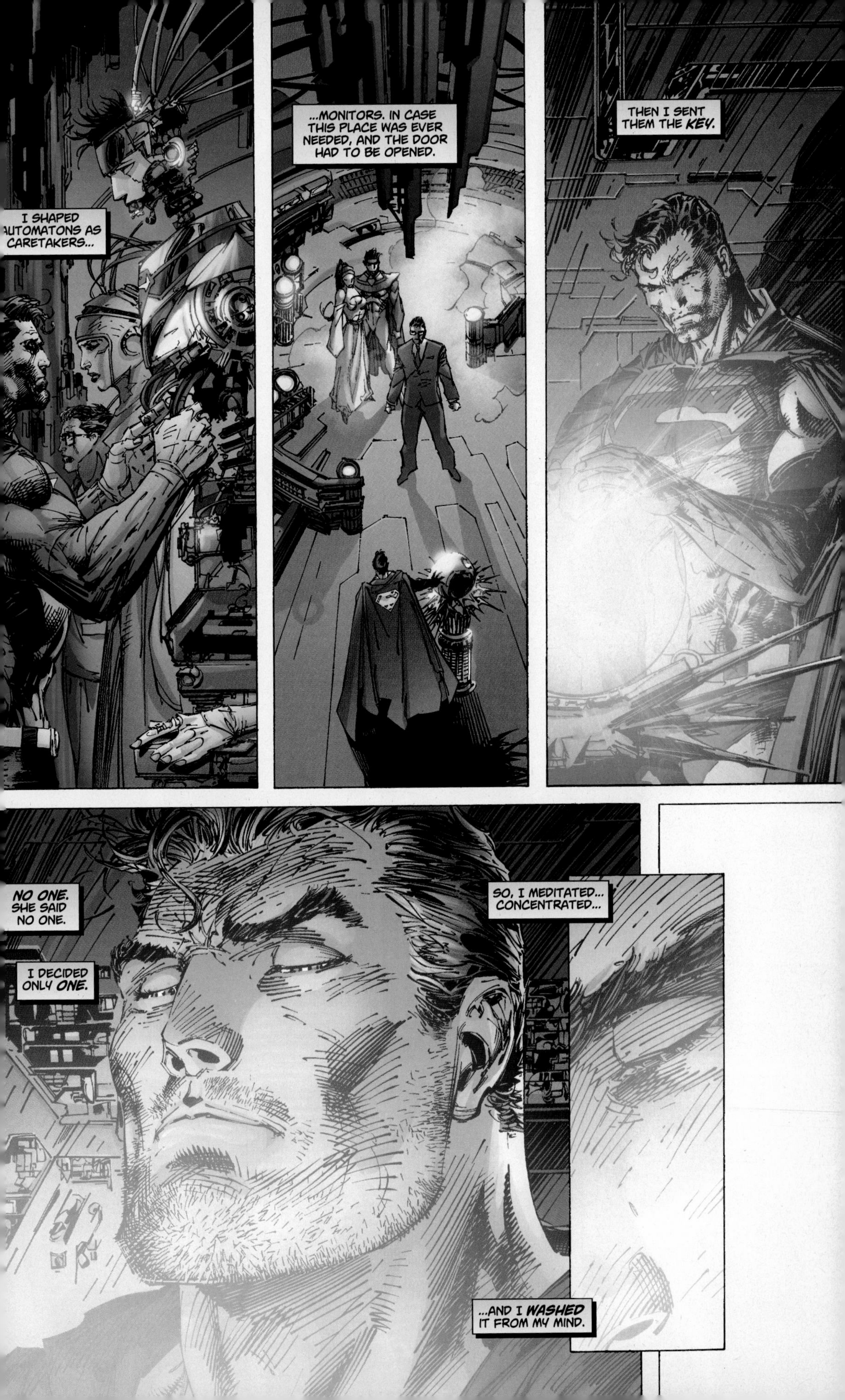
I SHAPED AUTOMATONS AS CARETAKERS...
...MONITORS. IN CASE THIS PLACE WAS EVER NEEDED, AND THE DOOR HAD TO BE OPENED.
THEN I SENT THEM THE KEY.
NO ONE. SHE SAID NO ONE.
I DECIDED ONLY ONE.
SO, I MEDITATED... CONCENTRATED...
...AND I WASHED IT FROM MY MIND.

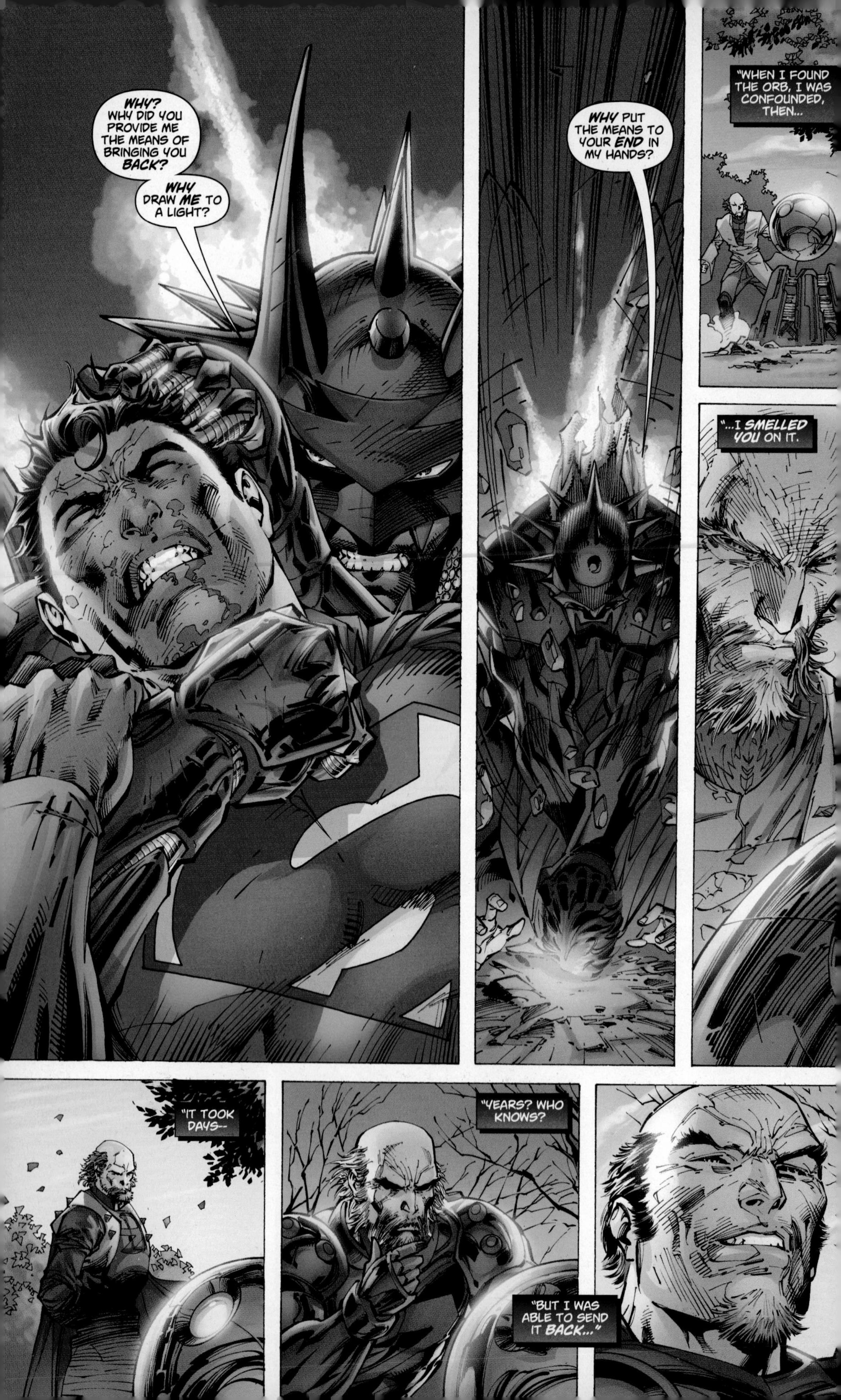
WHY? WHY DID YOU PROVIDE ME THE MEANS OF BRINGING YOU BACK?
WHY DRAW ME TO A LIGHT?
WHY PUT THE MEANS TO YOUR END IN MY HANDS?
"WHEN I FOUND THE ORB, I WAS CONFOUNDED, THEN...
"...I SMELLED YOU ON IT.
"IT TOOK DAYS--
"YEARS? WHO KNOWS?
"BUT I WAS ABLE TO SEND IT BACK..."

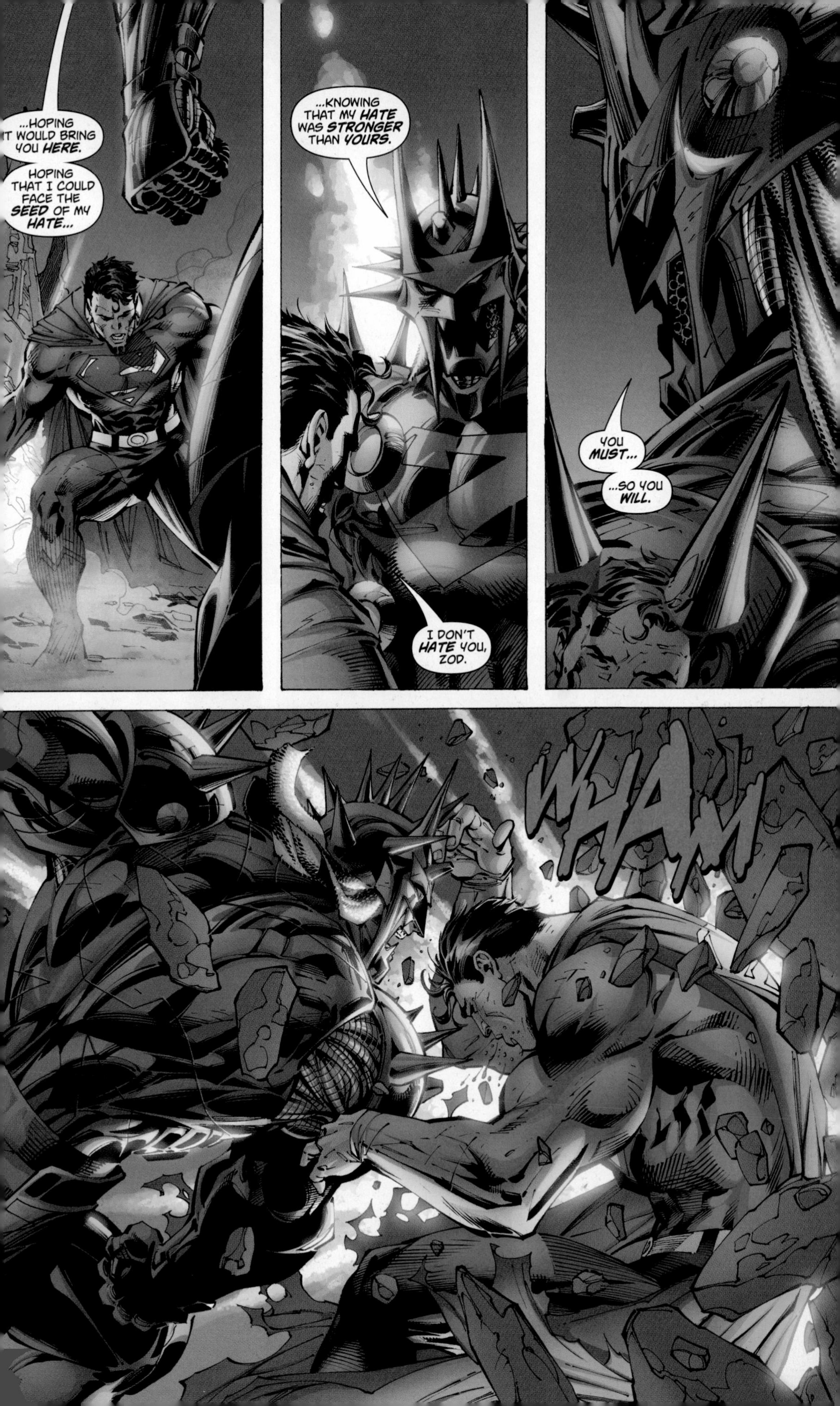
...HOPING IT WOULD BRING YOU HERE.
HOPING THAT I COULD FACE THE SEED OF MY HATE...
...KNOWING THAT MY HATE WAS STRONGER THAN YOURS.
I DON'T HATE YOU, ZOD.
YOU MUST...
...SO YOU WILL.
WHAM

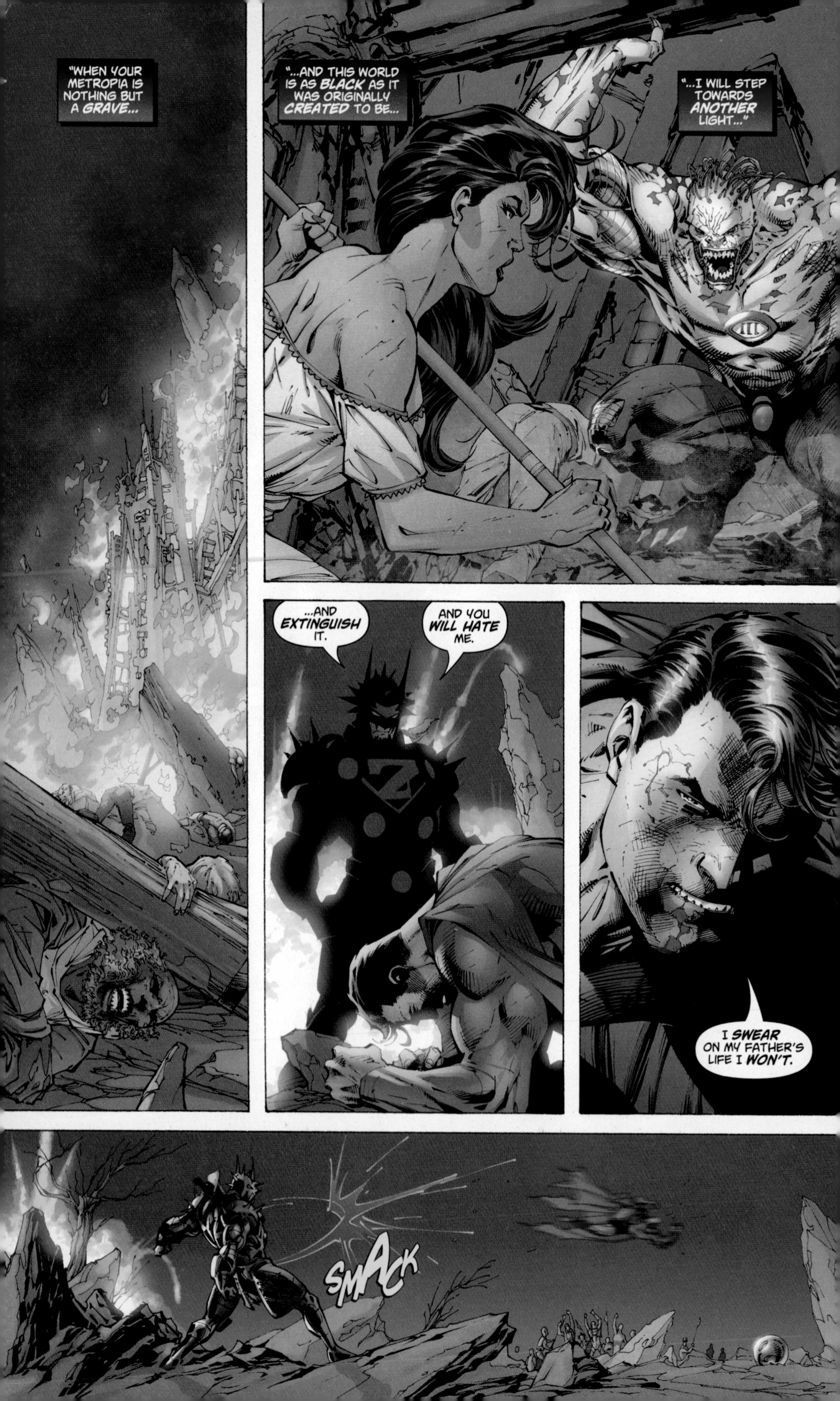
"WHEN YOUR METROPIA IS NOTHING BUT A GRAVE...
"...AND THIS WORLD IS AS BLACK AS IT WAS ORIGINALLY CREATED TO BE...
"...I WILL STEP TOWARDS ANOTHER LIGHT..."
...AND EXTINGUISH IT.
AND YOU WILL HATE ME.
I SWEAR ON MY FATHER'S LIFE I WON'T.
SMACK

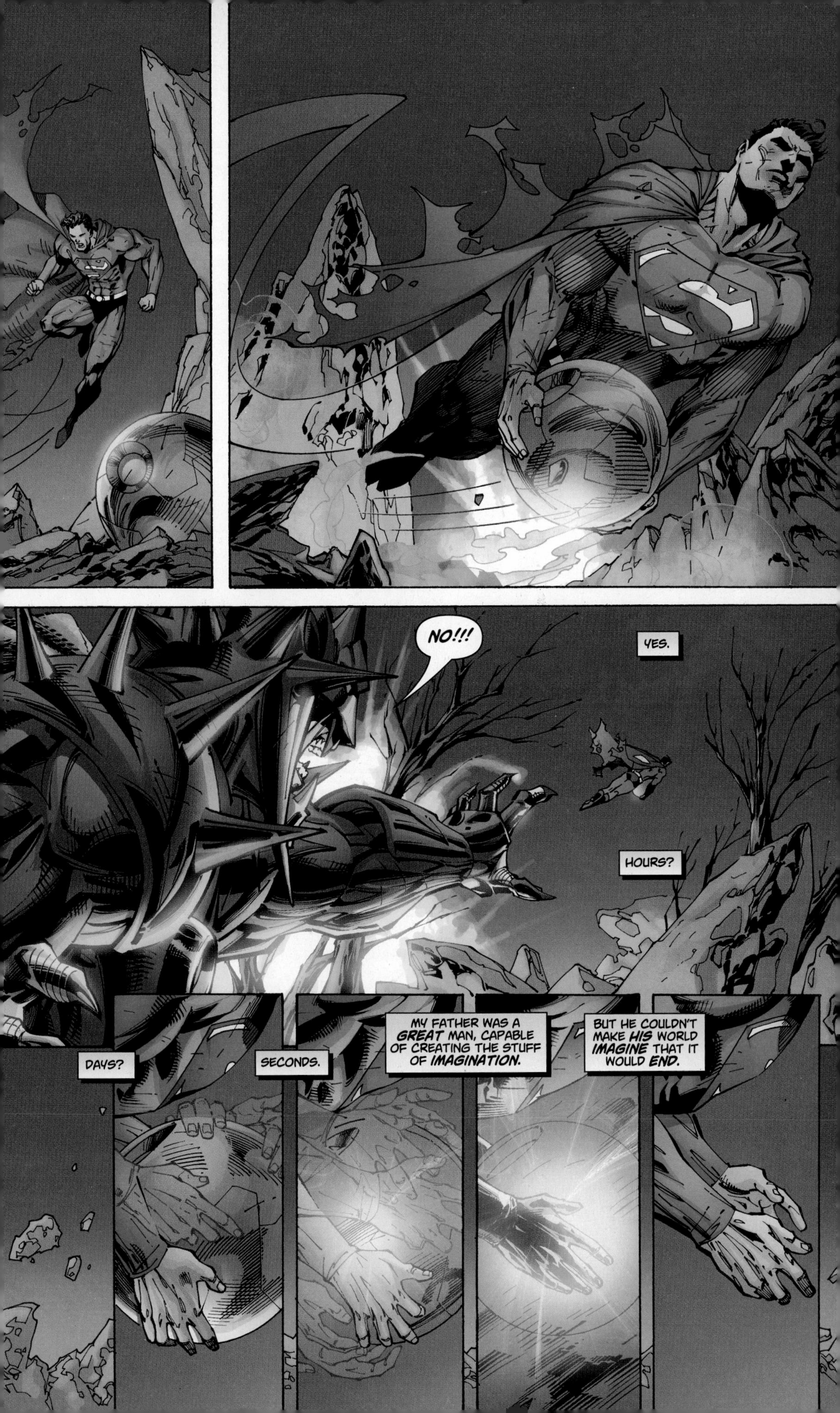
NO!!!
YES.
HOURS?
DAYS?
SECONDS.
MY FATHER WAS A GREAT MAN, CAPABLE OF CREATING THE STUFF OF IMAGINATION.
BUT HE COULDN'T MAKE HIS WORLD IMAGINE THAT IT WOULD END.

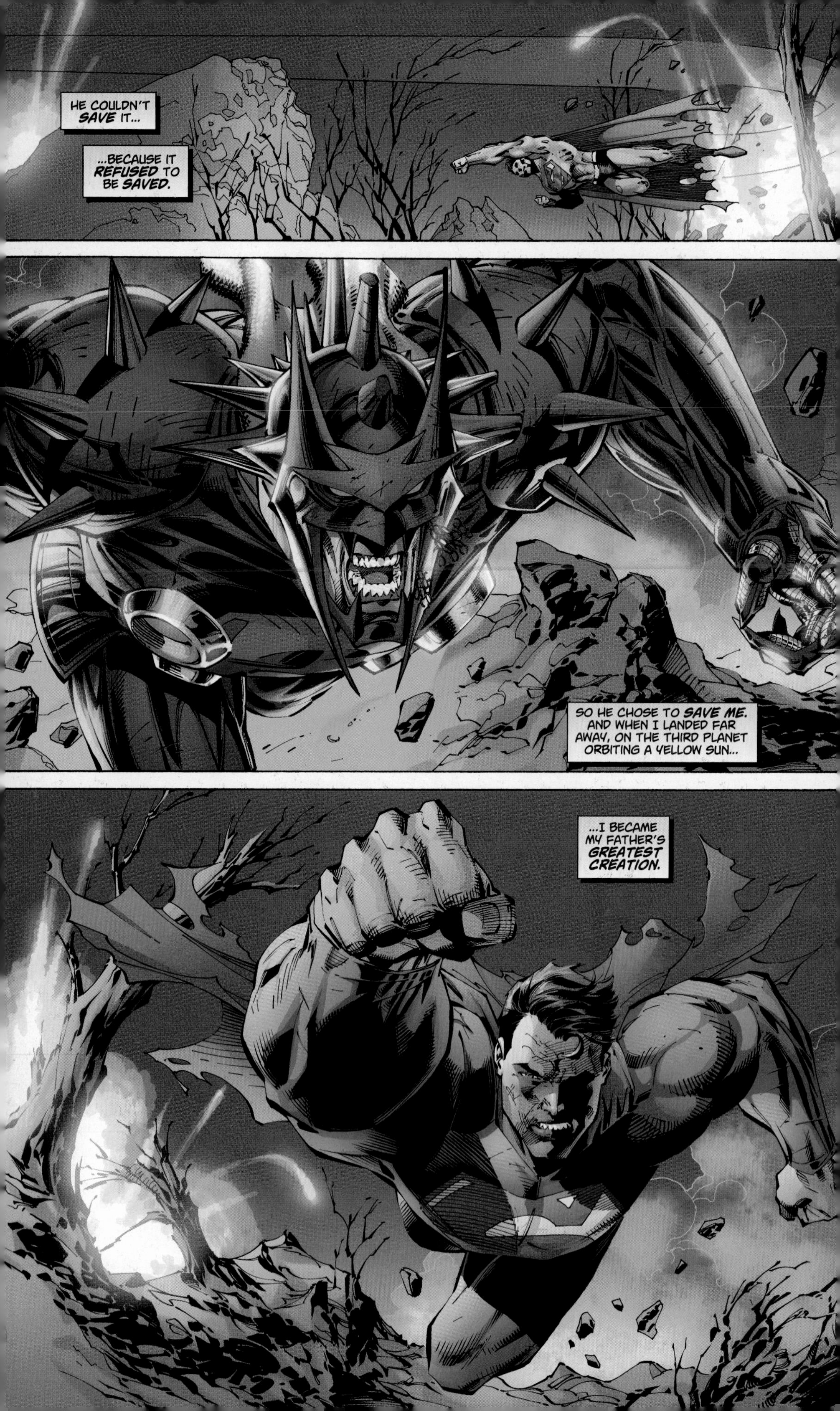
HE COULDN'T SAVE IT...
...BECAUSE IT REFUSED TO BE SAVED.
SO HE CHOSE TO SAVE ME. AND WHEN I LANDED FAR AWAY, ON THE THIRD PLANET ORBITING A YELLOW SUN...
...I BECAME MY FATHER'S GREATEST CREATION.

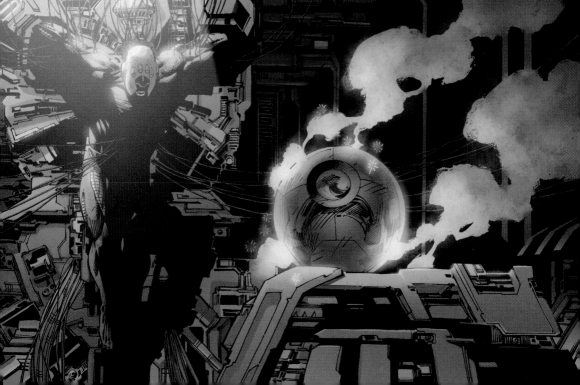

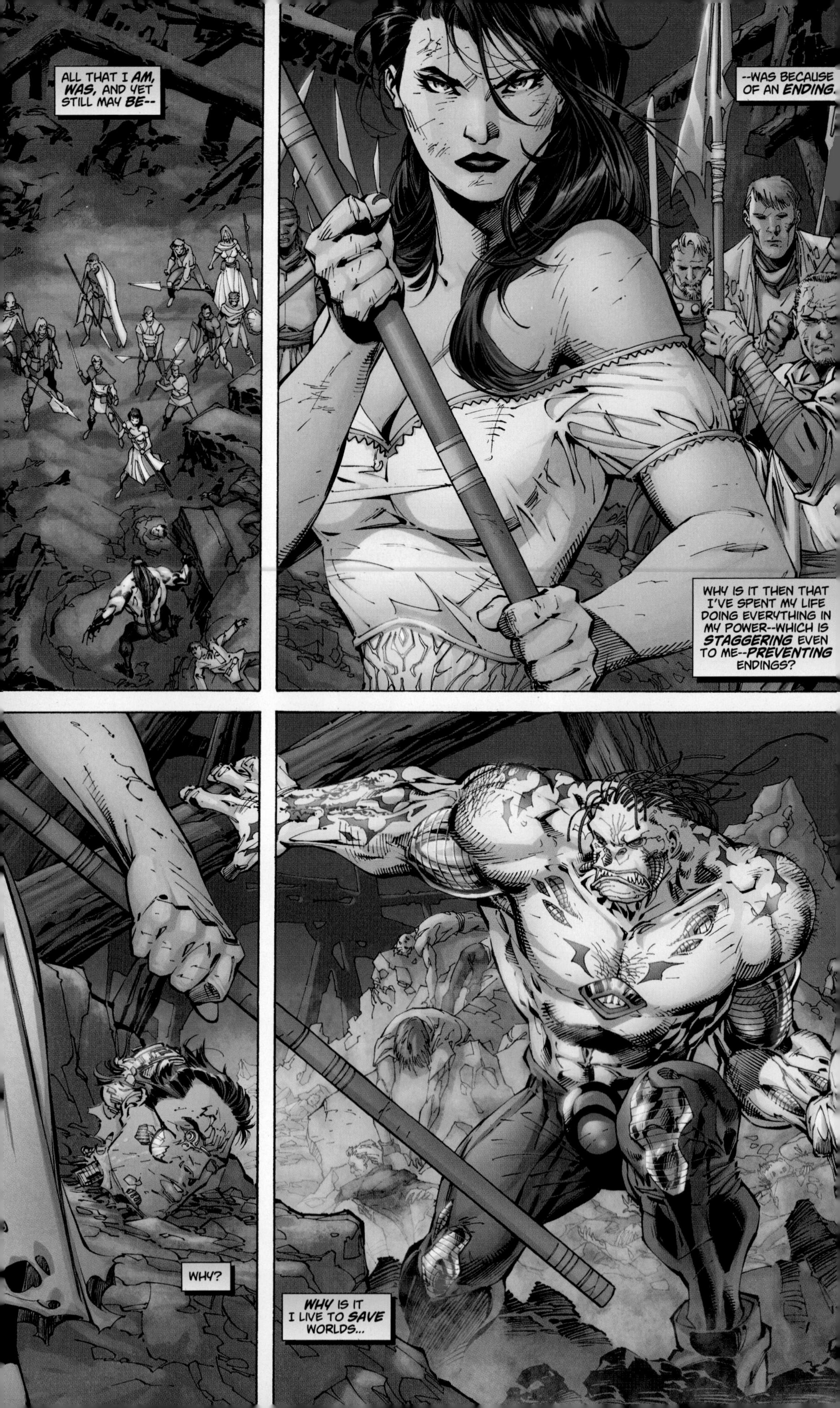
ALL THAT I AM, WAS, AND YET STILL MAY BE--
--WAS BECAUSE OF AN ENDING.
WHY IS IT THEN THAT I'VE SPENT MY LIFE DOING EVERYTHING IN MY POWER--WHICH IS STAGGERING EVEN TO ME--PREVENTING ENDINGS?
WHY?
WHY IS IT I LIVE TO SAVE WORLDS...

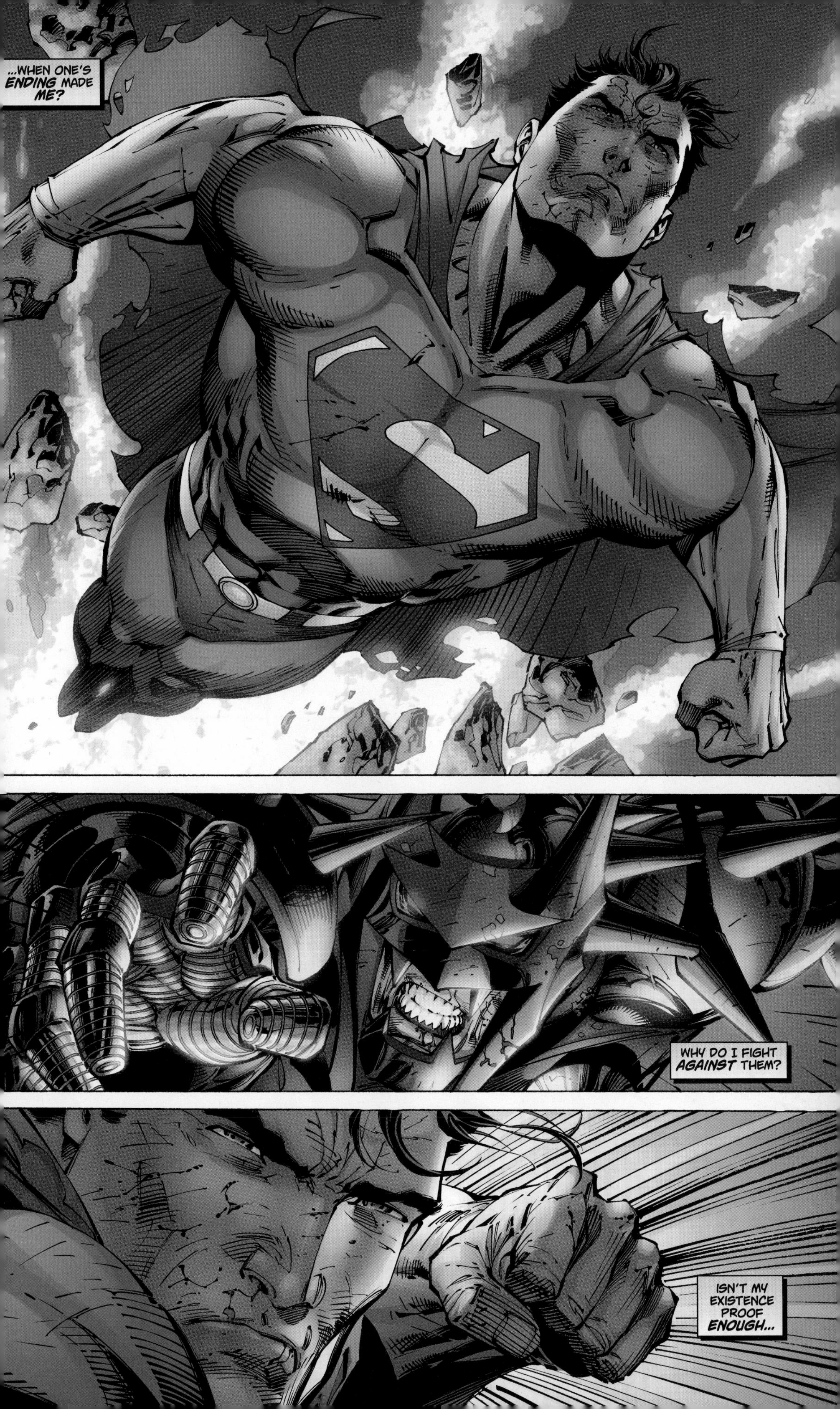
...WHEN ONE'S ENDING MADE ME?
WHY DO I FIGHT AGAINST THEM?
ISN'T MY EXISTENCE PROOF ENOUGH...

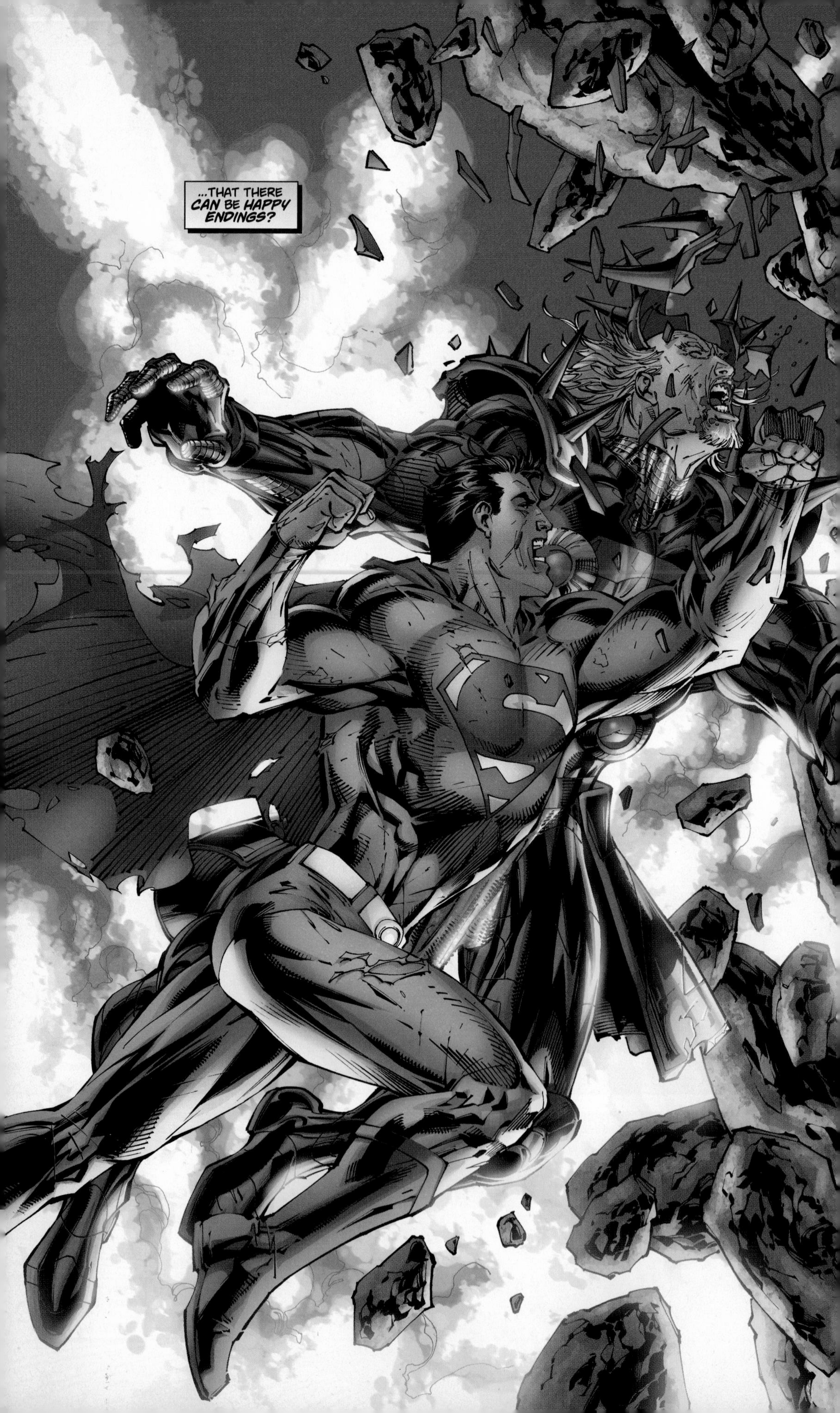
...THAT THERE CAN BE HAPPY ENDINGS?

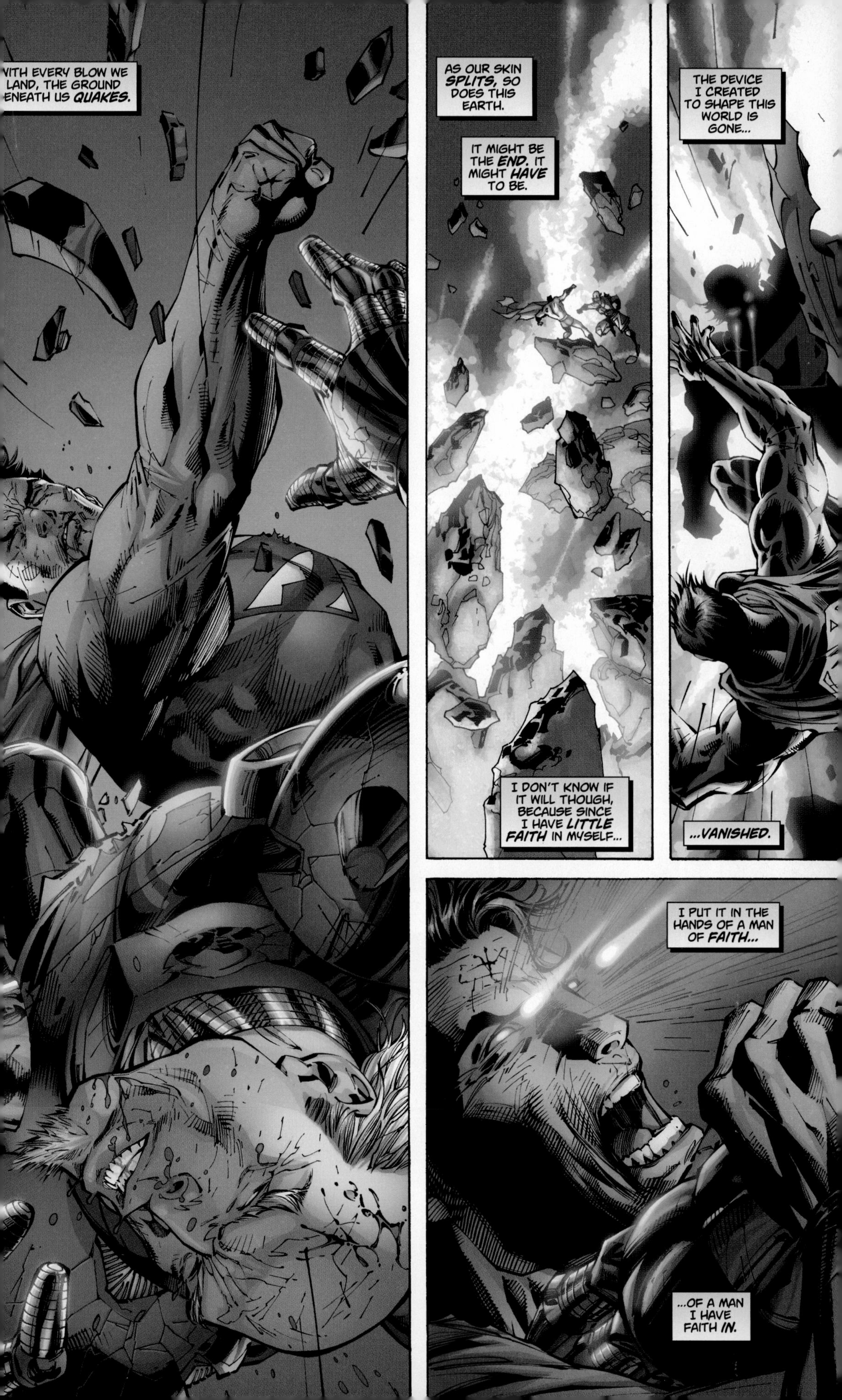

WITH EVERY BLOW WE LAND, THE GROUND ENEATH US QUAKES.
AS OUR SKIN SPLITS, SO DOES THIS EARTH.
IT MIGHT BE THE END. IT MIGHT HAVE TO BE.
I DON'T KNOW IF IT WILL THOUGH, BECAUSE SINCE I HAVE LITTLE FAITH IN MYSELF...
THE DEVICE I CREATED TO SHAPE THIS WORLD IS GONE...
...VANISHED.
I PUT IT IN THE HANDS OF A MAN OF FAITH...
...OF A MAN I HAVE FAITH IN.

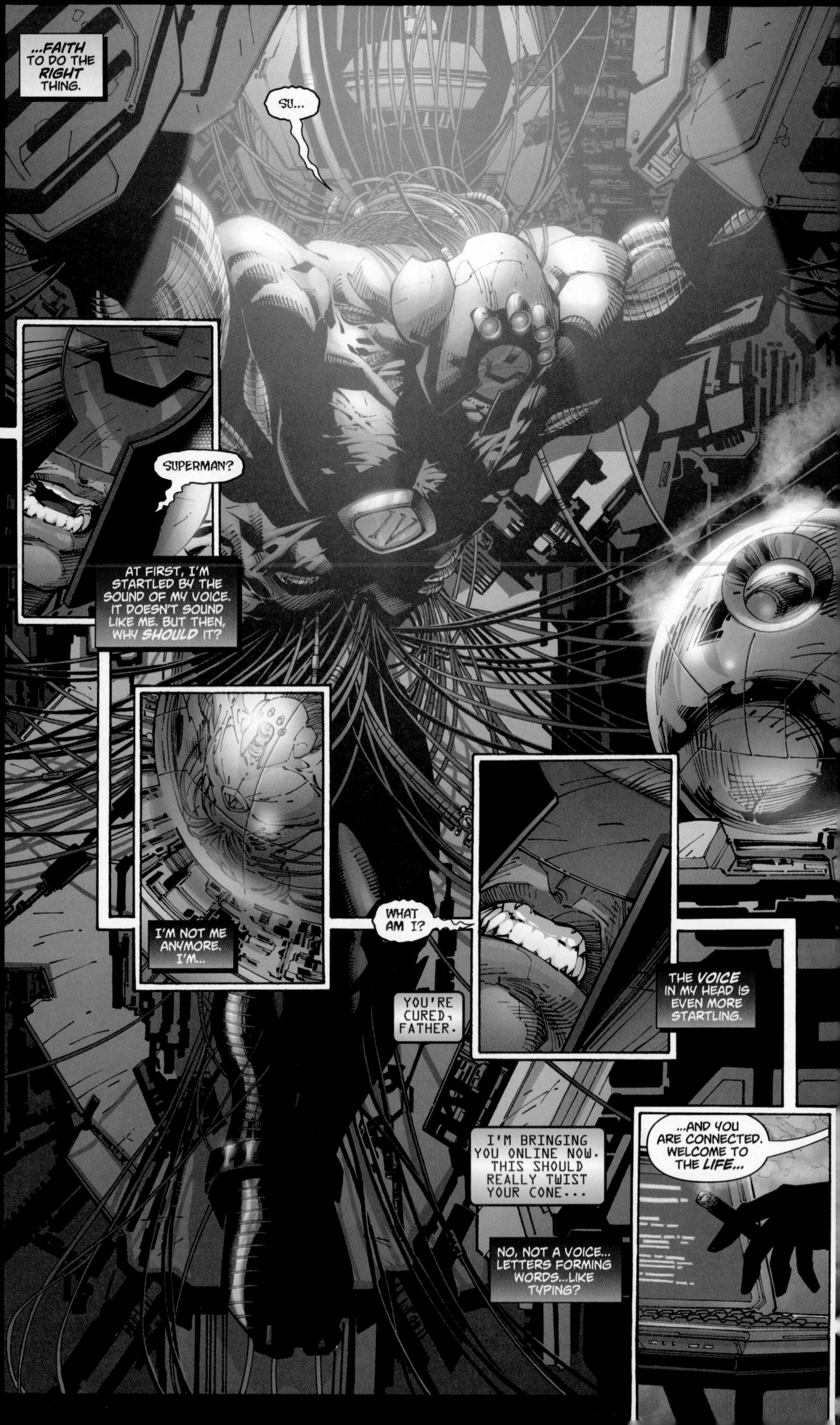
...FAITH TO DO THE RIGHT THING.
SU...
SUPERMAN?
AT FIRST, I'M STARTLED BY THE SOUND OF MY VOICE. IT DOESN'T SOUND LIKE ME. BUT THEN, WHY SHOULD IT?
I'M NOT ME ANYMORE. I'M...
WHAT AM I?
YOU'RE CURED, FATHER.
THE VOICE IN MY HEAD IS EVEN MORE STARTLING.
I'M BRINGING YOU ONLINE NOW. THIS SHOULD REALLY TWIST YOUR CONE...
NO, NOT A VOICE... LETTERS FORMING WORDS...LIKE TYPING?
...AND YOU ARE CONNECTED. WELCOME TO THE LIFE...

PILATE

MY NAME IS--

PILATE. THAT'S WHAT THE SYSTEM RECOGNIZES YOU AS. THINK OF IT AS A PASSWORD. NOW, THINK OF TEL AVIV...

UPLOADING...

WHAT'S SPILLING INTO YOUR HEAD IS ALL THE LATEST INTELLIGENCE, SATELLITE DATA, CITY MAPS--BOTH CURRENT AND HISTORIC--POWER GRIDS, SAFE HOUSE LOCATIONS AND MAYBE EVEN TEL AVIV'S KITCHEN SINK...

...EVERYTHING YOU'D NEED TO CARRY OUT A COVERT STRIKE IN THAT CITY.

NEAT, *huh?* IT GETS BETTER. YOU CAN SPEAK THE LOCAL DIALECTS, TOO.

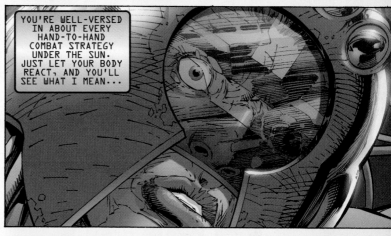

YOU'RE WELL-VERSED IN ABOUT EVERY HAND-TO-HAND COMBAT STRATEGY UNDER THE SUN. JUST LET YOUR BODY REACT, AND YOU'LL SEE WHAT I MEAN...

...ON YOUR WAY OUT.

OUT OF WHERE?

YOU *DON'T* WANT TO STAY WHERE YOU *ARE.*

F1

DISENGAGE MONITORS

PSSSSSSS

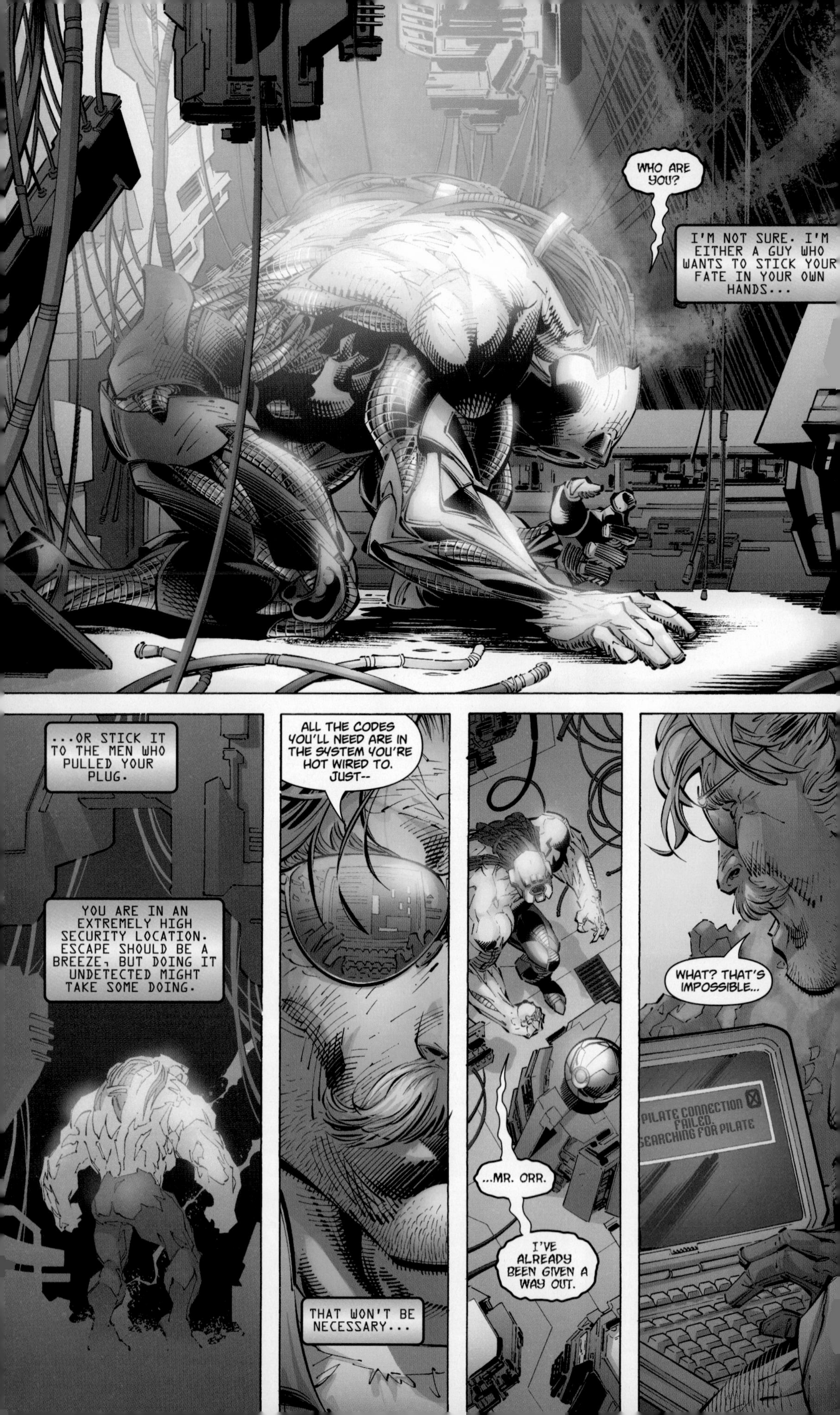
WHO ARE YOU?
I'M NOT SURE. I'M EITHER A GUY WHO WANTS TO STICK YOUR FATE IN YOUR OWN HANDS...
...OR STICK IT TO THE MEN WHO PULLED YOUR PLUG.
YOU ARE IN AN EXTREMELY HIGH SECURITY LOCATION. ESCAPE SHOULD BE A BREEZE, BUT DOING IT UNDETECTED MIGHT TAKE SOME DOING.
ALL THE CODES YOU'LL NEED ARE IN THE SYSTEM YOU'RE HOT WIRED TO. JUST--
THAT WON'T BE NECESSARY...
...MR. ORR.
I'VE ALREADY BEEN GIVEN A WAY OUT.
WHAT? THAT'S IMPOSSIBLE...
PILATE CONNECTION FAILED. SEARCHING FOR PILATE

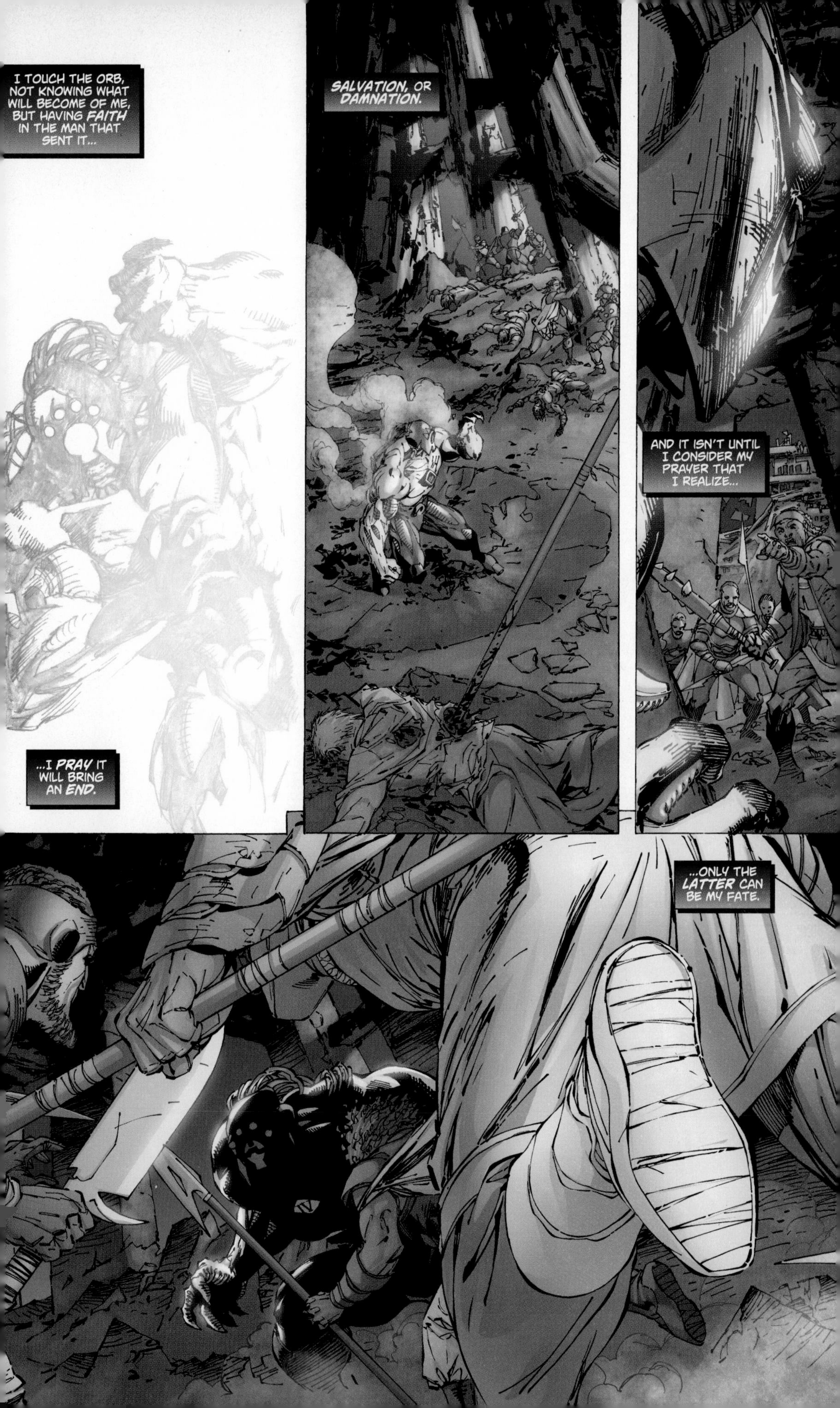

I TOUCH THE ORB, NOT KNOWING WHAT WILL BECOME OF ME, BUT HAVING FAITH IN THE MAN THAT SENT IT...
...I PRAY IT WILL BRING AN END.
SALVATION, OR DAMNATION.
AND IT ISN'T UNTIL I CONSIDER MY PRAYER THAT I REALIZE...
...ONLY THE LATTER CAN BE MY FATE.

FINALLY, SON OF JOR-EL...

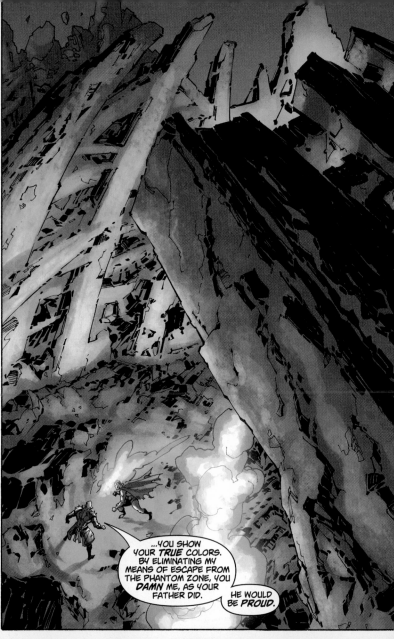

...YOU SHOW YOUR *TRUE* COLORS. BY ELIMINATING MY MEANS OF ESCAPE FROM THE PHANTOM ZONE, YOU *DAMN* ME, AS YOUR FATHER DID.

HE WOULD BE *PROUD.*

GENERAL, MY NAME IS KAL-EL...

...AND MY FATHER WOULD DO EVERYTHING IN HIS *POWER*--WHICH WAS *STAGGERING*-- TO *STOP* WHAT IS HAPPENING TODAY...

...THE *DESTRUCTION* OF A WORLD.

AND I *WILL* AS WELL.

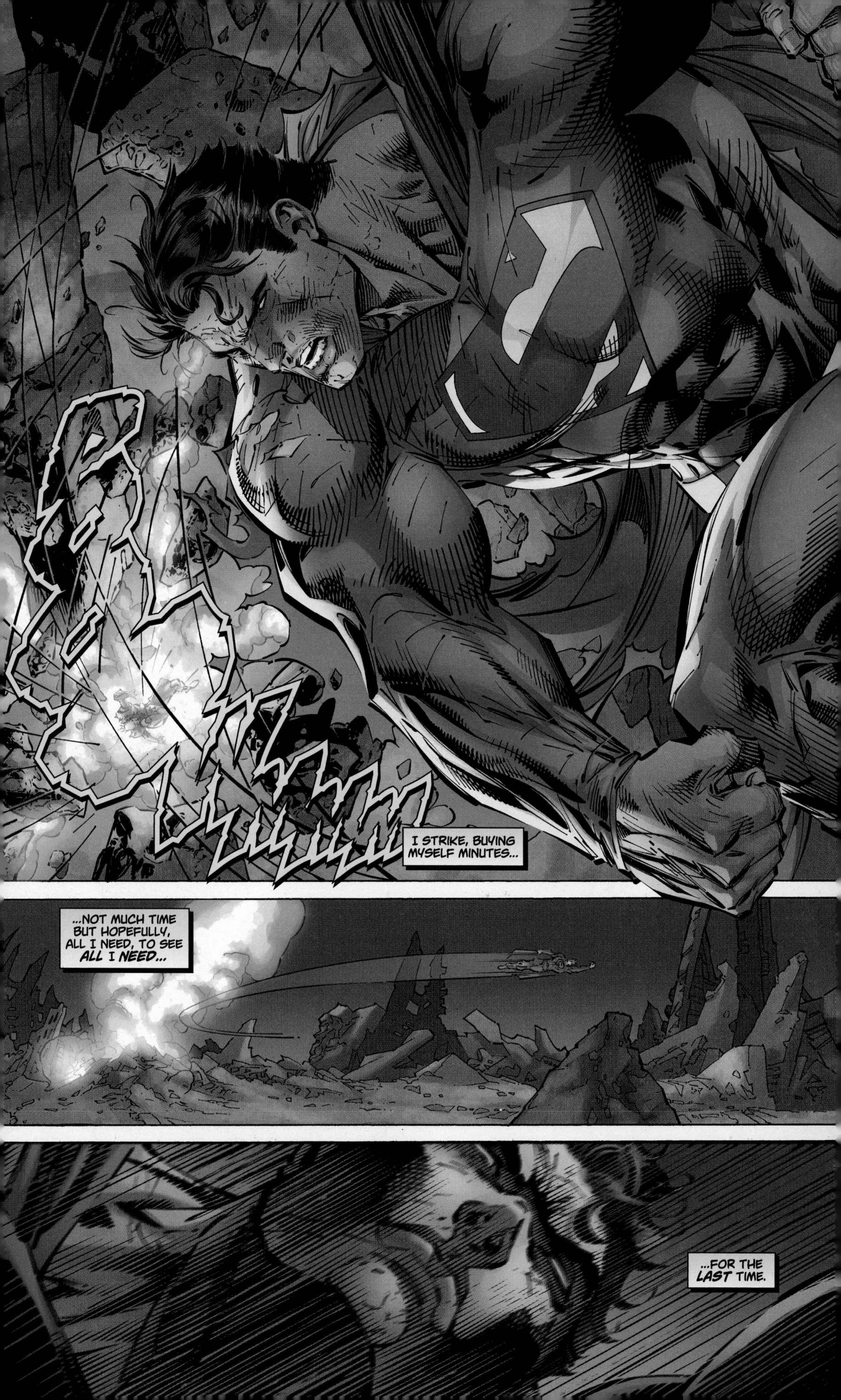
I STRIKE, BUYING MYSELF MINUTES...
...NOT MUCH TIME BUT HOPEFULLY, ALL I NEED, TO SEE ALL I NEED...
...FOR THE LAST TIME.

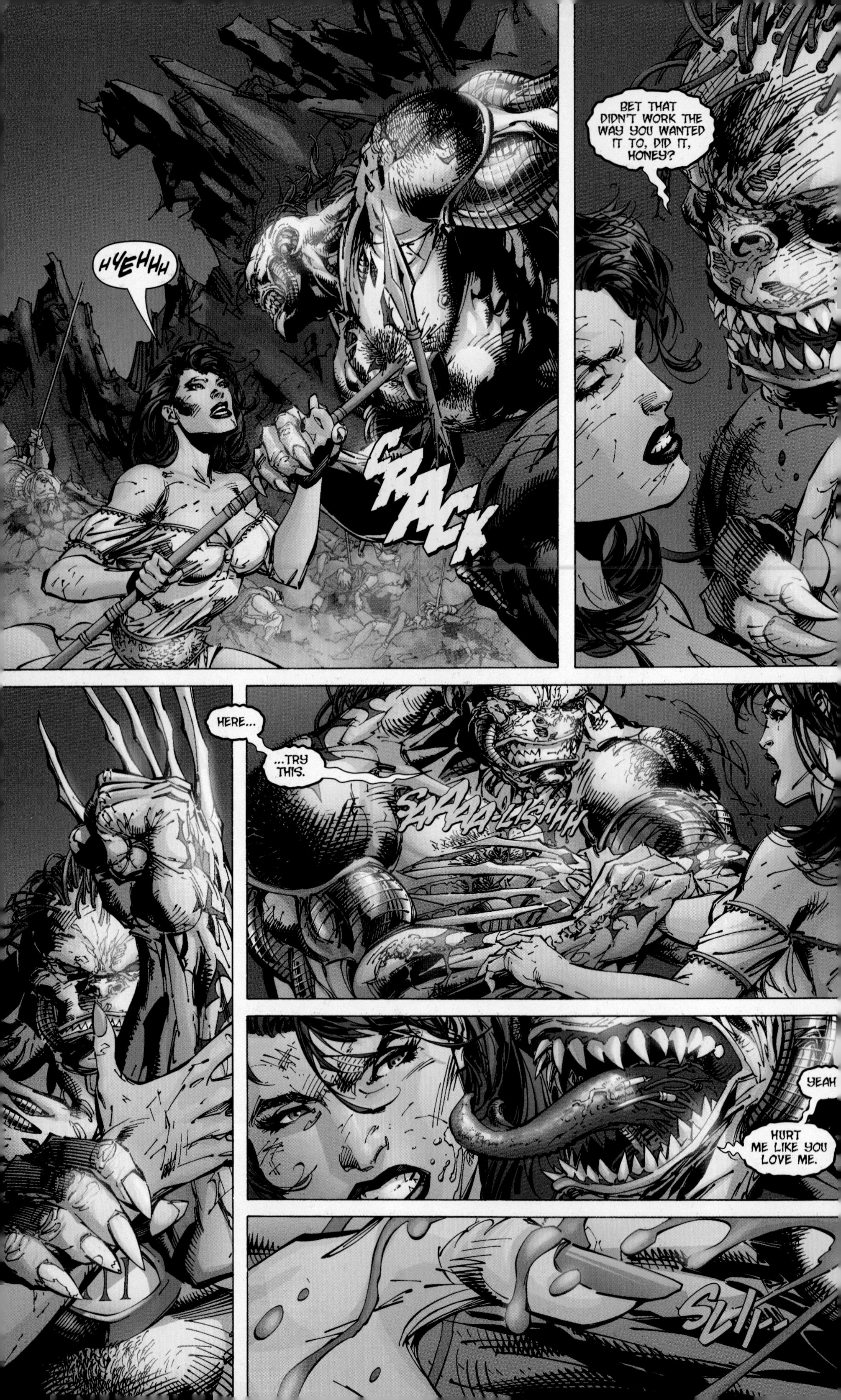
HYEHHH
CRACK
BET THAT DIDN'T WORK THE WAY YOU WANTED IT TO, DID IT, HONEY?
HERE...
...TRY THIS.
SHAAA-LISHHH
YEAH
HURT ME LIKE YOU LOVE ME.
SLI-

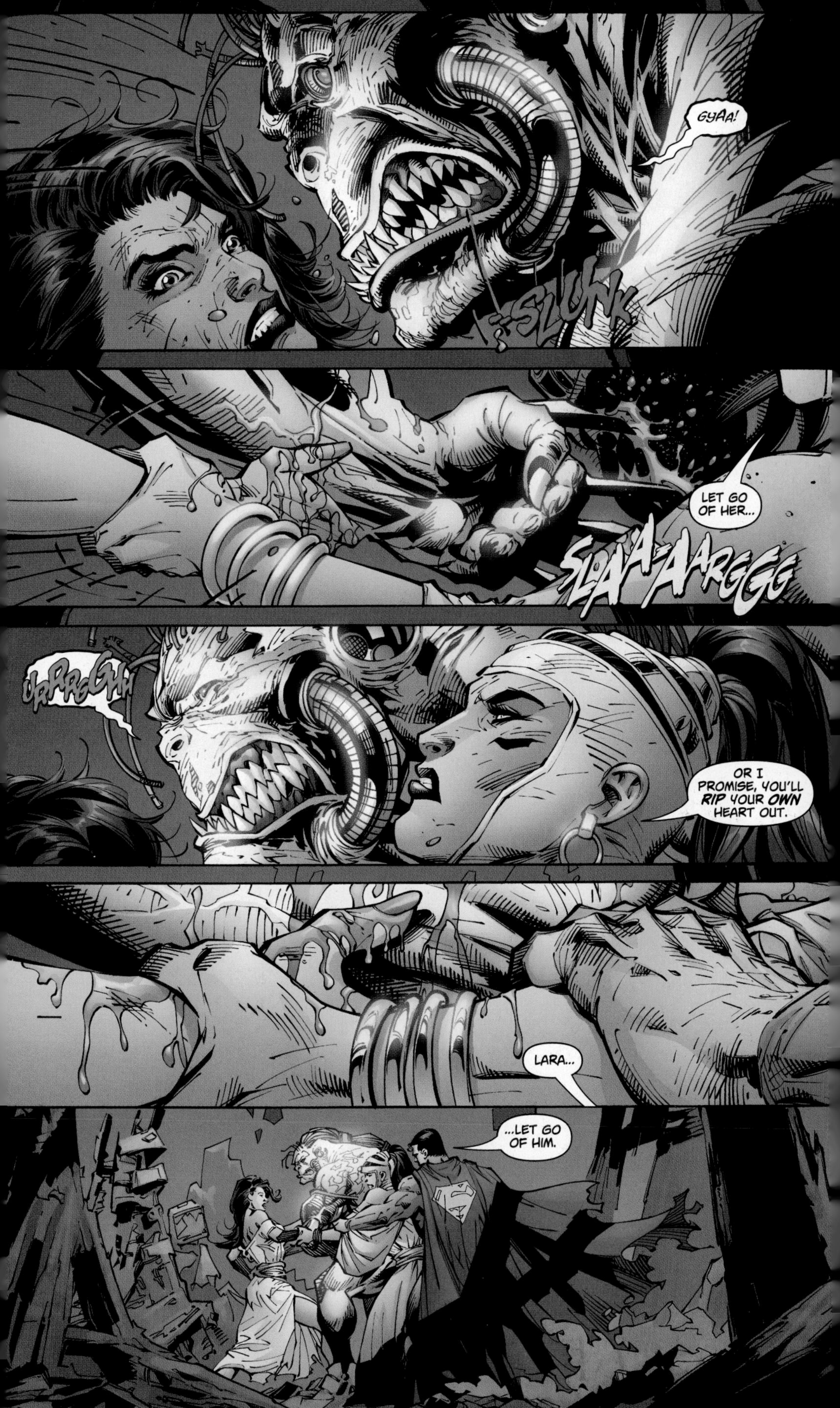
GYAA!
SLUNK
LET GO OF HER...
SLAAA-AARGGG
URRRGHH
OR I PROMISE, YOU'LL RIP YOUR OWN HEART OUT.
LARA...
...LET GO OF HIM.

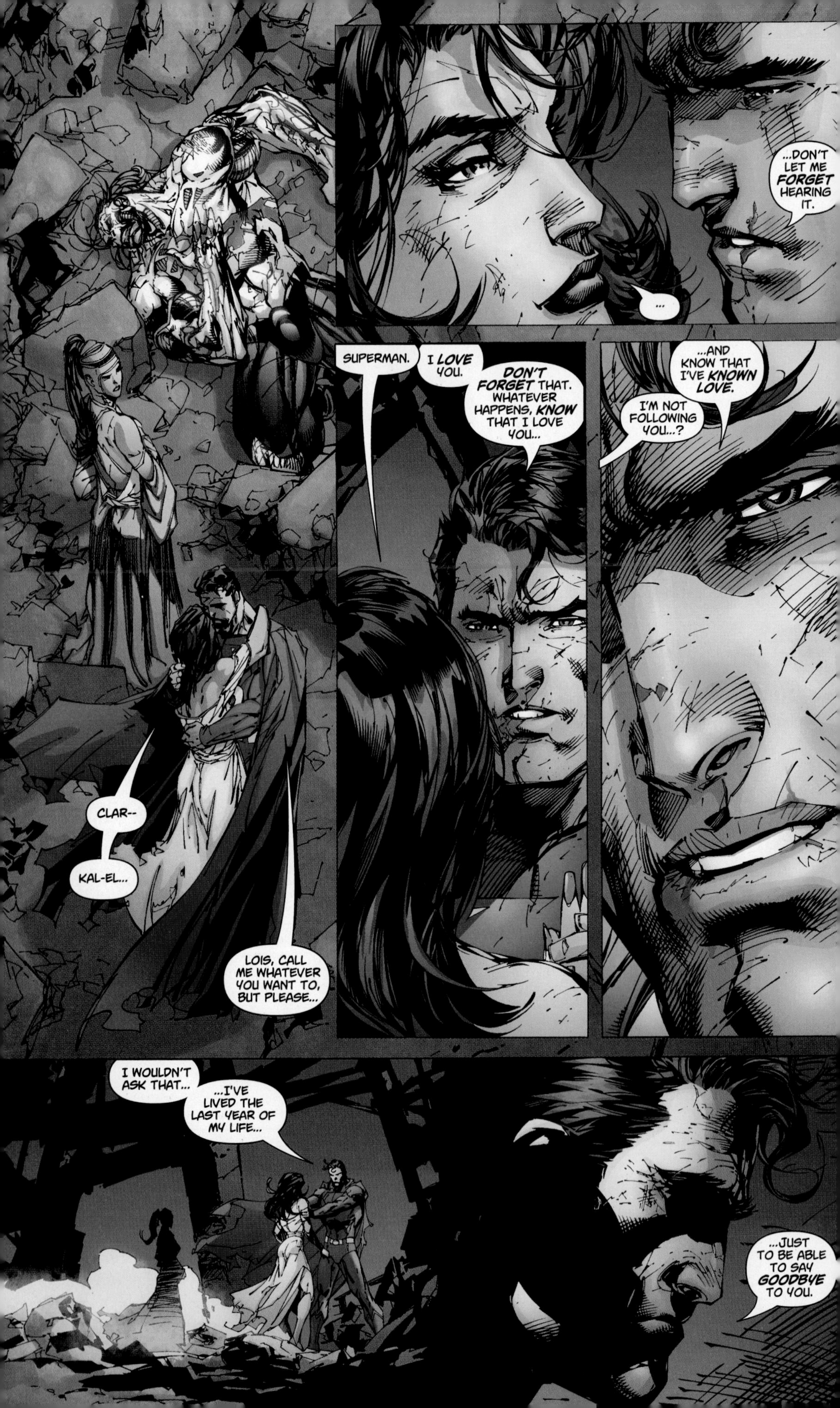
...DON'T LET ME FORGET HEARING IT.
...
SUPERMAN.
I LOVE YOU.
DON'T FORGET THAT. WHATEVER HAPPENS, KNOW THAT I LOVE YOU...
I'M NOT FOLLOWING YOU...?
...AND KNOW THAT I'VE KNOWN LOVE.
CLAR--
KAL-EL...
LOIS, CALL ME WHATEVER YOU WANT TO, BUT PLEASE...
I WOULDN'T ASK THAT...
...I'VE LIVED THE LAST YEAR OF MY LIFE...
...JUST TO BE ABLE TO SAY GOODBYE TO YOU.

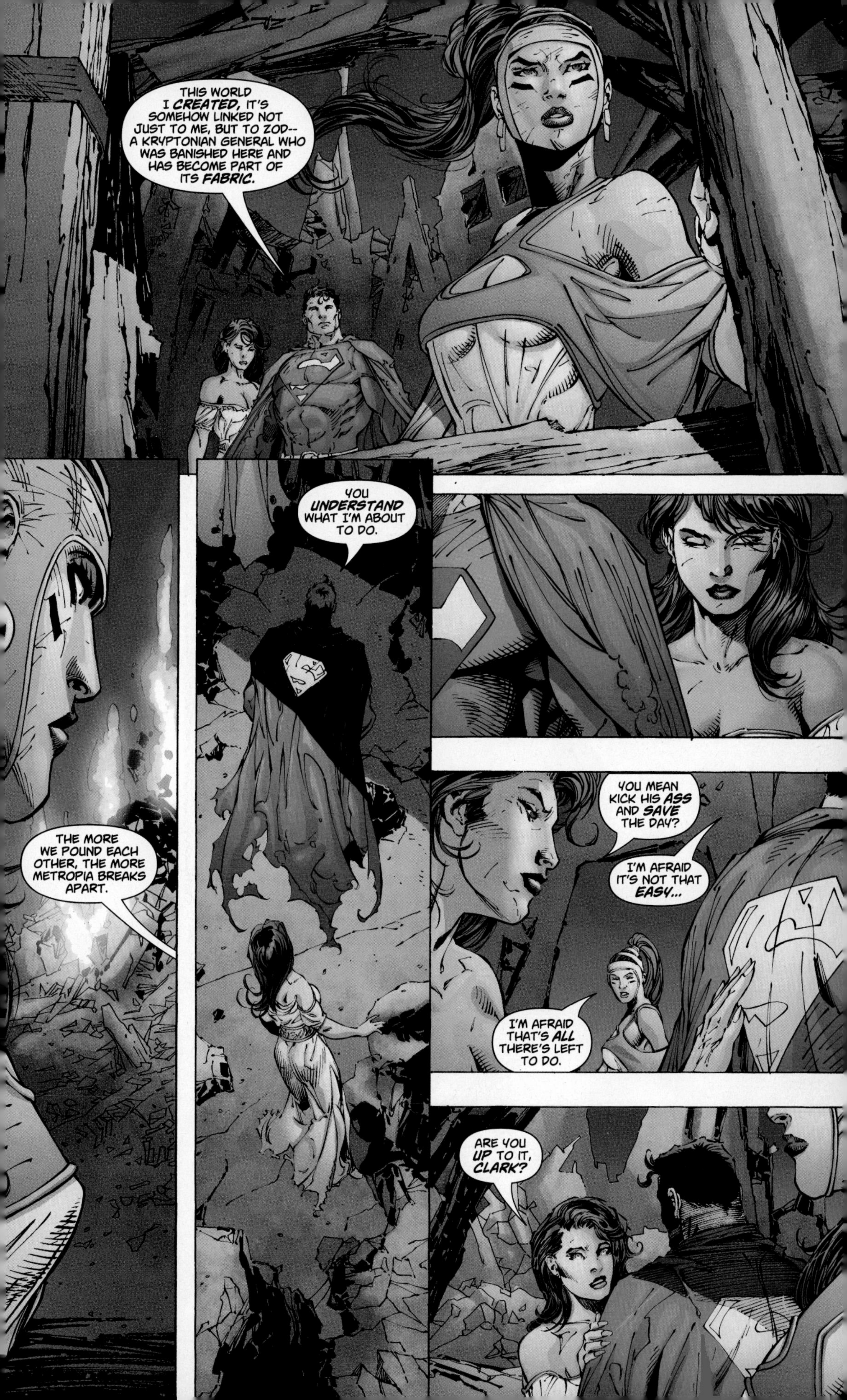
THIS WORLD I CREATED, IT'S SOMEHOW LINKED NOT JUST TO ME, BUT TO ZOD-- A KRYPTONIAN GENERAL WHO WAS BANISHED HERE AND HAS BECOME PART OF ITS FABRIC.
THE MORE WE POUND EACH OTHER, THE MORE METROPIA BREAKS APART.
YOU UNDERSTAND WHAT I'M ABOUT TO DO.
YOU MEAN KICK HIS ASS AND SAVE THE DAY?
I'M AFRAID IT'S NOT THAT EASY...
I'M AFRAID THAT'S ALL THERE'S LEFT TO DO.
ARE YOU UP TO IT, CLARK?

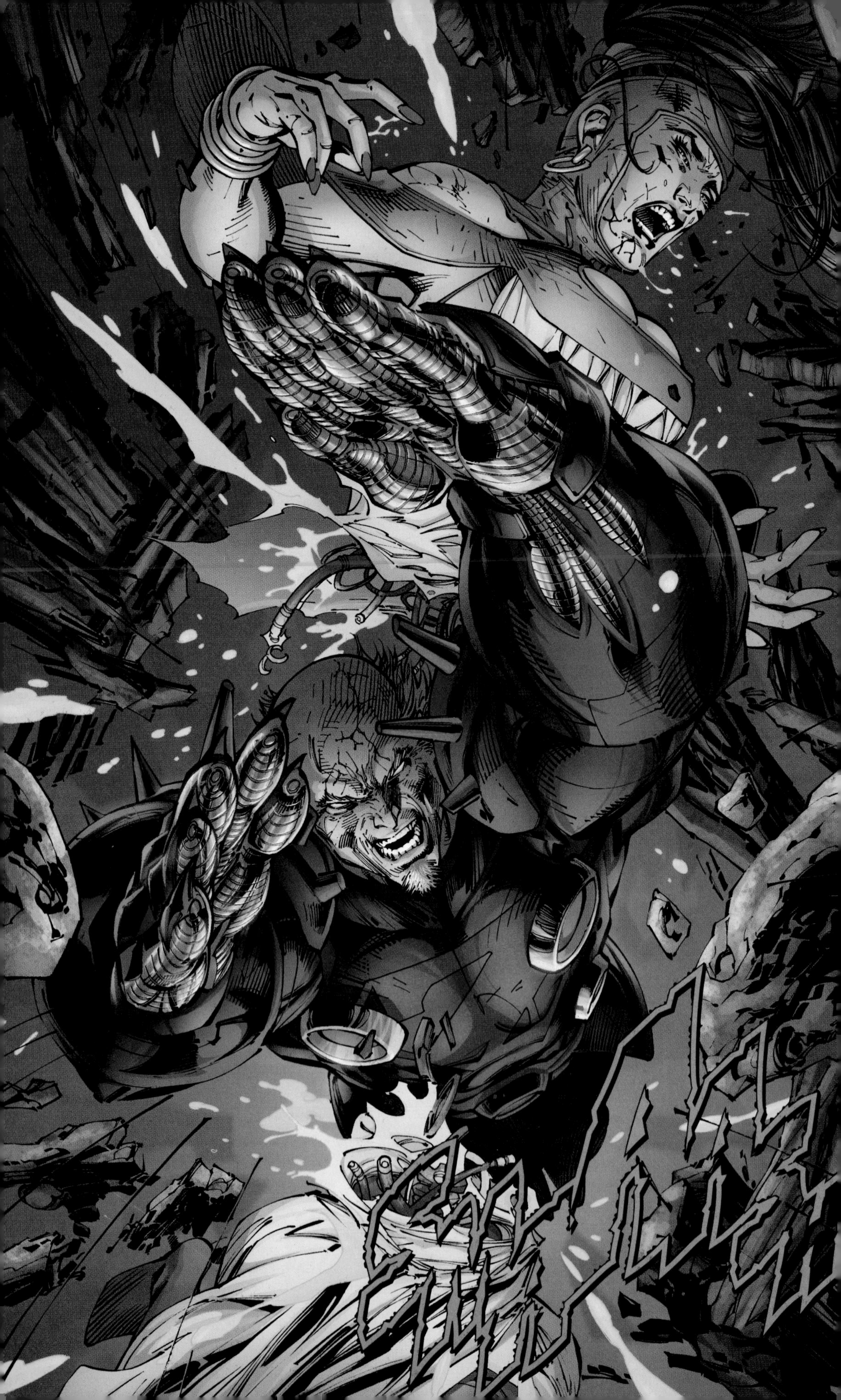

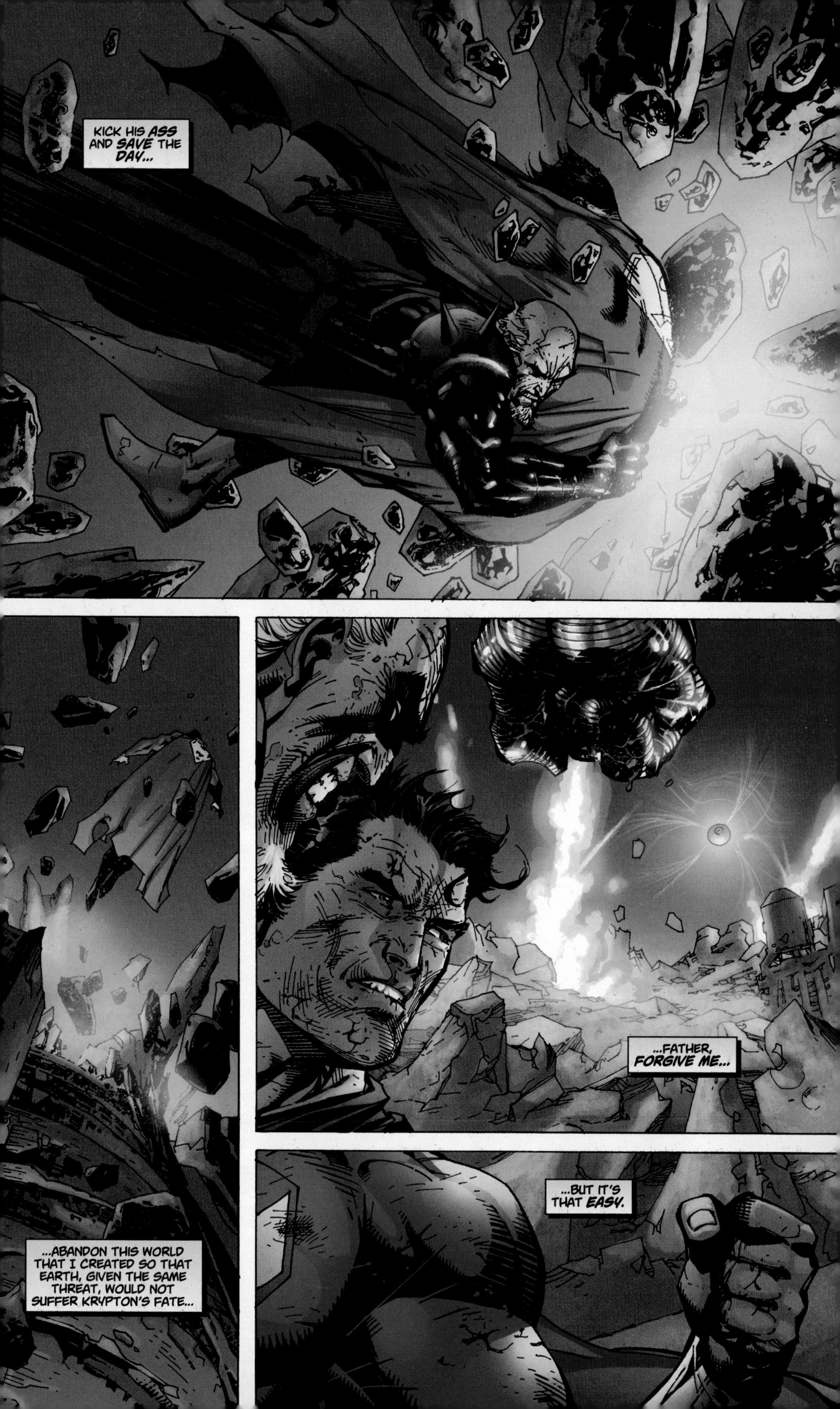

KICK HIS ASS AND SAVE THE DAY...
...FATHER, FORGIVE ME...
...ABANDON THIS WORLD THAT I CREATED SO THAT EARTH, GIVEN THE SAME THREAT, WOULD NOT SUFFER KRYPTON'S FATE...
...BUT IT'S THAT EASY.

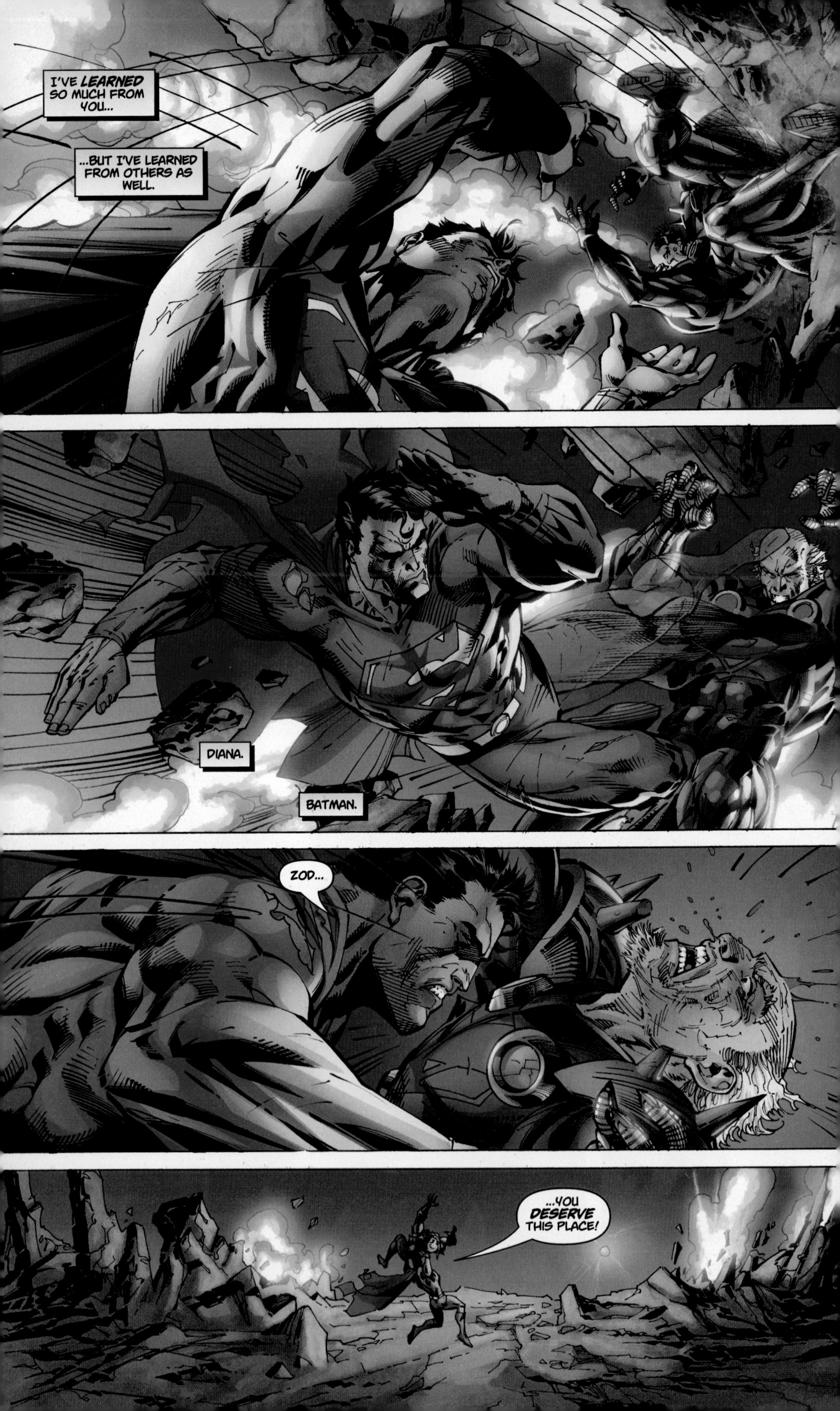
I'VE LEARNED SO MUCH FROM YOU...
...BUT I'VE LEARNED FROM OTHERS AS WELL.
DIANA.
BATMAN.
ZOD...
...YOU DESERVE THIS PLACE!

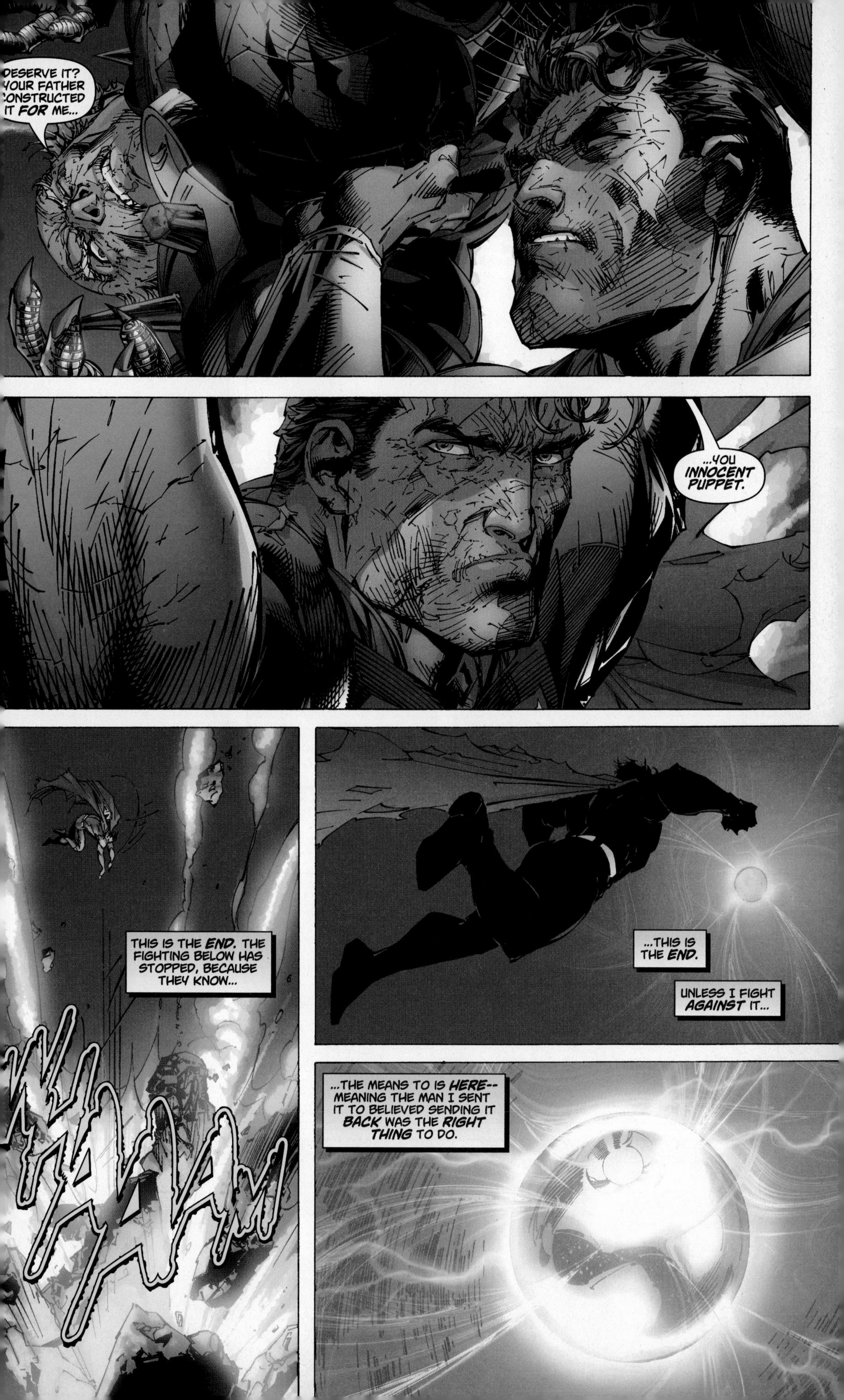
DESERVE IT? YOUR FATHER CONSTRUCTED IT FOR ME...
...YOU INNOCENT PUPPET.
THIS IS THE END. THE FIGHTING BELOW HAS STOPPED, BECAUSE THEY KNOW...
...THIS IS THE END.
UNLESS I FIGHT AGAINST IT...
...THE MEANS TO IS HERE-- MEANING THE MAN I SENT IT TO BELIEVED SENDING IT BACK WAS THE RIGHT THING TO DO.

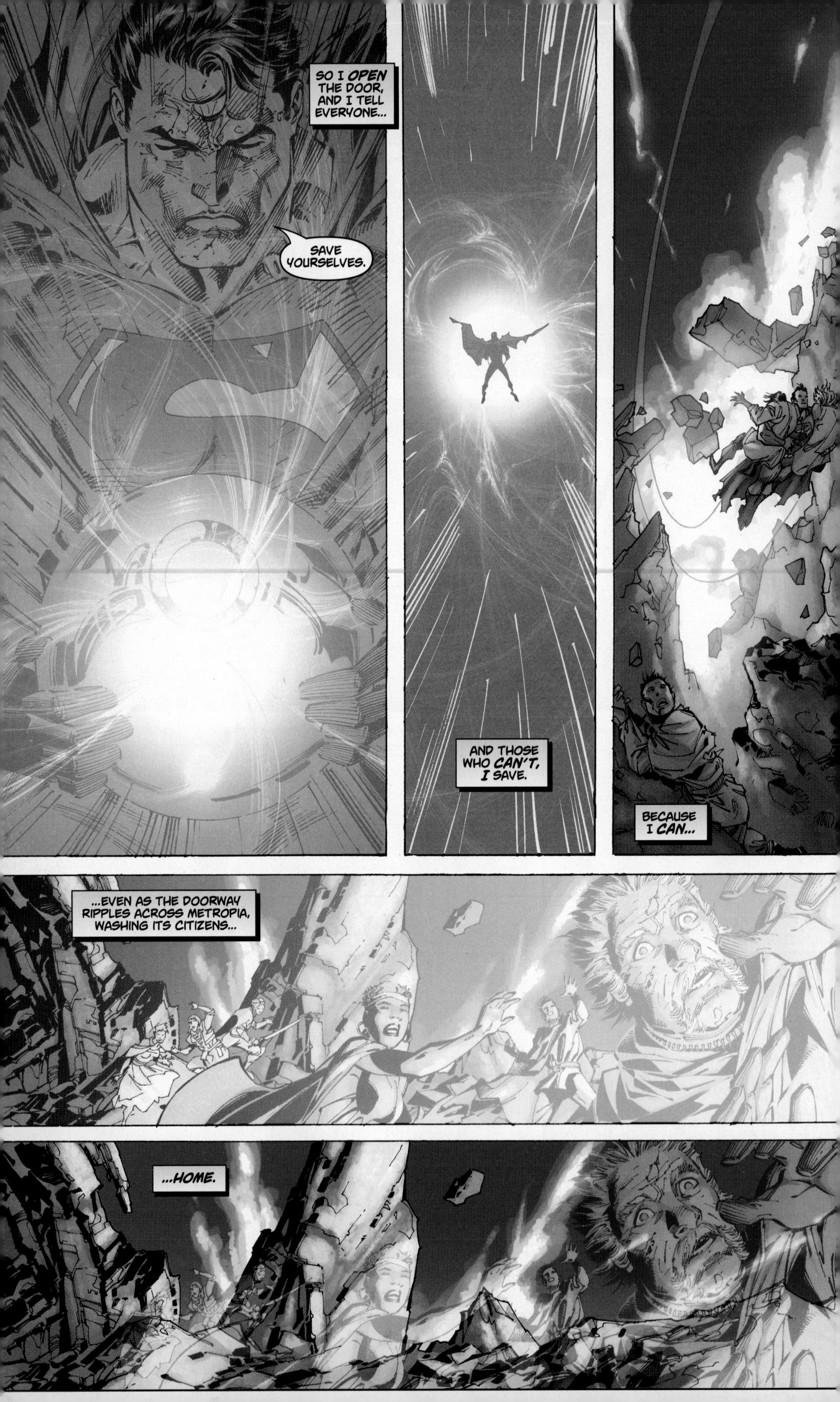
SO I OPEN THE DOOR, AND I TELL EVERYONE...
SAVE YOURSELVES.
AND THOSE WHO CAN'T, I SAVE.
BECAUSE I CAN...
...EVEN AS THE DOORWAY RIPPLES ACROSS METROPIA, WASHING ITS CITIZENS...
...HOME.

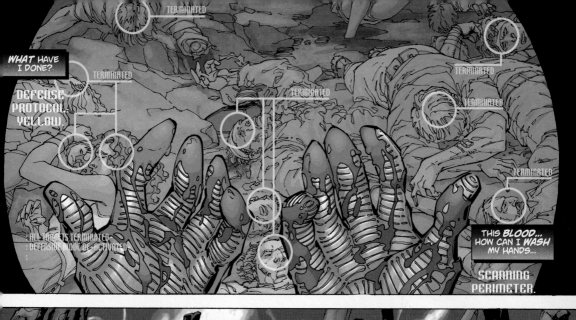

WHAT HAVE I DONE?

DEFENSE PROTOCOL: YELLOW.

TERMINATED

TERMINATED

TERMINATED

TERMINATED

TERMINATED

TERMINATED

: ALL TARGETS TERMINATED
: DEFENSIVE MODE DE-ACTIVATED
:

THIS BLOOD... HOW CAN I WASH MY HANDS...

SCANNING PERIMETER.

WATER TOWER 30 METERS NNE. STRUCTURE COMPROMISED.

I ALWAYS BELIEVED HELL WAS JUST A STORY, IMAGINED BY THOSE WHO NEEDED SOMETHING TO DISTRACT US FROM THE HELL THEY CREATED IN REALITY.

BUT I'M IN HELL... REAL HELL. AND DAMN ME, IT'S OF MY OWN DESIGN.

HOW DO I GET OUT?

INITIATING PILATE TO EYE IN THE SKY LINK-UP.

NO RESPONSE. RECONNECTING...

ALERT. DEFENSE PROTOCOL: ORANGE

SUPERMAN?

DEFENSE PROTOCOL: RED

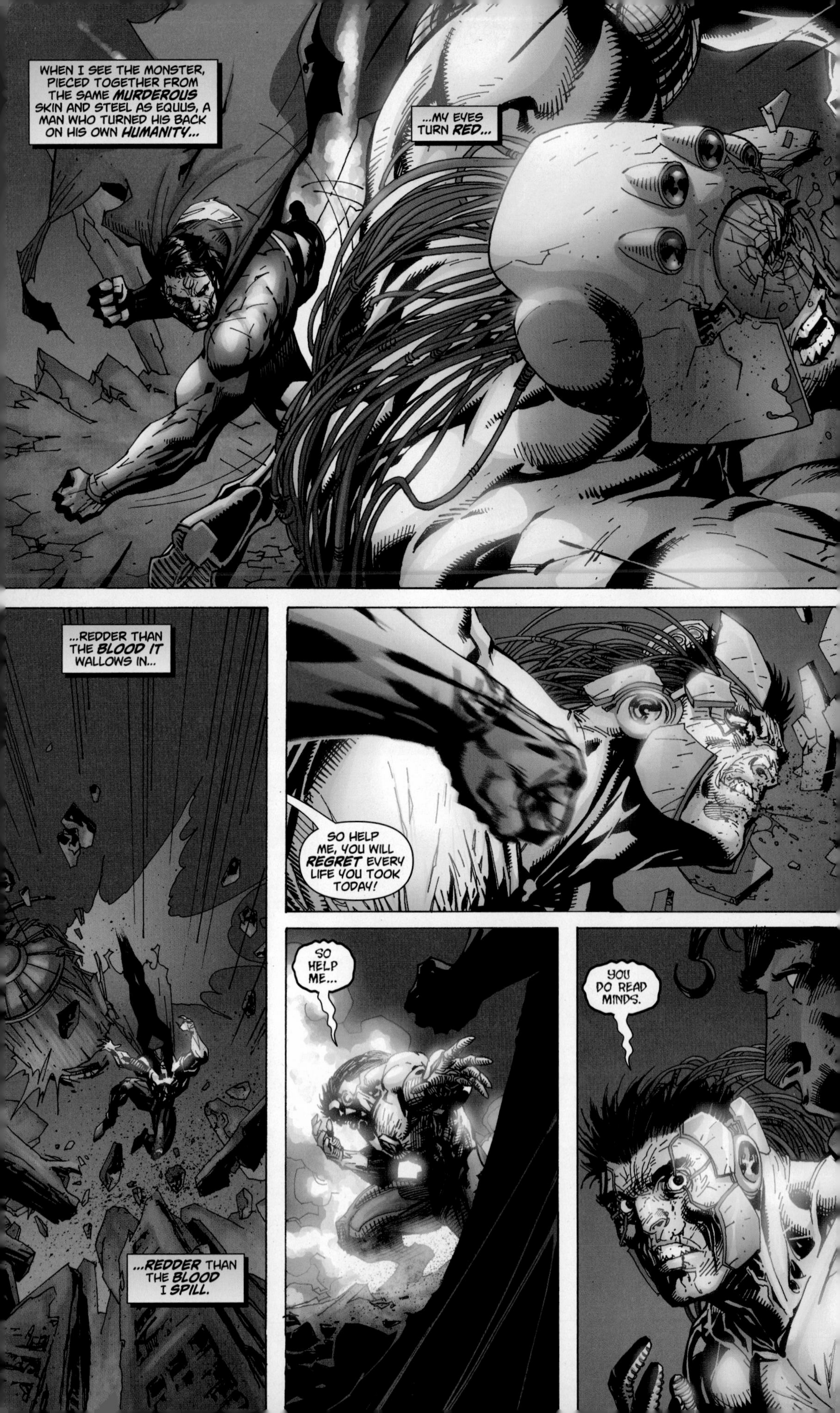
WHEN I SEE THE MONSTER, PIECED TOGETHER FROM THE SAME MURDEROUS SKIN AND STEEL AS EQUUS, A MAN WHO TURNED HIS BACK ON HIS OWN HUMANITY...
...MY EYES TURN RED...
...REDDER THAN THE BLOOD IT WALLOWS IN...
...REDDER THAN THE BLOOD I SPILL.
SO HELP ME, YOU WILL REGRET EVERY LIFE YOU TOOK TODAY!
SO HELP ME...
YOU DO READ MINDS.

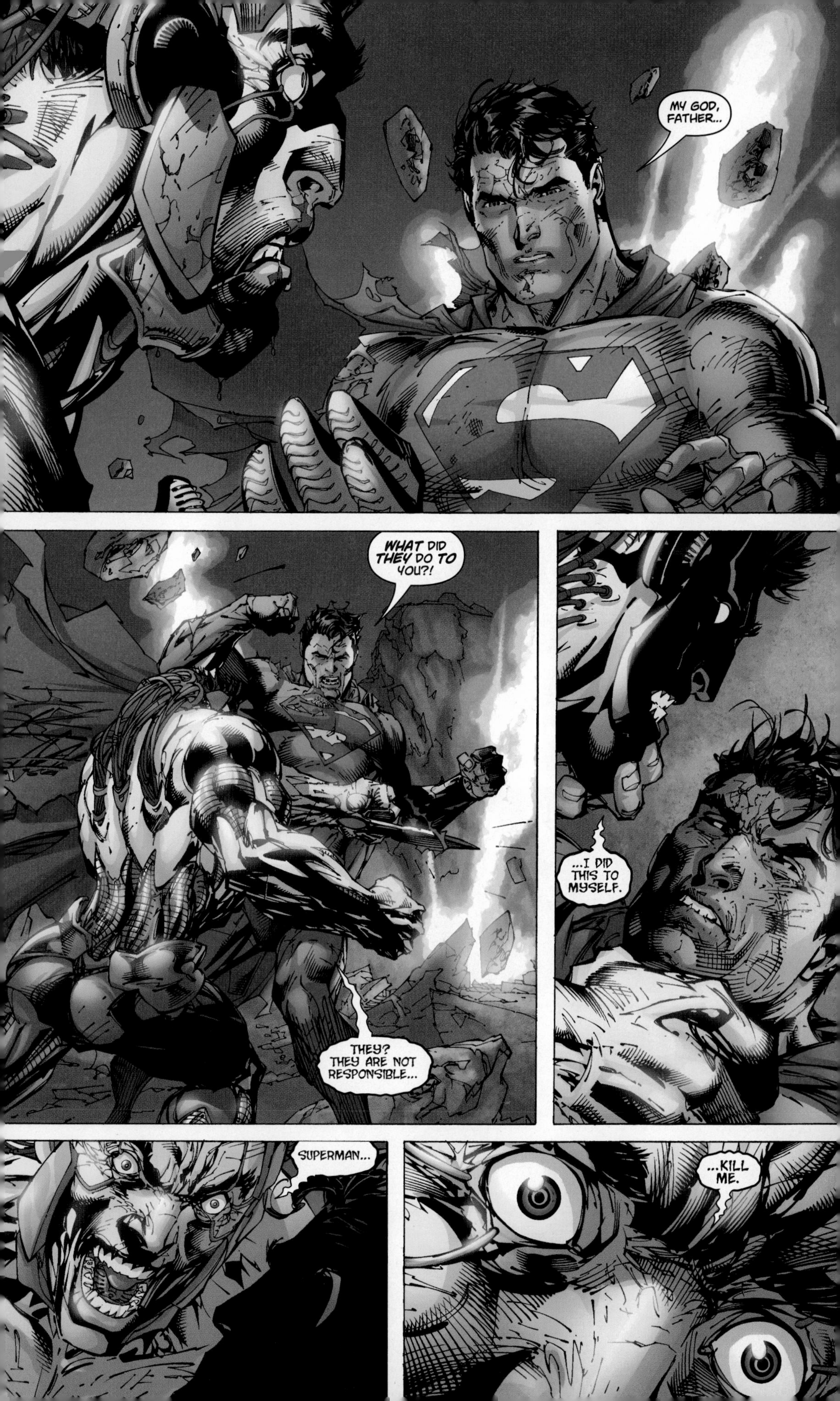
MY GOD, FATHER...
WHAT DID THEY DO TO YOU?!
THEY? THEY ARE NOT RESPONSIBLE...
...I DID THIS TO MYSELF.
SUPERMAN...
...KILL ME.

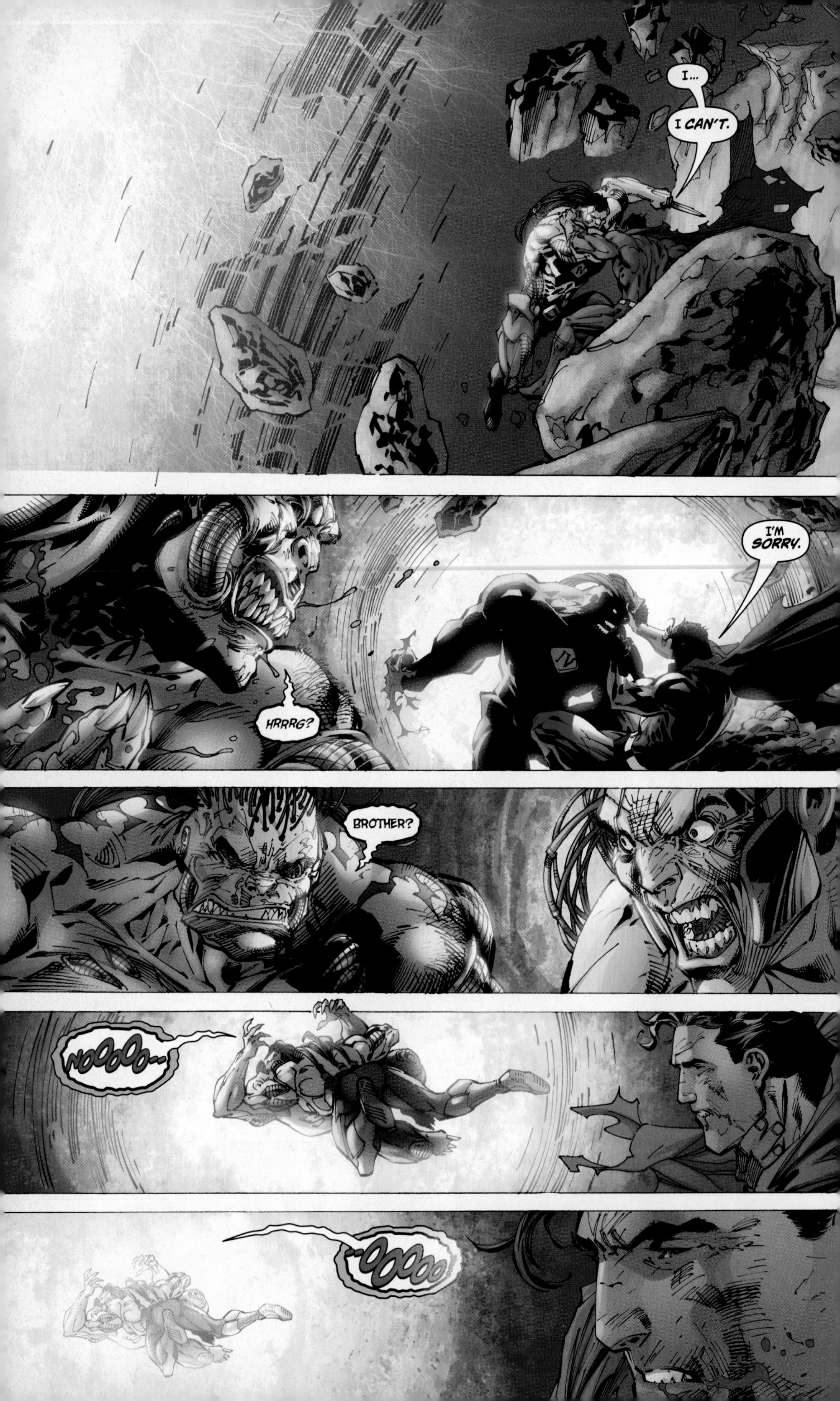

I...
I CAN'T.
I'M SORRY.
HRRRG?
BROTHER?
NOOOOO--
-OOOOO

WHAT DOES IT MEAN WHEN A MAN WHOSE LIFE IS BUILT ON *FAITH* SACRIFICES IT BY *SAVING* HIS OWN LIFE?

SUPERMAN...

...SAVE ME.

AND WHAT DOES IT MEAN WHEN A MAN IS WILLING TO SACRIFICE HIS OWN LIFE FOR WHAT HE *BELIEVES* IN?

ZOD...

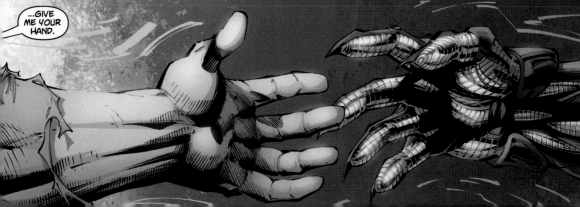

...GIVE ME YOUR HAND.

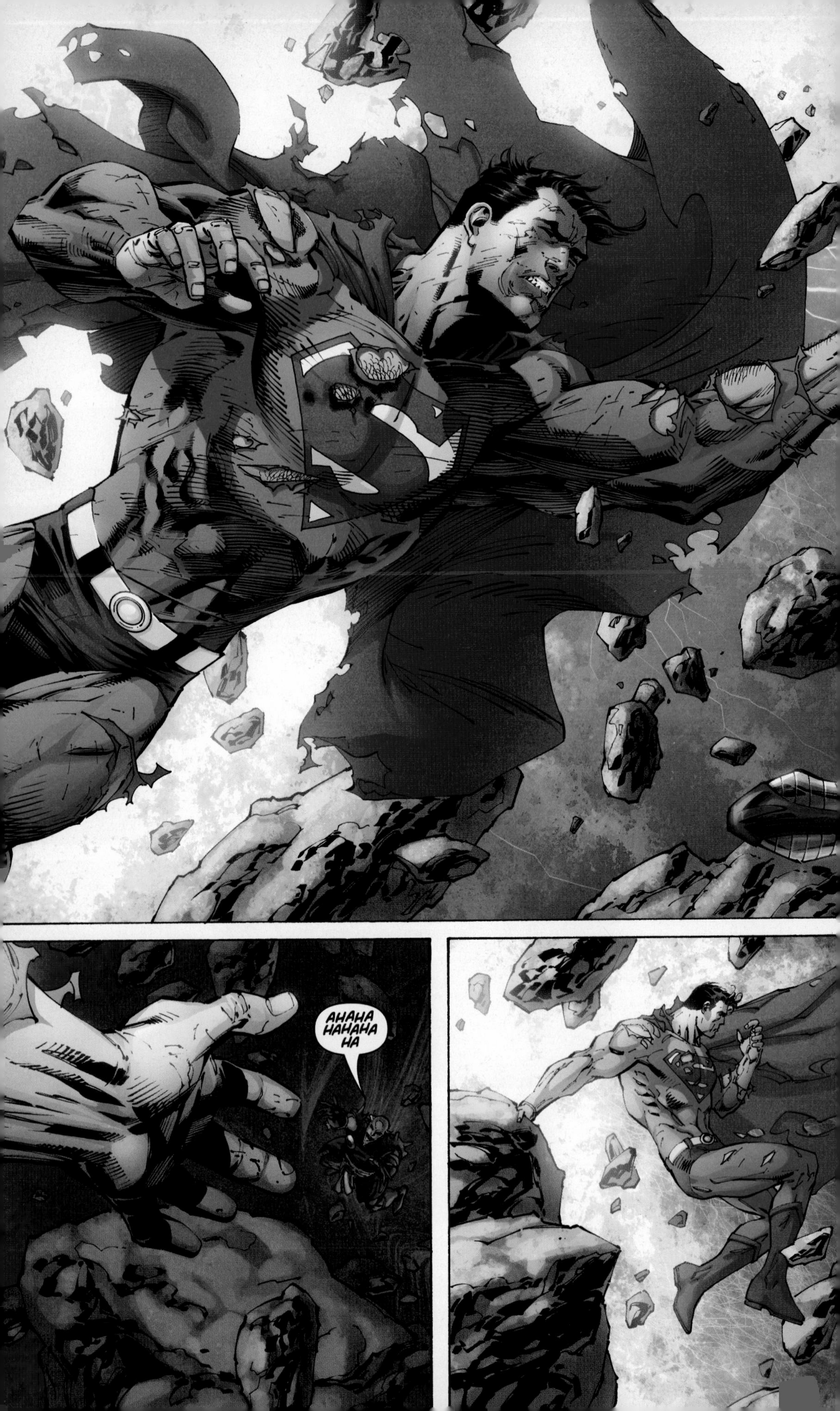
AHAHA
HAHAHA
HA

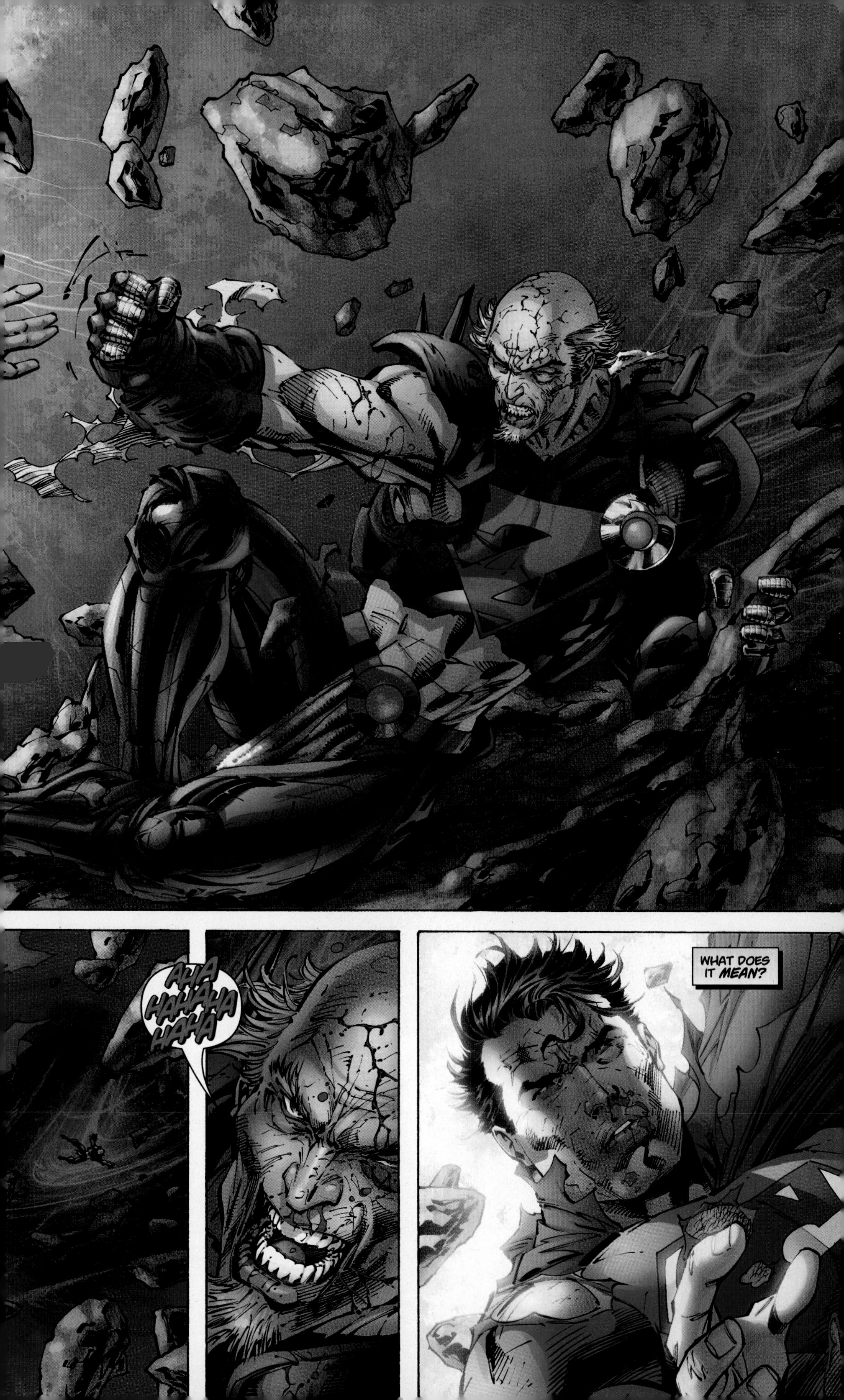
AHA HAHAHA HAHA
WHAT DOES IT MEAN?

I DON'T KNOW.

ALL OVER EARTH, THE VANISHED APPEAR. IT'S UNSETTLING...

...AND *NOT* JUST FOR THEM.

BUT AN *UNDERSTANDING* IS INSTANTLY *SHARED*...

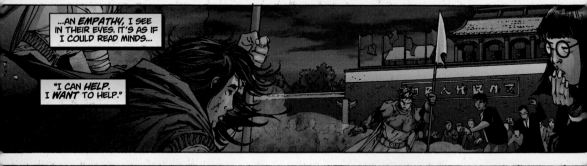

...AN *EMPATHY*, I SEE IN THEIR EYES. IT'S AS IF I COULD READ MINDS...

"I CAN *HELP*. I *WANT* TO HELP."

AND THEY DO.

THEY HELP EVERYONE...

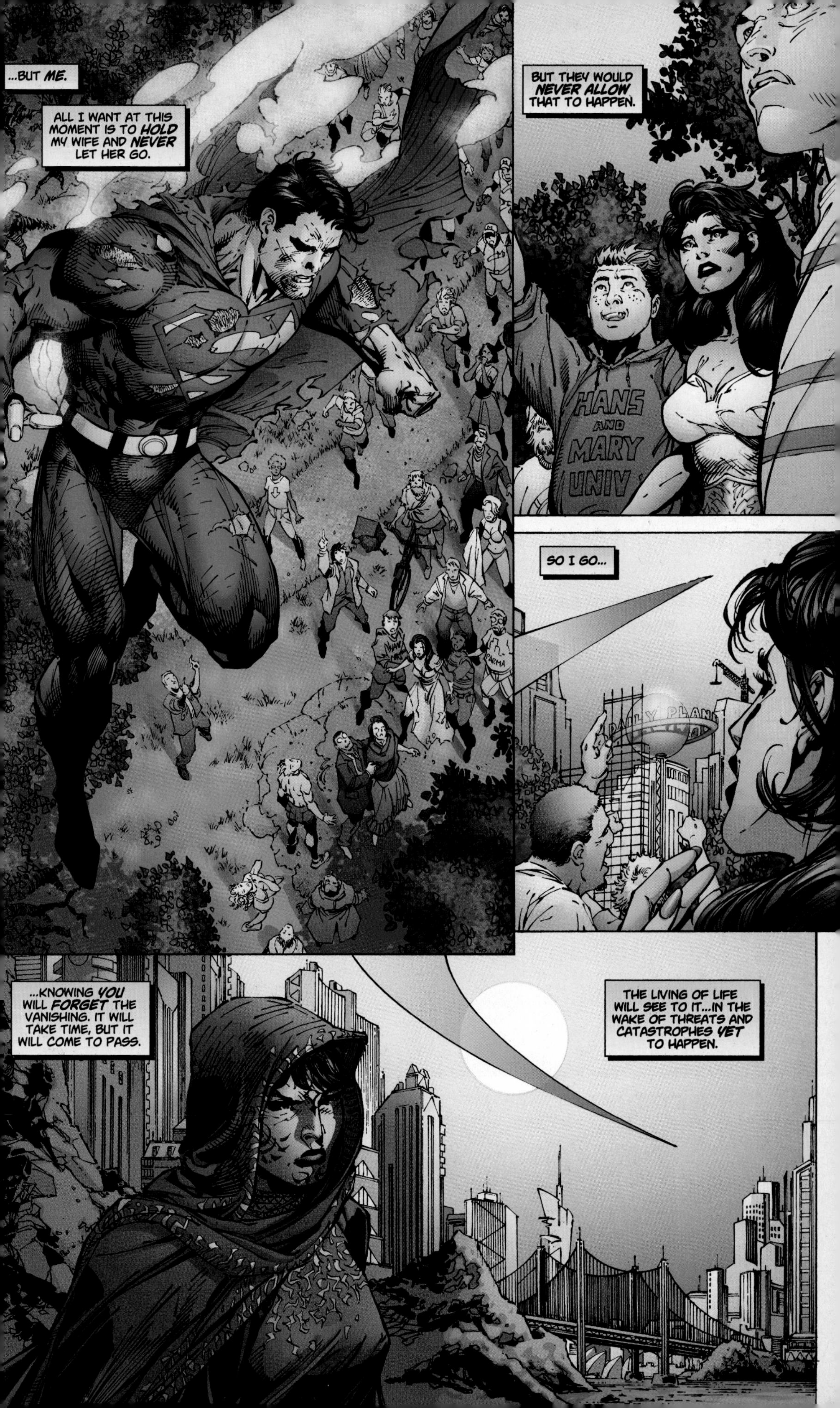
...BUT ME.
ALL I WANT AT THIS MOMENT IS TO HOLD MY WIFE AND NEVER LET HER GO.
BUT THEY WOULD NEVER ALLOW THAT TO HAPPEN.
HANS AND MARY UNIV
SO I GO...
...KNOWING YOU WILL FORGET THE VANISHING. IT WILL TAKE TIME, BUT IT WILL COME TO PASS.
THE LIVING OF LIFE WILL SEE TO IT...IN THE WAKE OF THREATS AND CATASTROPHES YET TO HAPPEN.

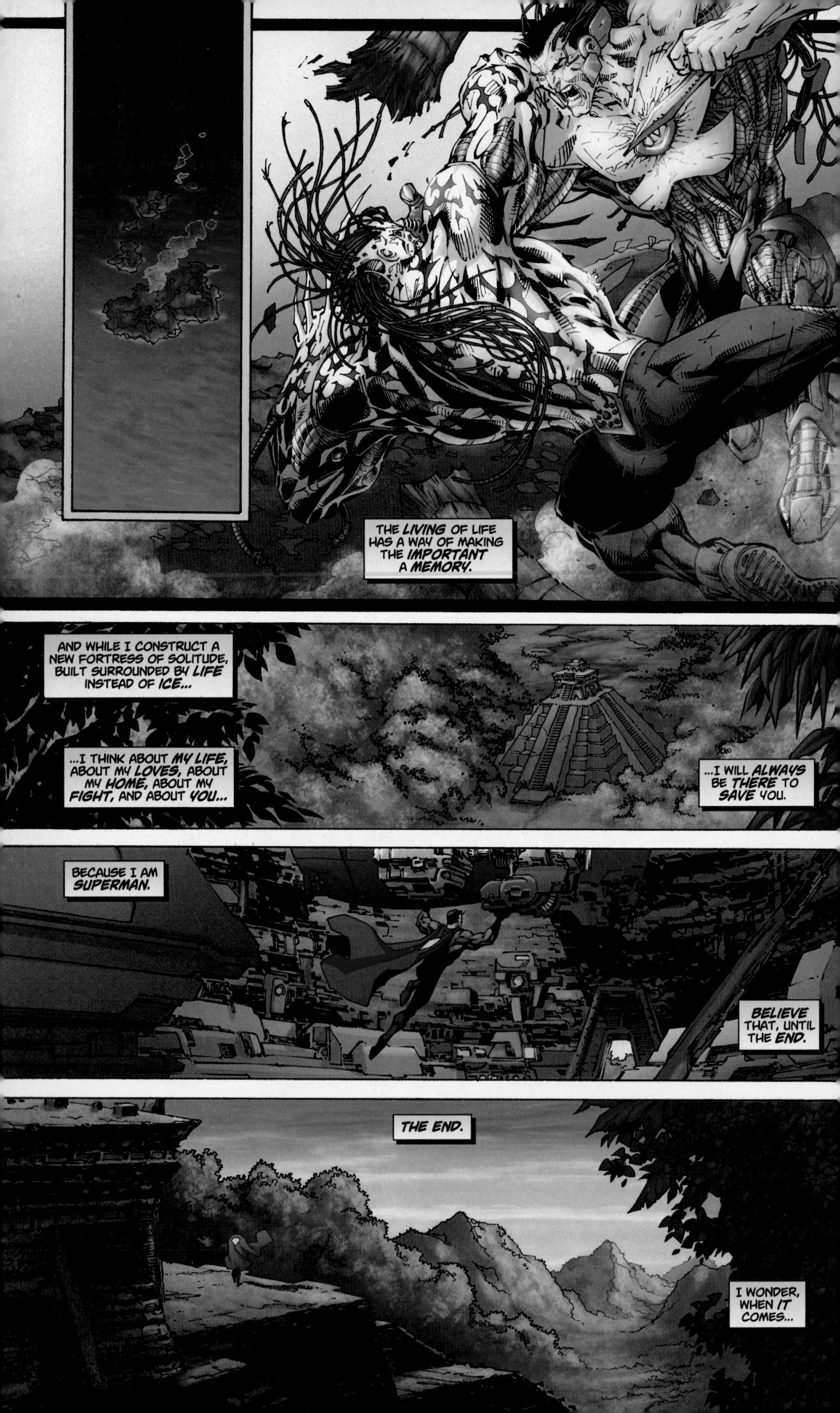
THE LIVING OF LIFE HAS A WAY OF MAKING THE IMPORTANT A MEMORY.
AND WHILE I CONSTRUCT A NEW FORTRESS OF SOLITUDE, BUILT SURROUNDED BY LIFE INSTEAD OF ICE...
...I THINK ABOUT MY LIFE, ABOUT MY LOVES, ABOUT MY HOME, ABOUT MY FIGHT, AND ABOUT YOU...
...I WILL ALWAYS BE THERE TO SAVE YOU.
BECAUSE I AM SUPERMAN.
BELIEVE THAT, UNTIL THE END.
THE END.
I WONDER, WHEN IT COMES...

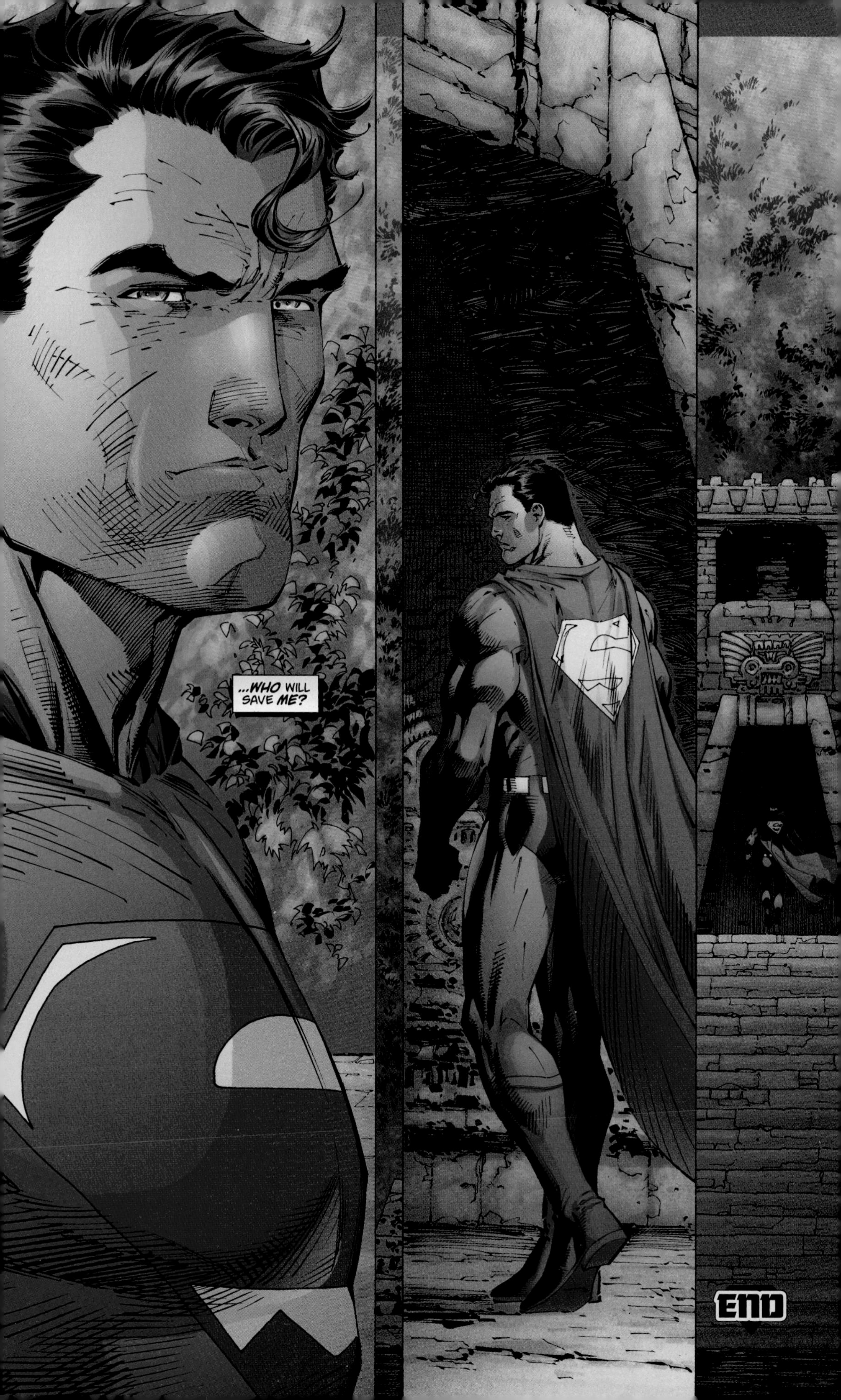
...WHO WILL SAVE ME?
END

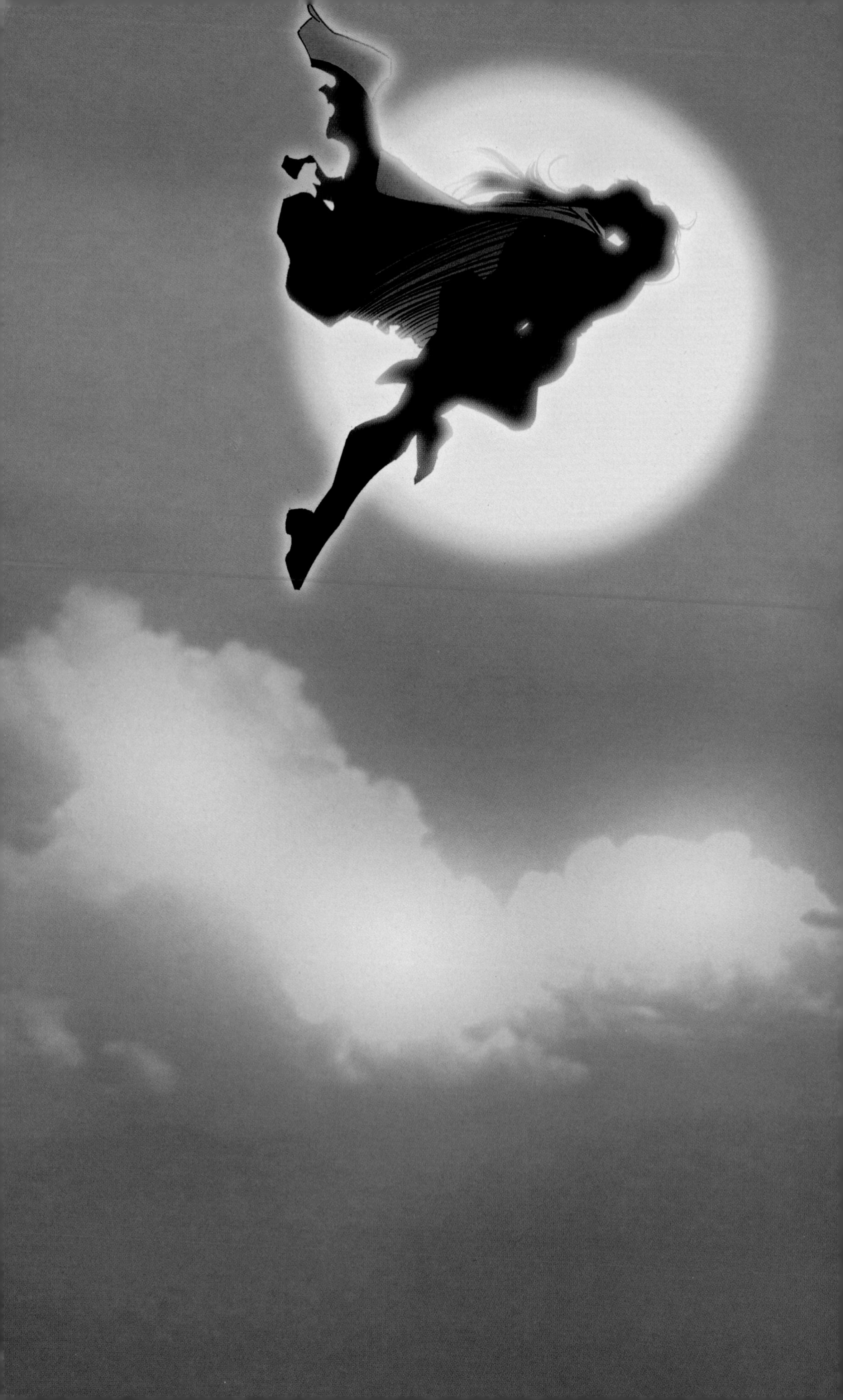

WE KNEW IT WASN'T GOING TO BE EASY.

Back in the spring of 2003, writer Brian Azzarello and I were sitting in a dark bar only a few blocks from the Moscone Convention Center in San Francisco, home of the Wonder Con, talking about our upcoming run on SUPERMAN. This is what we knew:

Superman was the ultimate symbol.

One of the best-known icons in the world, Superman was created by Jerry Siegel and Joe Shuster — two young Jewish teenagers from Cleveland growing up in Depression era America. The sole survivor of a dying race, Superman was sent by his father to Earth to protect and save us. With obvious religious overtones, Superman was a symbol of hope and salvation. For many fans growing up with the old black-and-white TV series starring George Reeves as the Man of Steel, Superman also came to represent Truth, Justice and the American way.

This lore we knew was immutable. Not that other creators had not given their best shot at change. In recent decades, although Superman had been portrayed in turn as the Ultimate Yuppie, a political lapdog, and even as a frazzled, therapy-seeking husband/super-hero who just happened to have the power to fly through the sun unscathed, he always remained, deep inside, the same. He was the ultimate Status Quo: literally and figuratively bulletproof!

So the dilemma we faced was simply this: How were we, as creators, going to say something new about this nearly 70-year-old character?

We knew our answer wasn't going to be cosmetic. *New green, purple and orange costume?* Nope.

We knew that we couldn't change the trappings of his world. *New job on Satellite Radio that will make him millions, allowing him to move on up to Beverly Hills?* Nope.

Our only recourse was to turn inward. To dig. We knew we had to penetrate beyond the symbol, past the shield to the character within. That's what attracted Brian to the project. And in the end, it really all comes down to characters. What drives them? What makes them tick? Why does one man choose to be a hero; the other, a villain? Is it even a choice?

AFTERWORD

BY JIM LEE

Known for his critically acclaimed work on his own title — 100 BULLETS — Brian had a way of reaching in deep into a character's psyche and finding that one *thing*, buried in a person's soul, which had the power of ripping that character apart or driving him on to greatness. As a fan of his work, I would marvel at how Brian always seemed to find that one thing and not only expose it for what it was but also managed to twist it and turn it in ways others before him had not.

Given that Superman was created in 1938, finding that *thing* in Superman was going to be a challenge. Like I said, we knew it wasn't going to be easy. Truth be told, once we started, we found a lot of *things*. They became *our* things. And we knew that for the story to work, the reader had to make the same discoveries and his own interpretations for the story to work and have lasting impact.

The gratifying part was that many did. While others were hostile to the pacing and the subtlety of the dialogue, a lot of fans, many of them new fans, welcomed and embraced what we were saying and made their own examinations and interpretations of the work. Brian always wanted part of the story to happen off-page, in the minds of the reader — and many, many fans took the challenge.

As did I. Every issue had dialogue which I realized I could interpret in many different ways: scenes which could be played for high drama or low laughs or both. It was a challenge trying to put across what I thought Brian meant, but I stubbornly refused to call him for his interpretation unless I was hopelessly divided.

As the issues came out and the big picture became clearer, more fans began to understand "For Tomorrow" was as much a story of Superman searching for some understanding of the father he never knew as it was a search for what he believed killed his wife. That it was a story not just about the limits of force as a means to enact change but the personal price of standing for Truth, Justice and the American way.

That it was about the power of guilt, the need for redemption and the hope and healing that Tomorrow brings.

Like I said, we found a lot of *things*. Hopefully you found some of your own too.

JIM LEE
La Jolla, 2005

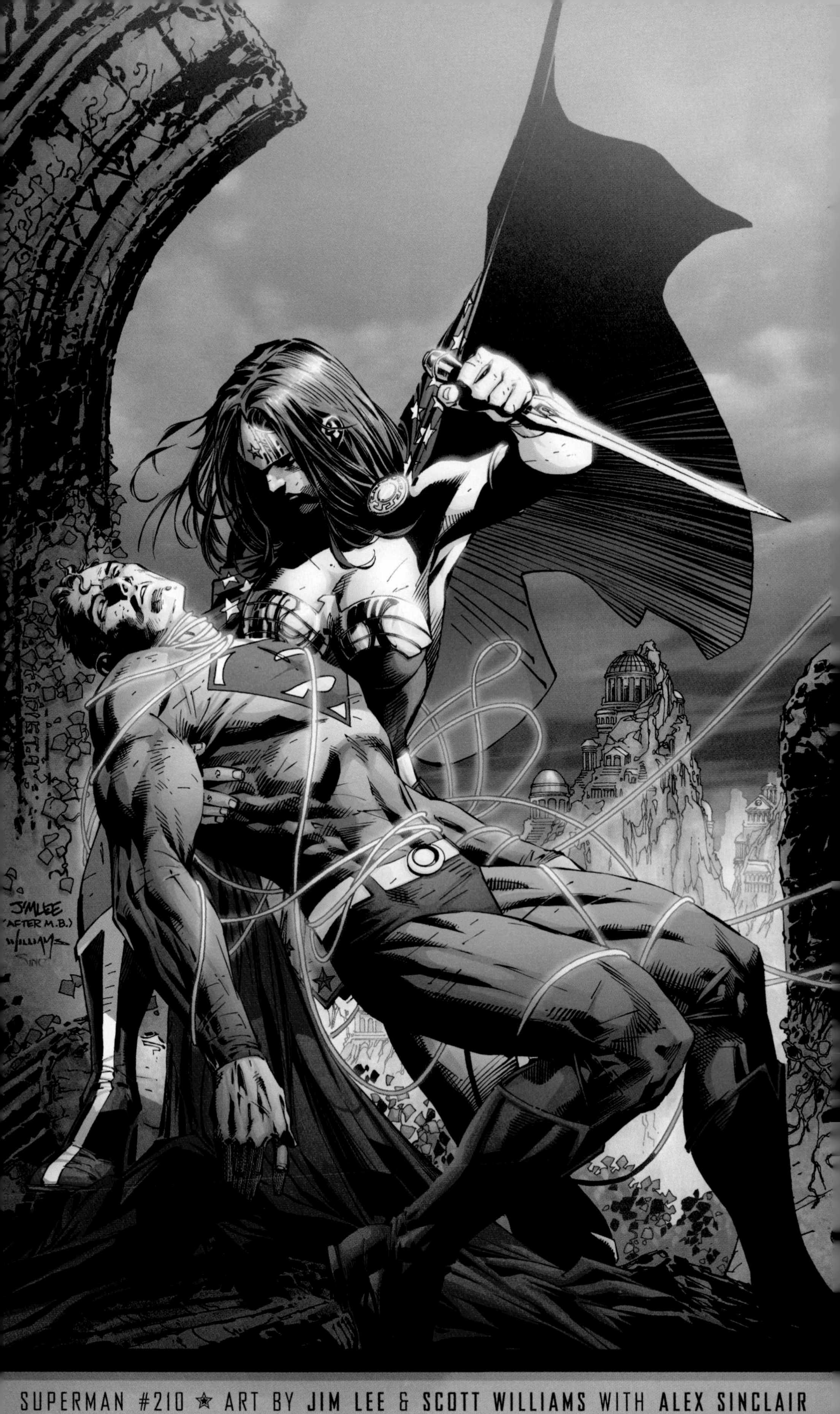
JIMLEE
(AFTER M.B.)
WILLIAMS

SUPERMAN #210 ✭ ART BY JIM LEE & SCOTT WILLIAMS WITH ALEX SINCLAIR

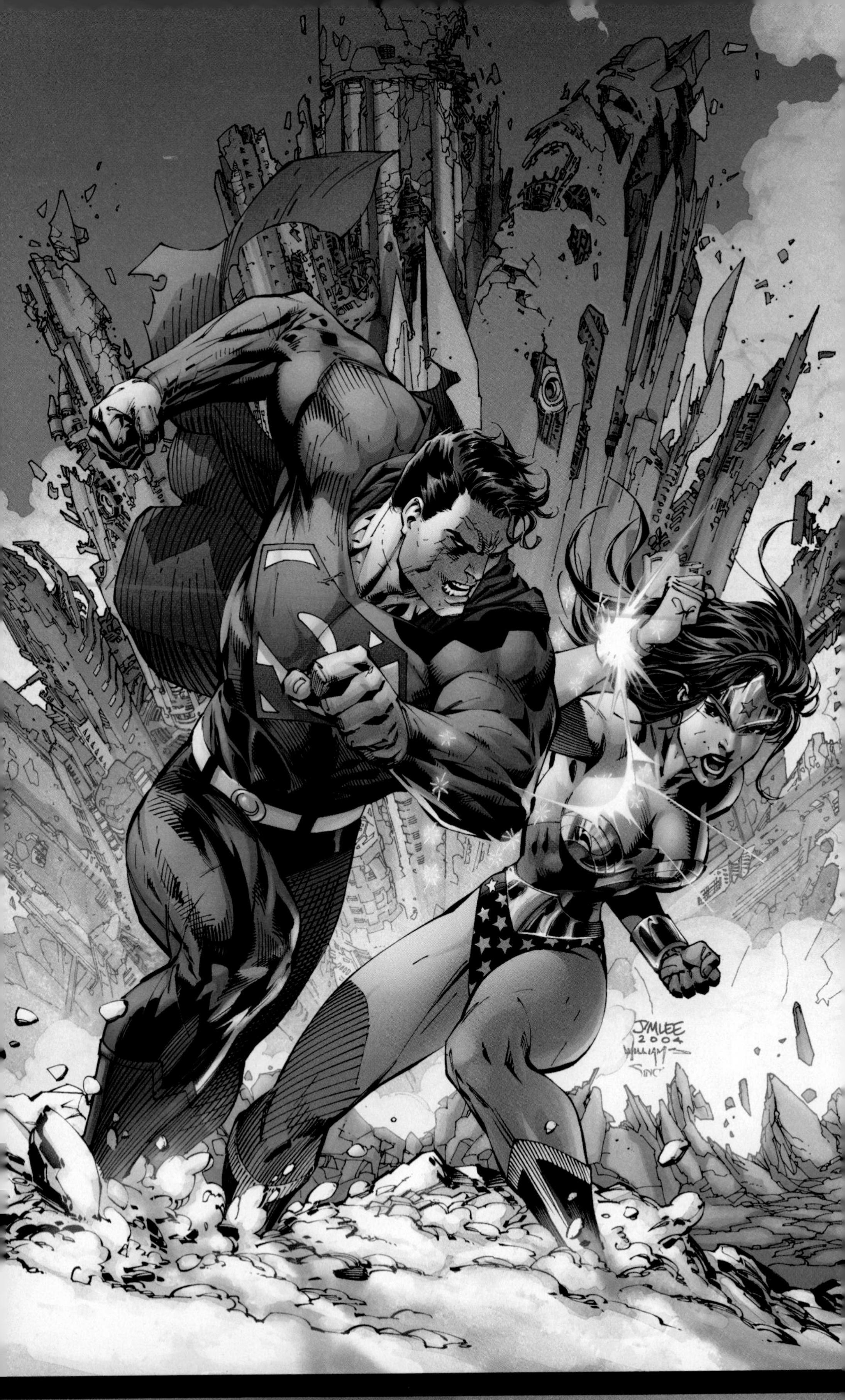
JIMLEE
2004

SUPERMAN #211 ✭ ART BY **JIM LEE** & **SCOTT WILLIAMS** WITH **ALEX SINCLAIR**

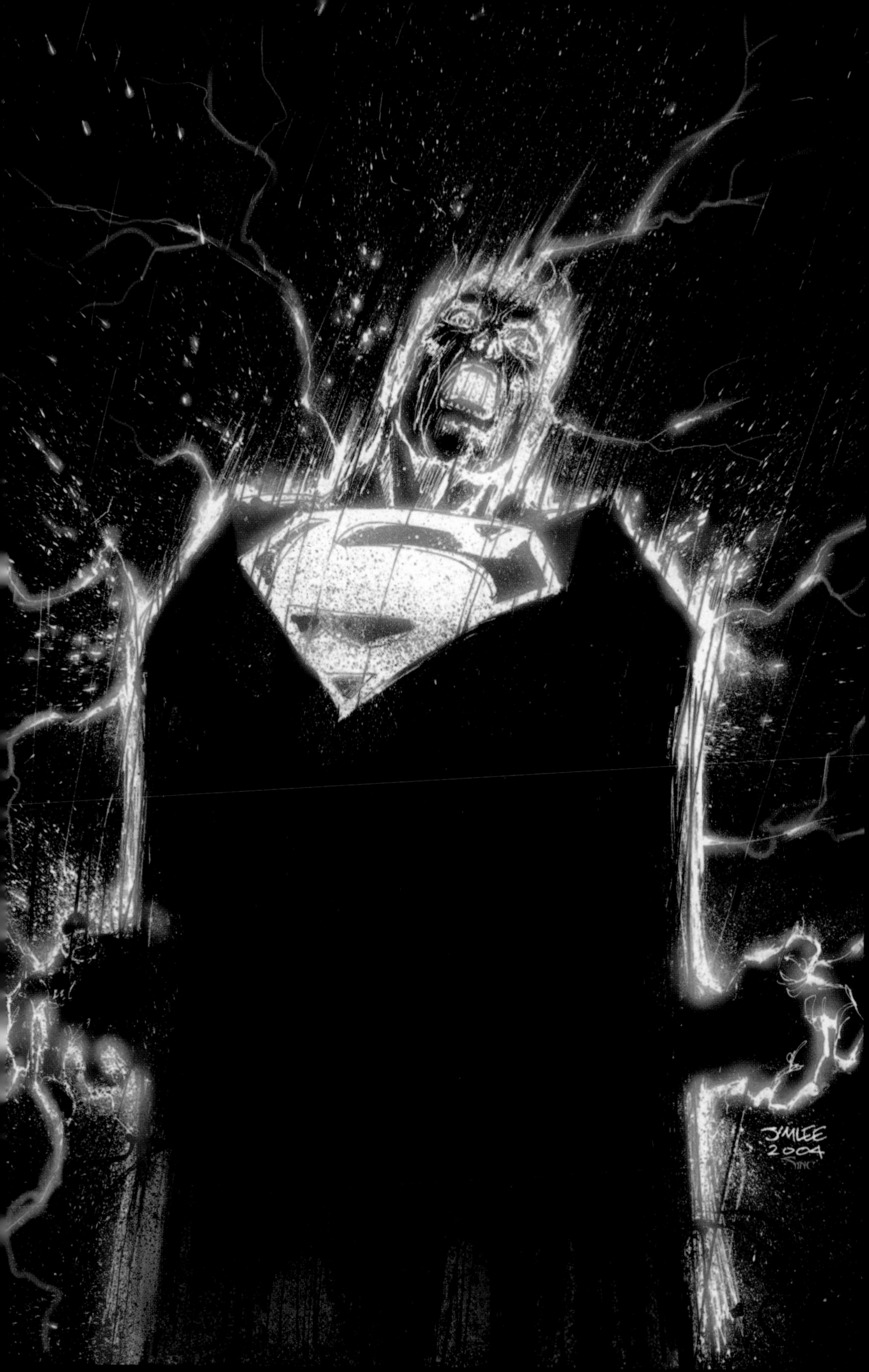
JIMLEE
2004

SUPERMAN #212 ✯ ART BY **JIM LEE** WITH **ALEX SINCLAIR**

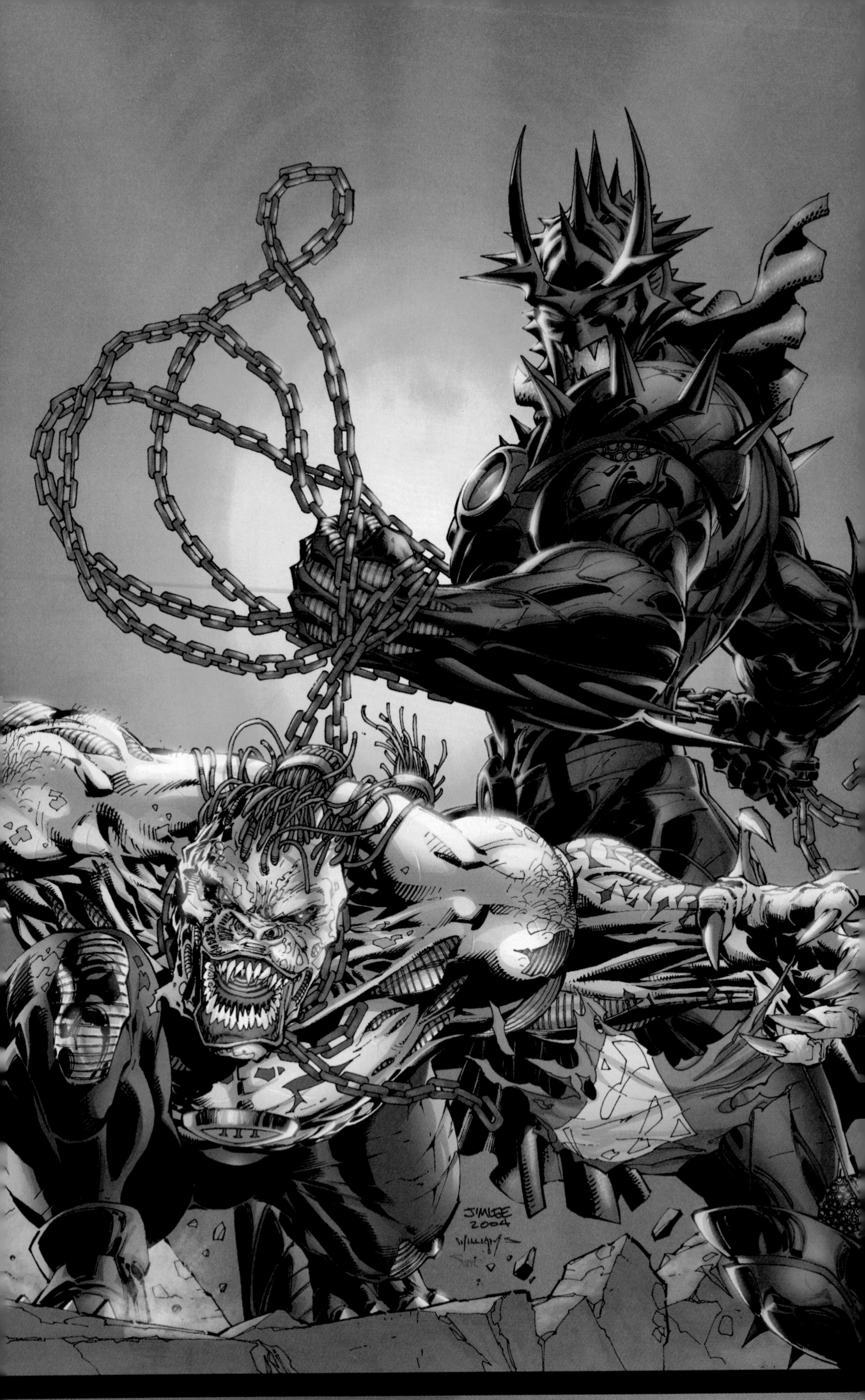

SUPERMAN #213 ★ ART BY **JIM LEE & SCOTT WILLIAMS** WITH **ALEX SINCLAIR**

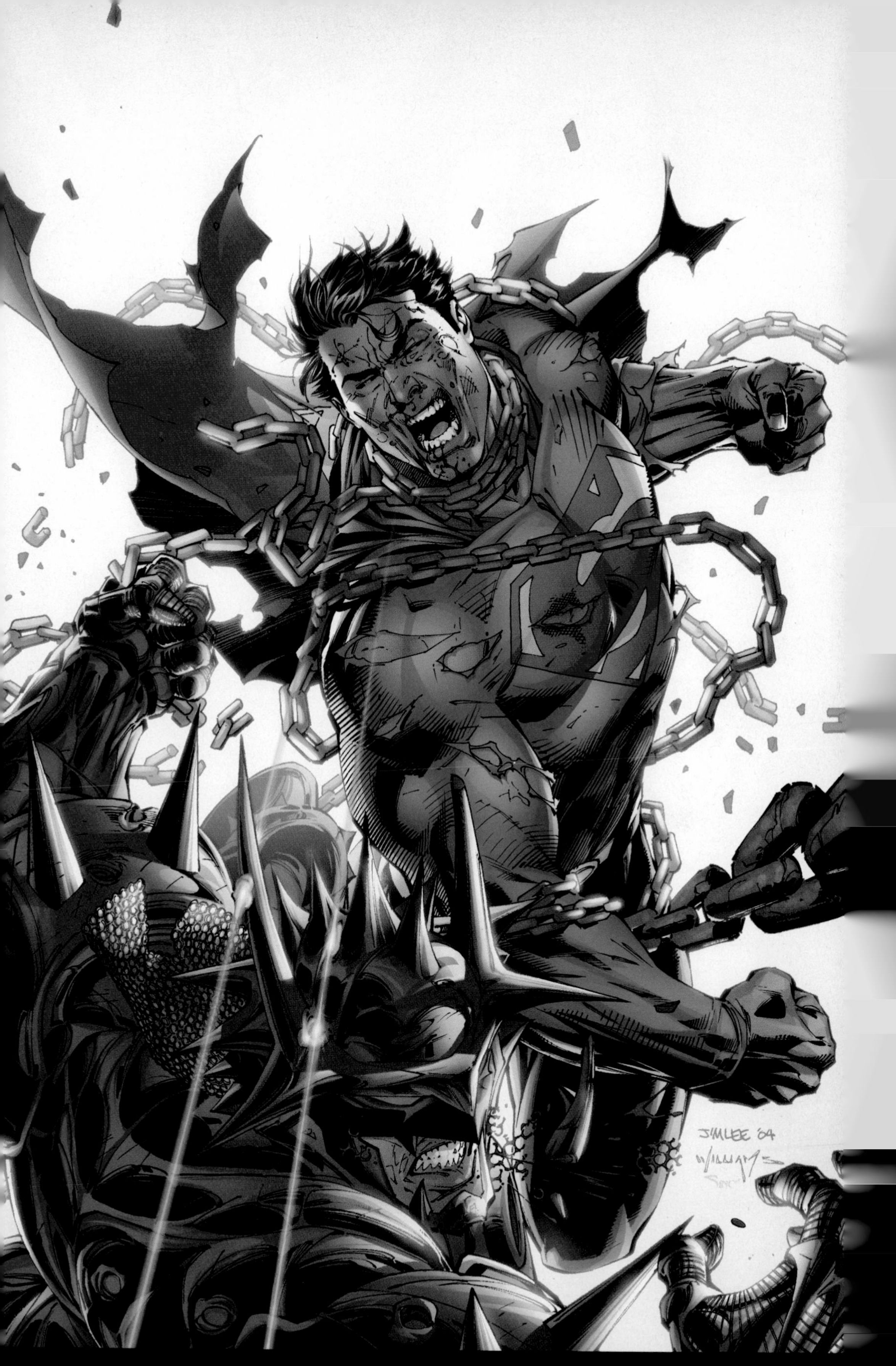
JIM LEE '04

SUPERMAN #214 ✭ ART BY JIM LEE & SCOTT WILLIAMS WITH ALEX SINCLAIR

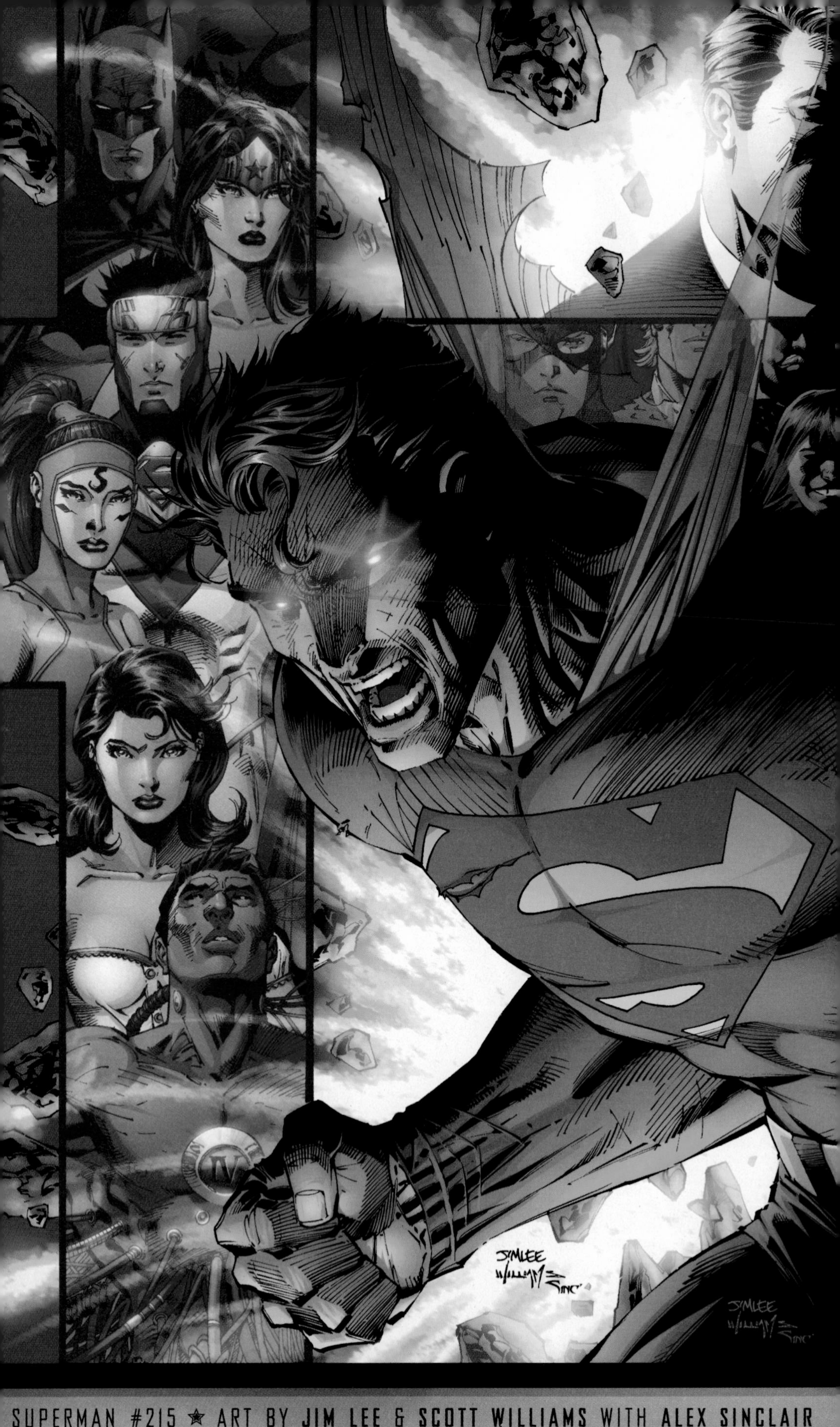

SUPERMAN #215 ★ ART BY JIM LEE & SCOTT WILLIAMS WITH ALEX SINCLAIR

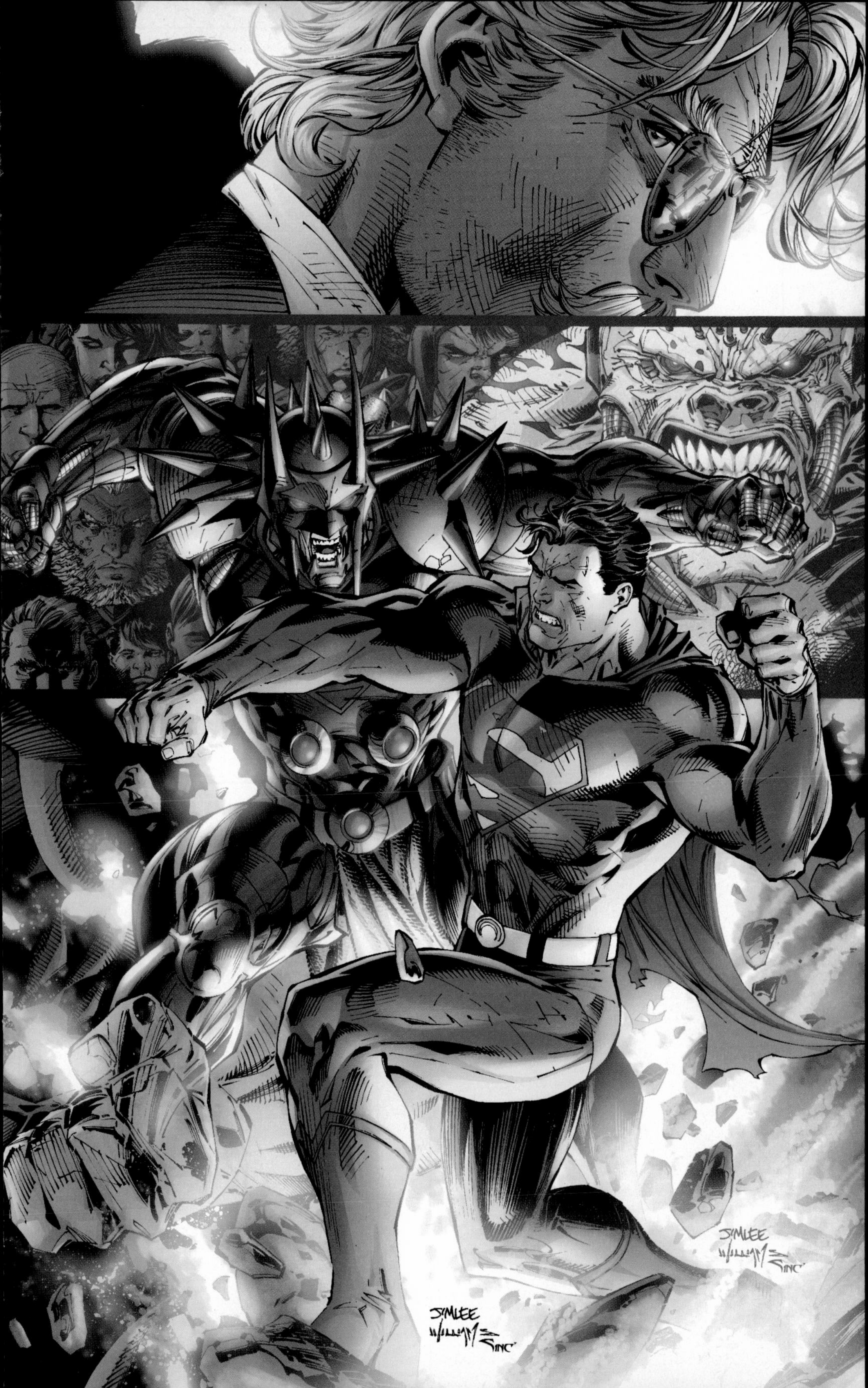

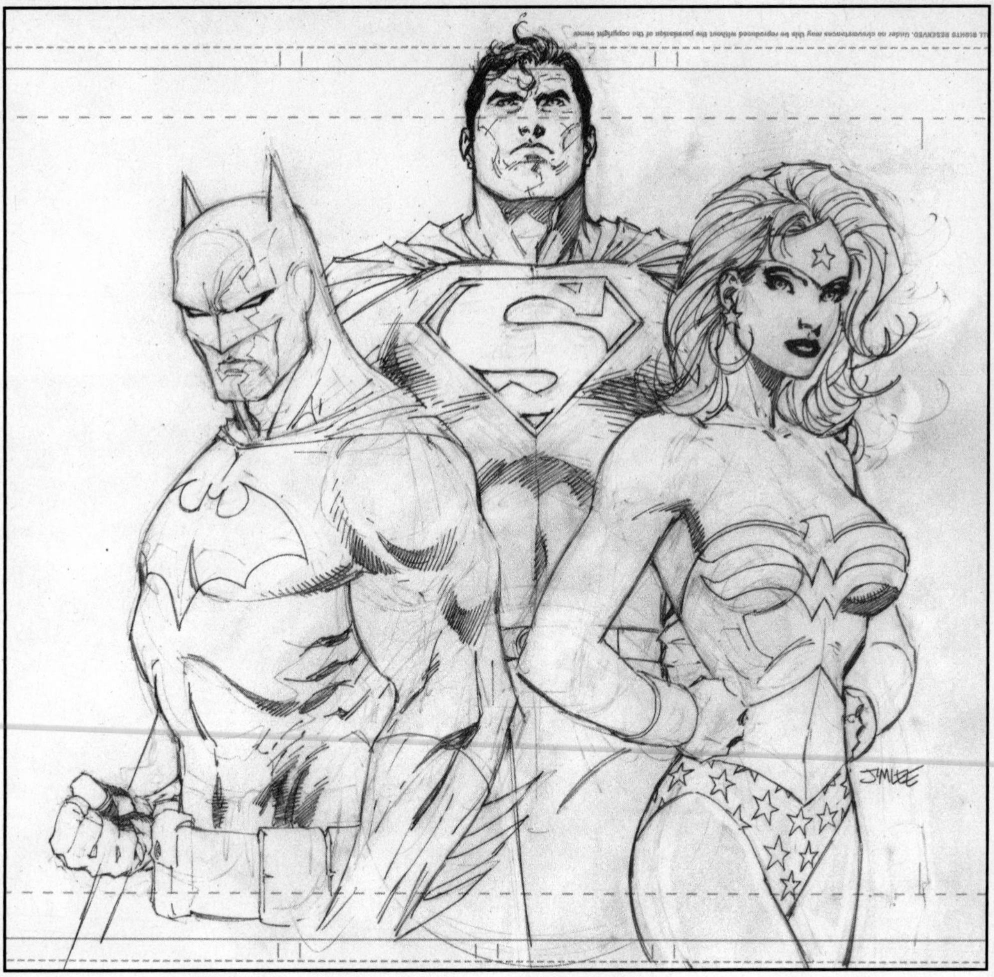
JIMLEE

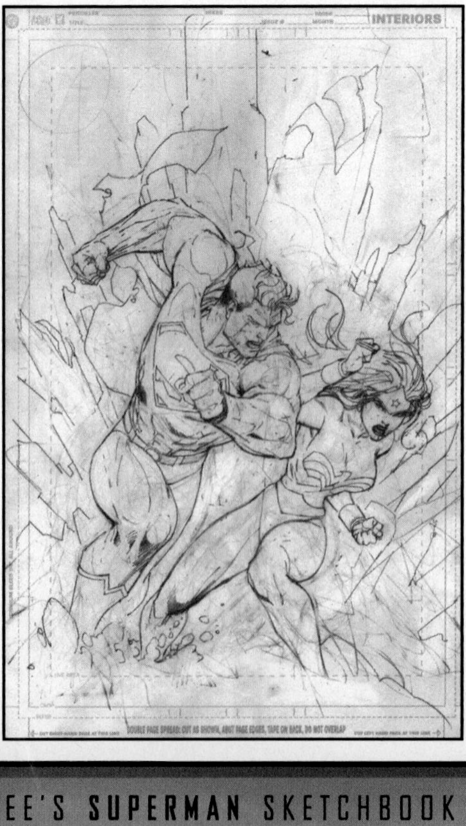
INTERIORS
DOUBLE PAGE SPREAD: CUT AS SHOWN, ABUT PAGE EDGES, TAPE ON BACK, DO NOT OVERLAP

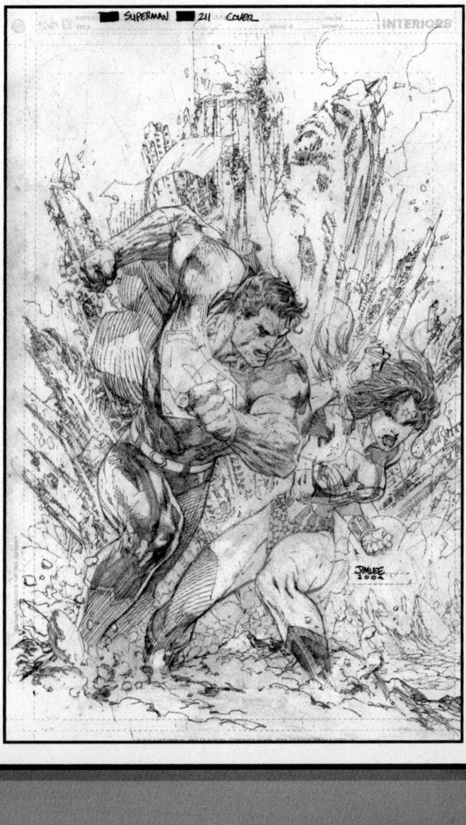
[redacted] SUPERMAN [redacted] 211 COVER
INTERIORS
JIMLEE

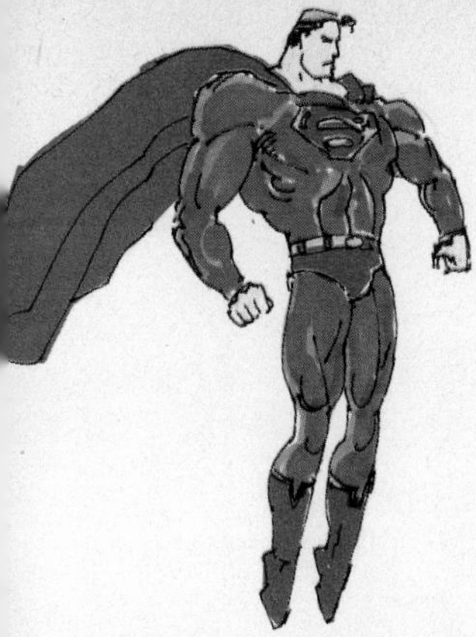

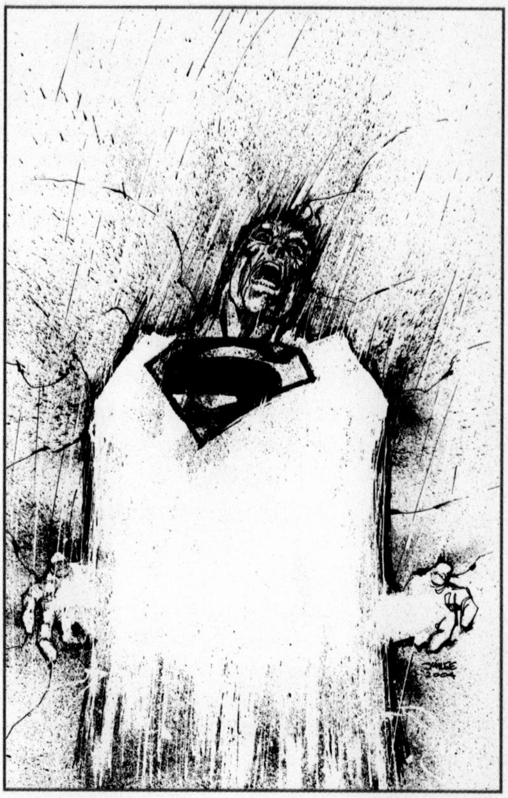

OPPOSITE PAGE
TOP: pencil art done for the animated version of dc comics' newest logo.
BOTTOM: sketch and final pencils for superman #211 cover.

THIS PAGE
TOP: a very, very early sketch of superman in color.
RIGHT: the inked version of the cover for superman #212.
the image was reversed (made "negative") for the final cover.
BOTTOM: a turnaround of superman.

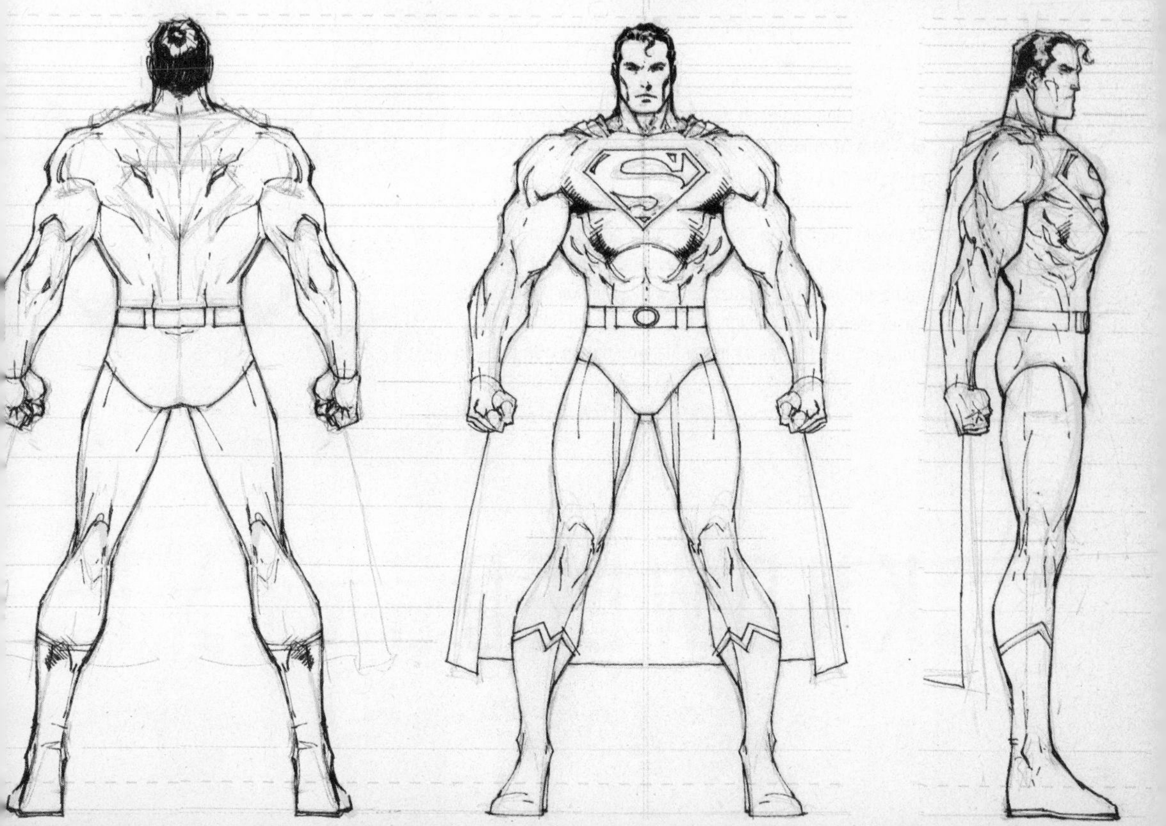

I'd like to thank any and all of you who kept the faith in Jim, Scott, Alex & myself throughout the year it took us to tell this story. You know who you are. It's ironic, how truth sometimes imitates fiction.

BRIAN AZZARELLO

While *By Tomorrow* was a popular deadline mantra amongst the creators on this run when pressed for delivery dates, *For Tomorrow* simply doesn't exist without the incredible dedication of Will Dennis and his assistant editor Casey Seijas who not only made it all work out in the end but did it with style.

I also want to thank Eddie Berganza and Tom Palmer for their tireless efforts, Dan DiDio for his good humor in the face of madness, Anton Kawasaki for his boundless patience and Amie Brockway-Metcalf for putting it all together in these dazzlingly designed volumes.

Finally, I am indebted to Scott Williams and Alex Sinclair for all the sacrifices they made to make sure *For Tomorrow* came out *Today*.

One simply cannot find better people.

JIM LEE

While patience is always a virtue when it comes to the publishing side of a project like *For Tomorrow*, it was nonetheless tested as all of my creative colleagues pushed to get things as "just right" as possible. My thanks to all for said patience and dedication in allowing Jim, Brian, Alex, Rob and myself to take deadlines to a new level of excitement to get this thing done. And of course the patience shown by my family in allowing me the long weekends and lost evenings to pursue my creative passions. Peace,

SCOTT WILLIAMS

Thanks to Jim and Scott, two guys who, in the eyes of everyone here at WildStorm, wear a big S on their chests. Every artist loves a great challenge, and now I know why Jim wanted to work with Brian. I am proud to say that I have too. Scott Iwahashi went above and beyond by helping and inspiring me with the Vanishing sequences. And the rest of the guys riding with me on this crazy train without brakes: Will Dennis, Casey Seijas, Rob Leigh, Chris Burns and Mike Komai. Finally, to the five ladies in my life who put up with my long hours in "the cave."

ALEX SINCLAIR

ACKNOWLEDGMENTS

BIOS

BRIAN AZZARELLO has been writing comics professionally since the mid 1990s. He is the writer and co-creator with Eduardo Risso of the acclaimed Vertigo monthly series 100 BULLETS, which won the 2002 Harvey Award as well as the 2002 and 2004 Eisner Award for best continuing series. Azzarello's other writing credits for DC Comics include BATMAN and JONNY DOUBLE (both with Risso), GANGLAND, BATMAN/DEATHBLOW, LEX LUTHOR: MAN OF STEEL, and an Eisner-nominated run on HELLBLAZER. He has also written *Cage* and *Banner* for Marvel Comics. Brian has been cited as one of *Wizard* magazine's top ten writers and has been profiled and/or reviewed in *Entertainment Weekly, GEAR, The Chicago Tribune,* and countless other publications. He lives in Chicago with his wife, artist Jill Thompson, and still does not have a website.

JIM LEE was born in Seoul, South Korea in 1964. He graduated from Princeton University with a degree in psychology but decided to try his hand at comic-book art — his childhood fantasy. He found work at Marvel Comics, where his work quickly proved so popular that the company created a new X-Men title just to showcase it. In 1992, Lee formed his own comics company, WildStorm Studios, which became one of the founding components of Image Comics. There, he launched the best-selling WILDC.A.T.S and helped to create many other characters. He also helped to discover and train a phalanx of writers, artists, and colorists. With its steady success, WildStorm as a business grew so demanding that Lee found he no longer had any time to draw, leading to his decision to sell the company to DC Comics. He remains WildStorm's creative director but now concentrates on his first love, art — including penciling ALL-STAR BATMAN AND ROBIN, THE BOY WONDER. He lives in La Jolla, California with his wife and three daughters.

SCOTT WILLIAMS has partnered with Jim Lee for more than ten years, and he was voted Favorite Inker for five years in a row (1990-94) in the Comics Buyer's Guide Fan Awards. His inking work can be found in BATMAN: HUSH, DANGER GIRL, GEN13, JUST IMAGINE STAN LEE..., WONDER WOMAN, WILDCATS/ X-MEN, *X-Men: Mutant Genesis*, and *X-Men: X-Tinction Agenda*.

ALEX SINCLAIR has previously worked on KURT BUSIEK'S ASTRO CITY, TOP 10, HARLEY QUINN, and, with Jim Lee and Scott Williams, on WILDC.A.T.S, GEN13, DIVINE RIGHT, and BATMAN: HUSH. Sinclair lives in San Diego with his sidekick Rebecca and their four hench-girls: Grace, Blythe, Meredith, and Harley. He would love to fight crime, but the weather's too nice. Instead, Sinclair became an editor at WildStorm in the spring of 2003.

ROB LEIGH is a graduate of the The Joe Kubert School of Cartoon & Graphic Art. His lettering first received critical notice in 1972, when he was sent home with a note for writing a four-letter word on the blackboard of Miss Tuschmann's second-grade class. In addition to lettering, Rob has inked many titles for DC. He lives in northern New Jersey with his wife, Vaughan, and homicidal cat, Barley.

NICK J. NAPOLITANO is also a graduate of the Joe Kubert School. Nick has worked for DC Comics, in one capacity or another, for nearly 13 years. Having pencilled, inked, lettered, edited, etc., he has finally settled down to manage DC's In-House Lettering Department, where he spends his quiet days surrounded by eccentric artists and frantic editors (he wouldn't trade it for anything). He lives on Long Island with his wife, Christine, his dog, Buffy, and about 30-40 of his goombata.

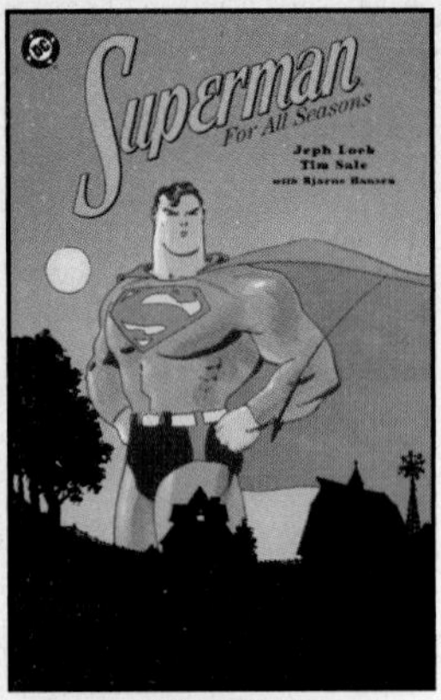
Superman
For All Seasons
Jeph Loeb
Tim Sale
with Bjarne Hansen

SUPERMAN
FOR ALL SEASONS

Jeph Loeb/Tim Sale

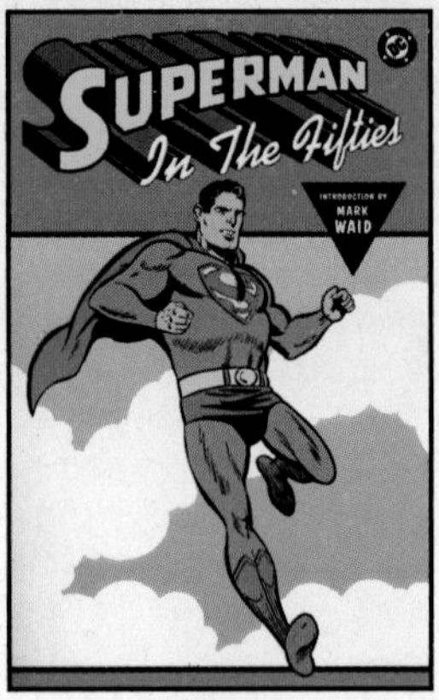
SUPERMAN
In The Fifties
INTRODUCTION BY MARK WAID

SUPERMAN IN THE FIFTIES
SUPERMAN IN THE SIXIES
SUPERMAN IN THE SEVENTIES

various

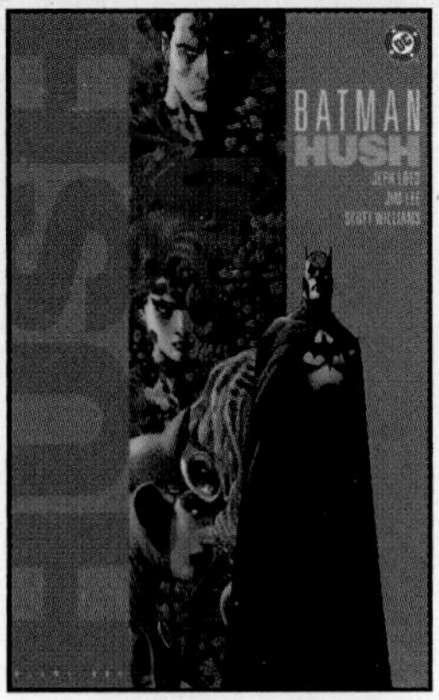
BATMAN
HUSH
JEPH LOEB
JIM LEE
SCOTT WILLIAMS

BATMAN: HUSH
VOLUMES 1 & 2

Jeph Loeb/Jim Lee/Scott Williams

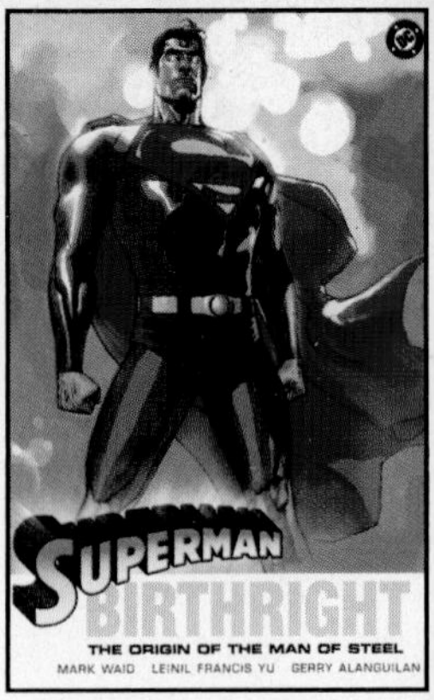
SUPERMAN
BIRTHRIGHT
THE ORIGIN OF THE MAN OF STEEL
MARK WAID LEINIL FRANCIS YU GERRY ALANGUILAN

SUPERMAN: BIRTHRIGHT

Mark Waid/Leinil Francis Yu/
Gerry Alanguilan

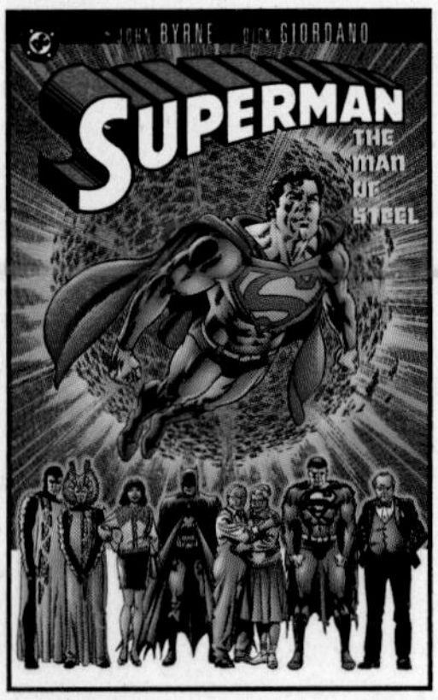
BYRNE
GIORDANO
SUPERMAN
THE MAN OF STEEL

SUPERMAN: MAN OF STEEL
VOLUMES 1 - 3

John Byrne/Marv Wolfman/
Jerry Ordway

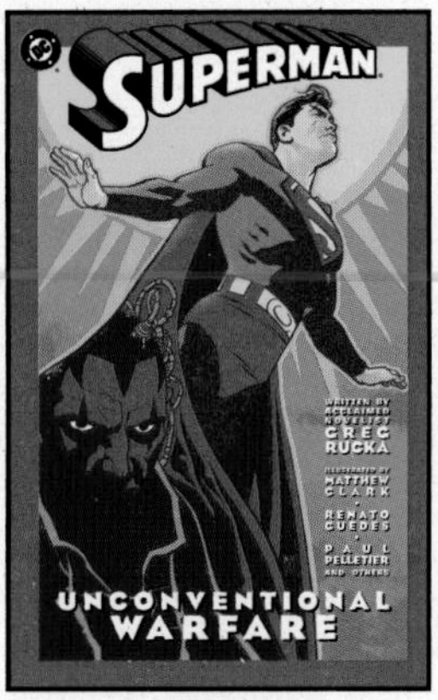
SUPERMAN
GREG RUCKA
UNCONVENTIONAL WARFARE

SUPERMAN:
UNCONVENTIONAL WARFARE

Greg Rucka/various

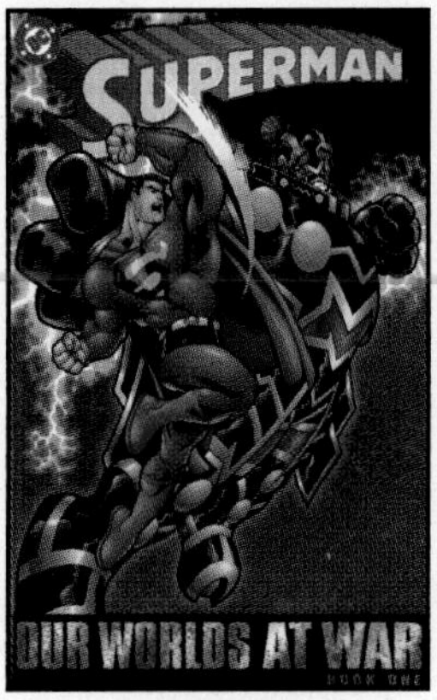
SUPERMAN
OUR WORLDS AT WAR
BOOK ONE

SUPERMAN:
OUR WORLDS AT WAR
VOLUMES 1 & 2

various

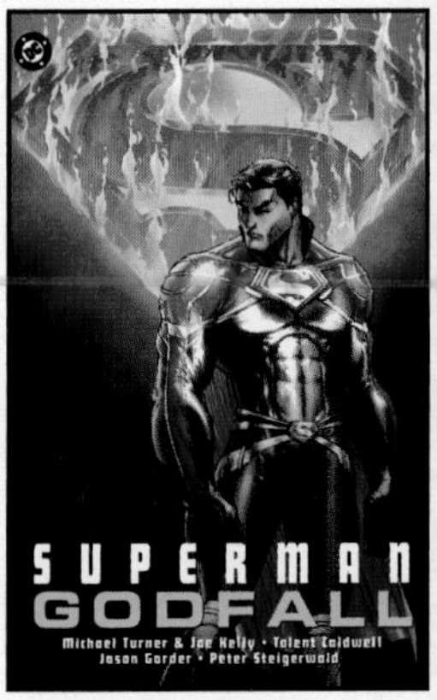
SUPERMAN
GODFALL
Michael Turner & Joe Kelly • Talent Caldwell
Jason Gorder • Peter Steigerwald

SUPERMAN: GODFALL

Michael Turner/Joe Kelly/Talent Caldw
Jason Gorder/Peter Steigerwald

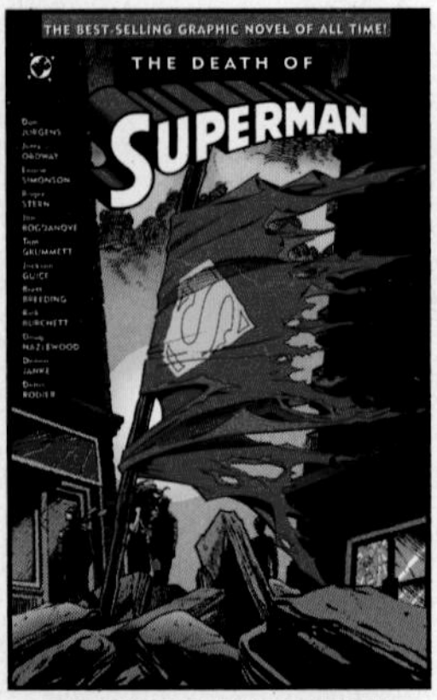
THE BEST-SELLING GRAPHIC NOVEL OF ALL TIME!
THE DEATH OF
SUPERMAN

DEATH OF SUPERMAN

various

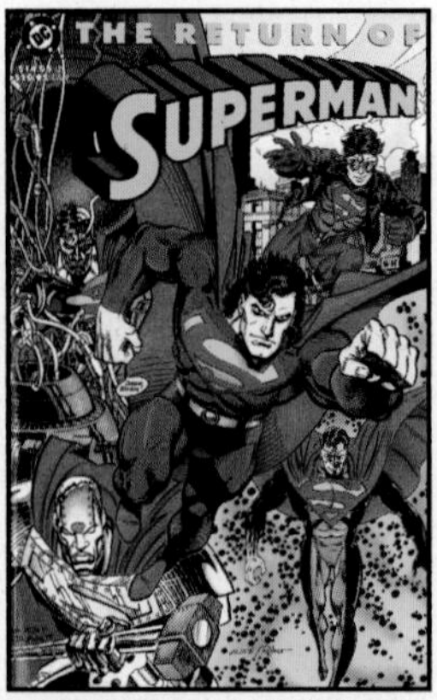
THE RETURN OF
SUPERMAN

RETURN OF SUPERMAN

various

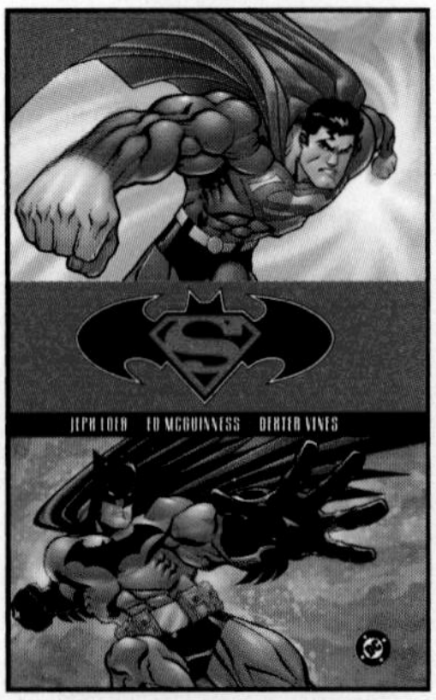
JEPH LOEB
ED MCGUINNESS
DEXTER VINES

SUPERMAN/BATMAN:
PUBLIC ENEMIES

Jeph Loeb/Ed McGuinness/
Dexter Vines

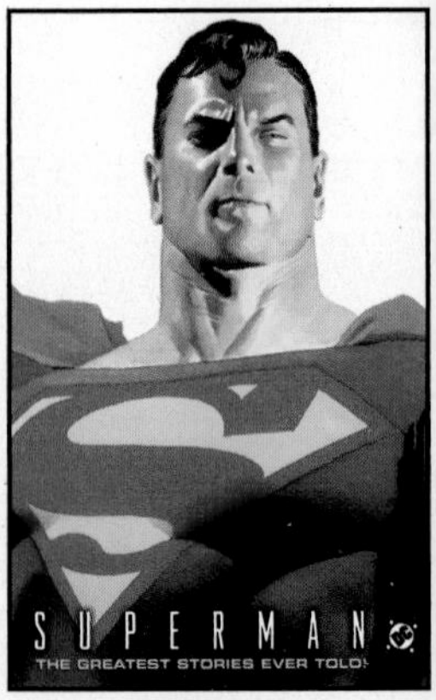
SUPERMAN
THE GREATEST STORIES EVER TOLD

SUPERMAN:
THE GREATEST STORIES
EVER TOLD!

various

OTHER COLLECTIONS FEATURING **SUPERMAN**